The British Light Infantry Arm

The British Light Infantry Arm
c. 1790–1815

its creation, training and operational role

David Gates

B.T. BATSFORD Ltd · London

In respectful and affectionate memory
of my friend and former tutor,
Ruth Talbot B.A.:
sadly missed

Printed in Great Britain
by Anchor Brendon Ltd., Tiptree, Essex

for the Publisher
B.T. Batsford Ltd
4 Fitzhardinge Street
London W1H 0AH

Contents

Preface

This book is an examination of the creation, training and combat role of the light infantry regiments that were added to the British land forces during the period of the French Revolutionary and Napoleonic Wars. Whilst reference is occasionally made to the light units of the militia and volunteer forces, the work is primarily concerned only with those of the regular Army.

The large-scale introduction of light forces into the Armies of the European powers was a turning point in the history of armed conflict. Essentially a response to a series of geographical, technological, social and political developments which, from around 1740, combined to gradually change the face of warfare, it was the embodiment of a revolution in military thought. The trained light infantryman – the type of highly versatile, free-moving, free-firing soldier that forms the backbone of present-day armies – along with the self-contained division – the organizational basis of those armies – were the principal products of that revolution; and the appearance of large numbers of such fast-moving, 'all purpose' troops provoked changes in tactics, strategy and logistical practices that helped make the Napoleonic Wars substantially different in scale and nature from any preceding conflict.

Thus, in the mosaic of the history of the development of land warfare, the specialist light forces of the late eighteenth and early nineteenth centuries form a key piece. That piece is, furthermore, one of the most colourful in the whole mosaic: the regiments that, for example, formed the Light Division of Wellington's Peninsular army constitute some of the most famous and flamboyant units in British military annals; and their role in Wellington's tactics made them of decisive importance on the battlefields of Spain, Portugal and, later, Waterloo. Indeed, the exploits of those regiments – and of Sir John Moore, General Robert Craufurd and some of the other legendary officers that led and trained them – have caught the imagination of generations of writers: the celebrated Captain Kincaid of the Rifle Brigade was one of the first of several Peninsular veterans to produce his military memoirs; during the latter part of the nineteenth century other professional soldiers such as W.H. Cope, R. Levinge, W.S. Moorsom and G. Rigaud all wrote histories of selected light infantry units ; and, more recently, authors like

S.G.P. Ward, Carola Oman and R. N. Buckley added further brief studies which, again, examined particular issues within the general subject.

Few of these works, however, provide the reader with anything more than a narrow – and often misleading – view of some dimension of this important topic. They are, moreover, increasingly dated and excessively reliant on other secondary sources. Indeed, other than the rather superficial studies produced by J.F.C. Fuller in the 1920s and by R. Glover in 1963, almost no primary research has been undertaken on Britain's first regular light infantry units and the developments that led to their formation. In writing this study, my aim has been, therefore, to produce a work which would be more accurate, comprehensive and scholarly than anything currently to hand; and, to this end, primary sources have been used as far as possible.

Indeed, a significant number of the sources used in compiling this study have gone quite unnoticed by previous historians and throw new light on many aspects of the subject. The Mackenzie and Graham Papers in the National Library of Scotland, for example, when linked with other primary sources, produced a rather different view of the work of Sir John Moore at the celebrated Shorncliffe camp than has traditionally been put forward. Similarly, manuscripts among the Earl Grey Papers at Durham University and in the War Office collections of the Public Record Office – notably the remarkable writings of General Dumouriez – yielded a large amount of novel material on the creation of the new light forces and the theory behind their training and organization. Likewise the analysis – pieced together from eye-witness accounts and period training manuals – of the battlefield and *kleiner Krieg* roles fulfilled by light infantry should prove useful to all those interested in the tactical details of Napoleonic period battles, particularly those of the Peninsular War. There are, furthermore, substantial sections on regimental history and on the development of weapons which, again, include appreciable amounts of original material.

But besides those interested purely in the military history of the Napoleonic Wars, this book should also prove of value to all students of the past and future development of land forces, strategy, tactics and military thought. Interest in light forces has, throughout history, followed a discernible cycle; and this work appears at a time when, just as it was in the 1790s, debate about the value of such units is rapidly intensifying: the US Army is currently engaged in forming a number of light divisions; the French have already established a 'Rapid Action Force'; and the Soviet Union and her allies are incorporating thousands of *Spetsnaz* – specialist light troops – into their armed forces. In parallel to these measures, written studies of various aspects of the theory underlying the training and role of light units appear with increasing frequency in defence journals.

But even when allowances are made for the effects of improved technology, few of the dimensions of this issue can fairly be described as new. The initial establishment of light regiments some 200 years ago was in response to a number of developments, most of which have resurfaced in today's debate about light forces. Pre-eminent amongst them is the reshaping of the European countryside – notably areas of West Germany – through enclosure, afforestation and urbanization. The same phenomenon affected much of the continent in the late eighteenth century and, as it did then, is again forcing changes in the manner in which troops are deployed. Just as, in the 1790s, infantry trained in the rigid, linear drills of the Frederickian school found their tactics ill-suited to operations in enclosed terrain, so too are current-day commanders perceiving topographical limitations on the formations and manoeuvres of their heavy forces. This – reinforced by the need to reduce the threat posed by tactical nuclear weapons and other modern forms of concentrated firepower – has given fresh impetus to interest in mobile warfare, carried out by relatively small, dispersed units of light troops.

Similarly, concern over 'rear area' capabilities is rising. A major part of any conflict between NATO and Warsaw Pact forces will consist of *kleiner Krieg* activities in the rear and on the flanks of the main armies – a traditional sphere of operations for light units. Besides making a major contribution in the field of patrol, screening, reconnaissance and outpost duties, Soviet light forces, for instance, would undoubtably attempt to neutralize NATO command, control and communication centres to, amongst other things, prevent any nuclear response to a conventional attack being effectively coordinated. Light, mobile units capable of reacting quickly to sudden threats will, therefore, be of vital importance. Indeed, their effectiveness may well decide the shape of any war – just as the early tirailleurs had so important an impact on the battlefields of the late eighteenth and early nineteenth centuries.

But the emphasis the Warsaw Pact places on avoiding a nuclear exchange by prosecuting a fast, fluent conventional war is symptomatic of a trend that is also affecting NATO. American and German military doctrine, for instance, now attaches increasing importance to mobile, defensive warfare techniques, including the extensive use of light forces. Besides *kleiner Krieg* functions on the fringes of major engagements, light troops could also play a significant role in the midst of pitched battles. Their transition from being auxiliary units – primarily intended for outpost work – to being integral parts of every battlefield formation first occurred in the 1790s; and today, operating in enclosed terrain with the devastating anti-tank weaponry at their disposal, light infantry could be instrumental in delaying, channelling or repelling attacks by hostile armour. The new US light divisions – being smaller and less heavily equipped than traditional mechanized forces – are, for example, seen as units that can be moved to any potential trouble spot with comparative ease and speed. As the US is seeking to play a more active role throughout the globe, this capability promises to be of increasing importance. Furthermore, as the costs of training, maintaining and airlifting heavy forces continue to rise, smaller, more lightly equipped units have financial advantages attached to them that have mounting significance at a time when defence expenditure is coming under harsher scrutiny.

Thus, light forces lie at the centre of the changes in military thinking currently sweeping through Europe and they promise to remain of major importance over the next few decades. But many of the issues relating to the basic training of such troops were also confronted by past generations of soldiers and military theorists; and, consequently their responses can be of great value to defence planners concerned with this field today. And of all the periods of modern history in which light forces have come to the fore, the years 1790–1815 are probably the most important: never before had light troops been seen in such numbers, nor had debate about them and the issues they gave rise to ever been so exhaustive. The Russians repeatedly look to their military history for guidance on today's defence issues; and, likewise, in the designing and training of their new light forces, the Western nations could profit from studying the wartime experiences of past generations.

It only remains for me to express my gratitude to all those who have assisted me in the production of this work. Its core was derived from the doctoral theses that I wrote while at Corpus Christi College, Oxford; and I owe a special vote of thanks to Professor Michael Howard who acted as my supervisor for that work, and to Dr Piers Mackesy who provided me with some additional guidance. I am also indebted to Earl Cathcart – who was kind enough to allow me to draw on his family's private papers – and Mr C.M. Woolgar, the archivist of the Wellington Papers at Southampton University. Among the many other people who assisted me in one form or another were the staffs of: the Codrington and Bodleian Libraries, Oxford; the Public Record Office, Kew; the British Library, London; the National Library of Scotland, Edinburgh; the Department of Palaeography and Diplomatic, Durham University; the Light Division's museum at Winchester; the *Militärgeschichtliche Forschungsamt*, Freiburg im Breisgau, West Germany; and the *Kriegsarchiv*, Vienna. I also owe a great debt of thanks to my friends Gill and Richard, who helped me in so many ways; and to Claudia, who gave me her invaluable encouragement and dutifully followed me around a dozen military museums on the continent and in Britain. Lastly, I would like to thank Miss Bridget Tanner, who typed the text so proficiently; the publishers who made the book possible; and my colleagues here at the University of Aberdeen for their support.

D.G.
Aberdeen

CHAPTER I

The European powers and the introduction of light forces, *c.* 1740–1815

By the end of the seventeenth century, improvements in the weapons of European foot troops had prepared the way for a series of major innovations in infantry tactics. The introduction of increasingly refined flintlock muskets fitted with socket bayonets gave individual soldiers an enhanced, independent capability both to give fire and to defend themselves in close combat. This development enabled detachments of troops to operate at a distance from the main body of their army in relative safety. Capable of resisting even superior forces until help could arrive or they were withdrawn, van, rear, and flank guards became increasingly commonplace features of European military forces on campaign.

However, the type of soldiers of which European forces were predominantly composed at this time were ill-suited to the *petite guerre* waged on the fringes of the main armies by these independent contingents. Often able to live off the land, such detachments were less concerned about lines of communication and supply than their larger parent formations, and thus were subject to far fewer restrictions on their movements.[1] The mode of warfare they practised – forced marches, 'hit and run' raids, fluid skirmishes in woods and enclosures, ambushes and other ruses – called for highly developed personal initiative, resourcefulness, intelligence and courage, coupled with an expert *coup d'oeil*. Such characteristics were rarely found amongst the traditional heavy infantry who were accustomed to fighting shoulder to shoulder in precise formations – usually of a linear construction – under the constant scrutiny of their officers. Here, discipline and unquestioning obedience to orders were regarded as paramount. To give the long, unwieldy lines a degree of manoeuvrability and tactical flexibility, complex evolutions were formulated; and to perform them required a clockwork-like precision on the part of the troops. Every action was regulated by formal drills and executed to the beat of a drum, musketry was delivered in controlled volleys – with the emphasis being placed on speed of fire, rather than on accuracy[2] – and any trace of initiative on the part of the troops was stifled.[3] Obedience and order were maintained by the threat of severe corporal punishment.

Nowhere had such a system been carried to greater perfection than in the Prussian Army of Frederick the Great, who once summarized his notion of the ideal infantry regiment as a 'moving battery'.[4] Whilst troops of this kind proved a perfect match for others of the same description fighting in a similar manner, they had no place in a *guerre des postes*. 'Where animation, *where the exercise of the faculties of the mind* are called for', noted one general, such soldiers were 'useless'.[5]

Thus, the need arose for specialist formations, equipped and trained for the waging of the *petite guerre*: units of light cavalry, highly mobile artillery and, above all, light infantry. The French were amongst the first to incorporate such troops into their army, and as early as 1692 their forces included a growing number of hussars – light horsemen of Hungarian origin.[6] Indeed, it was from the Hungarians and other ethnic groups in the eastern reaches of the Habsburg Empire that the first sizeable bodies of light troops to feature in campaigns fought in central Europe were drawn. When, in 1740, Frederick invaded the Austrian possession of Silesia, the Empress Maria-Theresa called on her Hungarian subjects for substantial military support. 'Then', wrote the great French tactical theorist Guibert,

> appeared in Germany the military of that nation, the Transilvanians, Croates, and other irregular and indisciplined corps, which the House of Austria never before attempted to unite to their armies either from political reasons, or because it found itself low in the zeal of that people. Marshal Saxe appointed Uhlans, and regiments were then raised . . . called *Light troops*. At the same time the king of Prussia made greater levies of hussars and dragoons, to act against the arrier-bans of Hungary . . .[7]

The hussars and other *Grenz* regiments of the Habsburg Empire were troops that were raised on a local basis. They were mostly employed in patrolling the eastern frontiers, and in raiding and reconnaissance missions. After lengthy campaigns against the Turks in south-eastern Europe, they had acquired an outstanding expertise as skirmishers and scouts, and the Imperial forces used them to good effect throughout the War of Austrian Succession.[8] Although dismissed by Maria-Theresa's opponents as thieves and murderers, these light troops, operating in the increasingly enclosed countryside of central Europe, proved a constant thorn in the side of Austria's enemies who were quickly compelled to raise similar formations of their own to counter them.[9] As the great soldier and military theorist Scharnhorst was to write in a 1794 essay on the need for light troops:

> Immediately after the Battle of Mollwitz, where [Frederick] . . . experienced and recognised his lack of such units, he made it his first task to strengthen his army with light troops. By the 2nd Silesian War he was able to oppose the Austrians with a relatively equal force. His example was followed by the French, the Hanoverians and the Saxons, all of whom founded units of this branch of the service. Nevertheless, the proportion of these troops to line formations remained extremely small, until the present war against the French Republic reminded us of the principle that one should always try to

regulate one's dispositions according to the enemy's methods.[10]

The battalions of *chasseurs* and *Jäger* raised by France, Prussia and other states to match the Austrian *Grenz* regiments were, as their titles suggest, predominantly recruited from hunters and gamekeepers. Skilled in marksmanship and accustomed to operating in forested and difficult terrain, such men made ideal light troops and, for camouflage purposes, usually retained the traditional green garb of huntsmen. Similarly, the musical trappings of the hunt – the use of horns and bugles to signal to men scattered across broken countryside – were adapted for military purposes.

In addition to the wars in Central Europe, the various campaigns in North America gave British, French and American soldiers experience in the skills of the *petite guerre*. The Battle of The Monongahela on 9 July 1755 provided an early demonstration of the limitations of European regular tactics in enclosed and wooded countryside. A British force of 1900 regular troops under General Edward Braddock was, while marching against Fort Duquesne, surprised by half as many French and Indian irregulars and utterly routed; the massed volley fire and close order tactics of Braddock's corps proving quite ineffective against their dispersed opponents who, from behind any suitable cover, poured a devastating, aimed fire into their adversaries' exposed, serried ranks.[11]

The British, however, learnt from this calamity and resolved to introduce specialist formations capable of combating enemy irregulars, carrying out scouting missions and protecting columns of heavy infantry on the march. Whereas, as we shall see, in Central Europe they were inclined to rely primarily on their German allies for such light troops, in America they were compelled to introduce forces of their own to supplement small bodies of Canadians and Indians who were past masters of the *guerre des postes*. Within a few months of Braddock's disastrous defeat, a new regiment, the 60th Foot, predominantly composed of Germans, was added to the army in America. Under the command of two Swiss-born soldiers of fortune, Colonels Henry Boquet and Frederick Haldimand, the four battalions of the new regiment were trained as marksmen and 'In order to qualify for the Service of the Woods, taught to load and fire, lying on the ground and kneeling.' Trained to 'march in Order, slow and fast in all sorts of Ground', they were also required to 'frequently . . . pitch & fold their Tents, and to be accustomed to pack up and carry their necessities in the most commodious manner.'[12]

At around the same time bodies of rangers were added to the regular forces in America to act as scouts and skirmishers. The most famous of these corps was 'Rogers' Rangers', who were named after their colonel, Robert Rogers of Connecticut. Colonel Rogers wrote a collection of *Rules for the Ranging Discipline*,[13] which were circulated amongst the parties of regular officers and NCOs that were occasionally attached to the ranger companies to receive tuition and practical experience in the *petite guerre.* These soldiers then returned to their own regiments to disseminate the principles and procedures they had acquired.[14]

Corps of Scottish Highlanders – who, as we shall see, many military theorists regarded as natural light troops – were also sent to serve in America and, after 1758, every regiment of foot included a company of suitably attired light infantry. The dress and accoutrements of these soldiers could not have contrasted more starkly with those of the infantry of the line. The latter wore a black felt hat, a red coat – the folds of which buttoned back to form lapels – a white waistcoat and breeches, and knee length gaiters. Their hair was worn plaited and tied with ribbon, and in addition to their flintlock they carried a cartridge box, a sword and bayonet, and a knapsack. On occasion they had to carry as much as 125 pounds of equipment, but even the more normal weight of some 60 pounds was an awesome burden.[15]

By comparison, the dress of most light infantry men at this time was, as one officer recorded, as follows:

The ground is black ratteen or frize, lapelled and cuffed with blue; . . . a waistcoat with sleeves, a short jacket without sleeves; only arm holes and wings to the shoulders (in like manner as the grenadiers and drummers of the army) white metal buttons, linen or canvas drawers; . . . a pair of leggins of the same colour with their coat which reach up to the middle of their thighs . . . and, from the calf of the leg downwards, they button . . .

The sleeves of the coat are put on the waistcoat, and instead of coat sleeves [the light infantry man] has two wings like the grenadiers, but fuller; . . . he has no lace, but . . . besides the usual pockets, he has two, not quite so high as his breast, made of leather, for ball and flints; and a flap of red cloth on the inside secures the ball from rolling out, if he should fall. His knapsack is carried very high between his shoulders, and is fastened with a strap or web over his shoulder, as the Indians carry their pack. His cartouch-box hangs under his arm on the left side, slung with a leathern strap; and his horn under the other arm on the right; . . . his canteen down his back, under his knapsack, and covered with cloth; he has a rough case for his tomahock, with a button; and it hangs in a leathern sling down his side, . . . between his coat and waistcoat. No bayonet; his leggins have leather straps under his shoes; . . . a cap with a flap and a button, and with as much black cloth as will come under his chin . . .[16]

Although this rather unglamorous dress only served to increase the disdain with which, as we shall see, some of the more traditionally minded officers in the British Army regarded the light service, it was far better suited to skirmisher work than the dashing, but less practical, uniform worn by the redcoats of the line. Indeed, the battalion light companies became quite accomplished skirmishers and were to operate with distinction until they were dissolved after the end of the Seven Years' War. Their polished performance against Pontiac's Indians in the 1763 uprising demonstrated above all the degree of professionalism that British skirmishers had acquired since Braddock's defeat some eight years before.[17]

With the outbreak of the American War of Independence in 1775, however, specialist British light troops were again in short supply. The 60th Foot had been halved in size and sent to garrisons in the West Indies and, although the regimental light companies dissolved after the Seven Years' War had been re-established during 1771, after nearly a decade of total neglect the skills of the *petite guerre* acquired in the previous conflict had been largely forgotten.

The need for such skills, however, was painfully demonstrated in early actions like Lexington and Concord, (April, 1775), and, above all, that of Bunker Hill the following June. Here, as one general observed, in a clash between 'undisciplined peasantry' and 'the best . . . regiments in the British service, the raw peasants of the country . . . killed and wounded, out of 2000, no less than 1054 British officers and soldiers.'[19] As in the case of Braddock's defeat some 20 years before, the limitations of European regular, tactical methods when opposed to dispersed, free-moving, free-firing skirmishers were made apparent. New specialist formations of light troops were necessary to protect columns on the march, perform scouting missions, strike at the enemy's flanks and rear and counter their irregulars on the battlefield – particularly in wooded or enclosed terrain.

As we shall see in the next chapter, many line regiments of the British Army were to make significant changes in their tactics and organization to cope with the style of fighting generally encountered in the American War of Independence. The enclosed nature of the countryside broke up large formations and prevented the employment of cavalry in appreciable numbers. These two factors led to infantry deploying in a far thinner and looser manner than the three-deep, close-order lines prescribed in most European drill books at this time. Troops regularly fought in only two ranks or in skirmish order and frequently scurried around rambling battlefields in relatively small bodies, fighting a series of connected but independent actions.

On and around these battlefields, a number of specially created light units carried out a *guerre des postes*. Having seen from the use made of 'Yagers in the woods of Westphalia in the German War, that such troops were the men wanted in America', and that 'Guards, and high-dressed corps, were not the troops . . . to take into the woods to fight Virginia Riflemen',[20] several British officers proposed that legions of light cavalry and infantry, supported by mobile artillery, should be formed. Of these legions, the two commanded by Lieutenant-Colonels John Simcoe and Banastre Tarleton were the most important. Dressed in green for camouflage,[21] Simcoe's 'Queen's Rangers' and Tarleton's 'British Legion' waged a lengthy *petite guerre* against the rebel forces and, after the war, both officers published exhaustive accounts of their operations. Simcoe's *Journal* was by far the finest English narrative of the daily work of a mixed light force to appear during the eighteenth century. Describing in minute detail the training methods, tactics and ruses employed by his men, it was full of useful instruction and observations.

Tarleton's *Southern Campaigns*[22] was also of great use to anyone interested in the work of light troops and the details of the *petite guerre* but, unlike Simcoe's work, was more of a broad narrative of operations than a detailed examination of the functions of one particular corps. Nevertheless, it provided an interesting account of the operations of the 'British Legion' and made a significant contribution to the available literature on the work of light troops.

Also of great importance was a work by a Brunswicker, Lieutenant Colonel Andrew Emmerich. He had served as a Jäger in Germany in the Seven Years' War and then in the American War of Independence where he had led a detachment of light troops. Such units, Emmerich believed, were indispensable: 'In war', he wrote,

> no army can act without light troops. Its operations and even existence depends upon them. Such light troops ought properly to be composed of select chasseurs with rifles, light infantry with bayonets, and light dragoons or hussars . . .[23]

'When an army is in motion', Emmerich continued,

> the business of the light troops is to form the advanced guard, to protect the flanks, and provide in every respect possible for the safety of its march . . . It is the particular duty of the light troops to prevent its being surprised, or disturbed, and alarmed by trifling causes. When the army retreats, the corps of light troops must form the rear guard, in order to cover its retreat . . .[24]

More in the style of Simcoe's *Journal* than Tarleton's *Southern Campaigns*, Emmerich's book was an examination of the work of light troops on campaign. Although it was limited in scope and, unlike later works, made little effort to provide instruction on battlefield tactics, it did contain many suggestions and observations that were potentially useful to officers leading light units, with small chapters devoted to such issues as day and night marches, spies, camouflage, and the duties of pickets and sentries.

Besides the legions under Tarleton and Simcoe, a number of smaller units of light troops were raised by the British for service in the American War. Several detachments of rangers, like those that had been formed during the Seven Years' War, were re-established. These included 'Butler's Rangers', 'Jessup's Loyal Rangers' and the 'King's Rangers'. The last of these units seems to have been a relatively small force of around 200 men commanded by Major James Rogers,[25] but Jessup's corps, on the other hand, consisted of nine companies and numbered nearly 600 men in February 1783.[26] Similarly, in March 1779, Butler's regiment had over 400 men divided into six companies.[27] These larger units of rangers were frequently split into detachments and attached to regiments of the line as skirmishers and scouts, just as they had been in the Seven Years' War.

Also of importance were 'Ferguson's Sharpshooters'; a small corps of American loyalist volunteers that were raised in 1776 and commanded by Captain Patrick Ferguson of the 70th Foot. Initially, at least some of the men in this force were equipped with a breech-loading rifle devised by the captain himself, but after the corps was roughly handled in the Battle of Brandywine in September 1779, most of these weapons were withdrawn from use. Over the next three years the sharpshooters regularly fought alongside the legions of Simcoe and Tarleton. However, in a disastrous engagement at King's Mountain, Carolina, on 17 October 1780, Ferguson was killed and his command effectively destroyed.[28]

Despite the important and impressive work of formations like Simcoe's 'Queen's Rangers', the end of major hostilities with the conclusion of the American War of Independence again led to a decline in the significance attached by the British Army to the light infantry service. As in 1763, the bulk of the light troops raised for the conflict were completely disbanded[29] and those few units that remained in being were increasingly neglected. The expertise gained by British troops in the various aspects of the *petite guerre* – and clearly demonstrated in actions such as that against the French at Vignie on St Lucia in 1778[30] – was rapidly lost once more, and by the 1790s few, if any, units retained the skills and training necessary for them to carry out such duties effectively.

Understandably, this development provoked considerable anxiety amongst those British soldiers and military theorists who had learnt from the experiences of recent wars and who observed certain martial trends that were taking place in continental Europe with mounting concern. In presenting a copy of his *Journal* to King George III, Lieutenant-Colonel Simcoe added a 12-page manuscript to the printed text. In this document, he called for the reintroduction of legions organized and trained like his own 'Queen's Rangers' had been, and capable of countering those that were currently being raised by the French.[31]

Similarly, a General Money, noting the absence of trained light infantry in the British Army and the increasingly enclosed nature of the European countryside, called for the raising of more 'Irregulars' and pointed to the bitter lessons of the American War. 'What', he asked in 1799,

> was the army that captured General Burgoyne's but an army of Irregulars? What other appellation can be given to Militia untrained to any species of evolution, and undisciplined, but that of Irregulars? At Saratoga the finest army in the world . . . laid down their arms to what Mr Rigby in the House of Commons called an 'undisciplined rabble': but they were all Woodsmen; that is, marksmen. . . . An old Colonel, who commanded a regiment in General Burgoyne's army, . . . declared to me, that if there had been in that army about a thousand well-trained Chasseurs, that army would not have

been lost. I will venture to say, had half of them been Chasseurs, it would have marched to Albany, even to New York. . . . Such an army as he had was not fit to fight in woods, composed of heavy useless Germans, and high-dressed British Infantry – those were not the species of troops he wanted. The troops in Canada are at this day composed of just such regiments. If they were never to be removed from the walls of Quebec, or out of works, there could not be better men; but if they should unhappily be called into woods again to meet the Americans, that province will be over-ran [sic] in as short a time as it was before by Generals Arnold and Montgomery. No less than three or four battalions or Riflemen, call them by what name you please, ought to be stationed here; the colour of their clothing ought to be that which comes nearest to the bark of trees.[32]

After outlining how he himself had planned a legion of *chasseurs à cheval* and riflemen for duty in America, Money explained that this plan had been rejected by the government. 'But', he continued,

a corps was raised by . . . Tarleton, . . . somewhat similar to it; he knew my plan and was to have been a Captain in my legion had it been raised. The good effect of this corps was often seen; and it would have been fortunate for us if we had raised more such legions; it would have saved the life of many a brave man, who lost it in the unequal contest between high-dressed corps and corps of skilful marksmen. Seldom were the Americans' Riflemen seen, the report of his gun you heard but his ball was felt.

'My blood ran cold in my veins', Money continued,

after that unhappy war, when it occurred to my mind the cruel situation my brave countrymen, through ignorance, had been placed in . . . where bravery was unavailing; yet it is a doubt with me at this moment, notwithstanding the experience we have had in that war, whether we should not fight it over again in the same manner from the cheapness with which Riflemen and Irregulars are still held.[33]

In Europe as well as in America, the British had been slower than their adversaries to introduce units of light troops and develop the specialized instruction and equipment they required. In the Wars of the Austrian Succession, the British had no regiments of this description whatsoever and depended instead on the legions, hussars and *Jäger* of their German allies. Heavy losses, notably at Fontenay in 1745, at the hands of French skirmishers such as De Graffin's *Regiment des Arquebusiers*, eventually led to the British raising light units of their own and, in 1759, a battalion of light infantry, 'Keith's Highlanders', was sent to Germany. They were subsequently joined by another regiment, 'Campbell's Highlanders', and a corps of light dragoons. Though not as experienced, they fought alongside the army's Hessian and Hanoverian light troops, and made an important contribution to the *guerre des postes*.

Similarly, though primarily for service in the West Indies, the British formed two other regiments of light troops at this time. These were 'Colonel Morgan's Irish Light Infantry' and the two battalions of the

'Royal Volunteers Light Infantry'.[36] As had been the case in America, however, at the end of the Seven Years' War all of these light regiments, having been created to meet a specific need, were effectively done away with: the 'Royal Volunteers' and Morgan's regiment were completely disbanded – although they were both re-established on the outbreak of war in America in 1775 – whilst 'Keith's Highlanders' and 'Campbell's Highlanders' discarded their function as skirmishers and were assimilated into the Army's line troops as the 87th and 88th Regiments of Foot respectively.

This policy of raising light regiments on an *ad hoc* basis whenever war broke out and then, on the return of peace, either dissolving them completely or retaining them – and 'standardizing' them – as ordinary line troops was a fairly widespread practice in European armies and reveals a good deal about the way light formations were regarded. As we have seen, substantial numbers of such troops were first introduced into the forces of most European states during the 1740s, and this expansion of the light service continued throughout the Seven Years' War and, in many countries, beyond the end of that conflict. In 1756, for example, no less than 40,000 men of the Austrian Army – nearly one quarter of the whole – were designated as *Grenzer*[37] and by 1808 there were some 62 battalions of troops that were regarded as light infantry, plus thousands of light cavalry, in the Austrian service.[38] Similarly, in March, 1787, shortly after the death of Frederick the Great, the Prussians added ten *Schützen* – marksmen equipped with crudely rifled weapons – to each company of their infantry,[39] and the following June raised 20 battalions of fusiliers – troops that were clothed in green and similar to the Army's existing 2000 *Jäger*.[40] These fusilier units were another example of the trend to standardize light infantry corps, having been largely formed from *Freibataillone* who had been raised on a temporary basis in previous years.[41]

From the 1760s in particular, the French, too, increased their forces of light cavalry, artillery and infantry. Companies of *chasseurs* were added to each line regiment in 1760 and by 1788 there were also twelve *chasseur* battalions in the Army.[42] Similarly, the Russians introduced more light horsemen and designated increasing numbers of foot units as *Jäger*.[43] Indeed, of the major European states, only Britain failed to permanently expand her light forces in a substantial way. Apart from the restoration of the regimental light companies in 1771,[44] there were no efforts to add permanent bodies of light infantry to the British Army until the very end of the eighteenth century.

However, as one general remarked to Lord Amherst – the Commander-in-Chief of the British Army in the early 1790s – 'It is not a Short Coat or Half Gaters that makes a light Infantry Man, but . . . a confidence in his Aim, & that Stratagem in a personal conflict which is derived from Experience.'[45] Whilst, after the Seven Years' War, the various European armies did introduce corps that were labelled as 'light troops', in a great many cases the differences between these formations and those of the line were purely cosmetic. They were, as one critic observed, '*Jäger* in name alone',[46] and, as we shall see, were to prove a poor substitute for genuine light infantry. There was, for example, no comparison between the *Jäger* of the Prussian Army and those found in the Russian Service. Whilst the former were a small, *élite* body of professional marksmen, armed with highly accurate rifled weapons and skilled in scouting and skirmishing, the Russian *Jäger* were totally different. Except for two *élite* battalions who were equipped with rifles, they were armed with poor quality smoothbore muskets and had little ability in skirmishing and other independent activities. Although the Archduke Charles, the great Austrian general of the Napoleonic era, once remarked that the 'ordinary Russian soldier is brave and his courage unsurpassed', he nevertheless dismissed both officers and men as being of limited use in the *kleiner Krieg* due to their lack of training and tactical skill.[47] Likewise, General Philibert Duhesme – one of the most eminent of French theorists on the subject of light troops – having seen Russian *Jäger* regiments in action, commented that:

> The skirmish lines that they occasionally tried to deploy in their front or flanks did not know how to spread out or to maintain proper direction. The majority of their NCO's are not capable of fending for themselves, and there are few who understand how to lead even a small patrol.[48]

Thus, very few of the 50 Russian *Jäger* regiments seem to have had any practical ability as skirmishers and they invariably functioned like ordinary line troops.[49] Indeed, William Surtees, a British light infantry-man who fought alongside the Russians in Holland in 1799, noted that their *Jäger* were not even suitably dressed for the work of light troops: 'Their rifle men', he wrote,

> were shod with boots very much resembling those of our fishermen, coming up considerably higher than the knee; thus rendering them . . . incapable of celerity of movement, one of the chief requisites of a rifle corps . . .[50]

There were also substantial distinctions to be made between the Prussian *Jäger* and the fusiliers of the same army. Although dressed in similar uniforms, the latter units lacked expertise as marksmen and had little ability in open-order tactics and the other preserves of true light infantry.[51] Furthermore, they did not carry rifles, but were equipped in much the same way as the Russian *Jäger*. This was also the case with the bulk of Austria's *Jäger* regiments, where only the rear (third) rank and NCOs actually carried rifled weapons.[52] Indeed, although more accurate than the common flintlock musket, the rifle remained very much a sniper's weapon throughout this period and was issued to only a few hundred troops. More expensive, difficult to maintain in good order and of restricted tactical value, they were, as we shall see, not as popular as the ordinary smoothbore weapons. In the French Army, for example, their general use by light troops was discontinued after the Consulate, though a few were retained as weapons for the personal use of officers and NCOs.[53]

So far, we have discussed two principal ways in which light troops were added to European armies: the creation of *élite* regular units such as the *Jäger* of Prussia and the *chasseurs* of France; and the conversion of temporary, irregular light corps – like 'Campbell's Highlanders', and the Prussian and Austrian *Freibataillone* – into permanent, regular formations. Besides these methods, there was a third that was also commonly employed, and this was the addition to line regiments of a few soldiers trained, to varying degrees, in sniping and open-order tactics.

One of the earliest examples of this practice was the establishment of light companies by the British in their regiments serving in America in 1758. As we have seen, such flank companies were eventually introduced into every battalion of the British Infantry and, simultaneously, other European states also took steps to provide their line regiments with bodies of skirmishers; the French added companies of *chasseurs* to each regiment in 1760,[54] and the Prussians added a handful of *Schützen* to every company.[55] On the whole, however, the British, just as they had with the introduction of light troops in general, were to lag behind the continental powers in this field. As early as 1756, Marshal Count Maurice de Saxe had suggested that a tenth of each infantry regiment should be trained to act as skirmishers,[56] and by the 1780s some military theorists and officers were calling for up to 30 per cent of a unit to be so instructed.[57]

One such officer was *Oberst-Leutnant* Von Ewald of the Hessen, and, later, Danish Army. He first wrote a detailed study of the duties of light troops in the early 1780s following extensive service in America, and much of his work was subsequently adopted by the *Jäger* of Hessen – some of the most celebrated skirmishers in Europe – as the basis for their training and tactics. In an extended version of the same book produced for the Danish service in 1790, Von Ewald criticized the policy of raising *Freibataillone* on the outbreak of war to serve as skirmishers. He believed that the work of light infantry was too important to entrust to poorly trained irregulars, raised for the duration of the war, and that as the handful of regular *Jäger* could 'not be everywhere', substantial bodies of light troops should be permanently established in every regiment to ensure that there would no shortage of such soldiers at any point.[58] Skilled in marksmanship, 'highly trained and capable of any function',[59] they would, by their tactical versatility, be a match for a force of many times their strength.[60]

Similarly, in 1781, the great French tactical theorist Guibert attacked the raising of temporary, unskilled bodies of skirmishers for the duration of hostilities and called for the institution of permanent units each consisting of 1200 men. 'Exercised in the same manner', he continued,

> they should know how to fight in line, as well as in detail or straggling parties. Care should be taken to compose these corps of chosen and veteran

soldiers. . . . The same choice should be made of the officers of these corps; . . . those of experience and enterprising dispositions, men whose merit has been proved, . . . men who know that these kind of corps are destined to be harassed and sacrificed in time of need; in short not to fear being beaten, when they know by being so they are of real service to the army.[61]

In concluding, Guibert added that such units should be 'practised in swimming, running, everything that can increase their bodily activity and strength.[62]

Within eight years of Guibert writing these words, the French Army had twelve such battalions of *chasseurs d'élite*[63] and, furthermore, only half a decade later, most French line regiments could operate quite successfully as skirmishers. As Duhesme observed, 'By the end of 1793, the French armies had only light infantry'.[64] Indeed, as we shall see, the skill and numerical strength of the French light service was eventually to lead to major reforms in the organization and tactics of other European armies.

The Germanic powers also made considerable efforts to introduce more flexibility into their infantry's tactical capabilities by training parts of every regiment as skirmishers. In 1804, Hermann von Boyen – who was later to become Prussia's Minister for War – noted that the Hessians had earmarked the third rank of every infantry battalion as light troops. Von Boyen, supported by Scharnhorst, who was the commandant of the Berlin Military Academy at this time, subsequently advocated that the Prussian infantry should do the same, and, over the next few years, the practice was gradually adopted and finally, in 1812, included in the *Reglement* as official policy.[65]

Similarly, the Austrians took to designating the third rank of their infantry battalions for skirmisher work. The idea was first tried in 1804 by General Mack, and developed in the *Reglement* of 1807. These laid down that the rear rank of every battalion was henceforth to be composed of the 'brightest, most cunning and reliable' troops in the regiment.[66]

However, whilst this measure did ensure that each infantry corps included an adequate proportion of light troops and thus extended the tactical scope of the units, the utility of these skirmishers was somewhat limited. Both the Prussian and Austrian regulations relating to their deployment gave them little opportunity for independent action in true light infantry style. The Austrian rear rank skirmishers, for example, were largely relegated to a purely defensive role. Their function was seen as one of protecting the line regiments from harassment by hostile *tirailleurs*, and they rarely ventured more than 300 yards from the parent force which retained a rigid grip on their activities by transmitting directions on the battalion drums.[67] However, in that they merged the specialist functions of the line and light troops into one service, these soldiers were the embodiment of the most advanced doctrine of the period: trained, all-purpose infantrymen.

In the late 1790s and early 1800s, British officers were also to call for some efforts to increase the tactical versatility of their line troops as part of the response to the alarming build-up of France's light infantry forces. As early as 1789, Lieutenant-Colonel Andrew Emmerich had written:

> As it is often difficult, in time of war, to find select chasseurs, who are active, good marksmen and well acquainted with the use of a rifle, I submit . . . whether it might not be attended with great convenience and benefit to the service, if two active men, of every company of every regiment . . . were taught the use of the rifle . . . and the other points of duty belonging to light troops; in order, that when occasion required, they might be formed into a corps for the use of the army.[68]

Likewise, some years later, Colonel George Hanger commented that:

> The French have 192,000 light troops in their army, which, rating their army at 600,000 is nearly one *third* of the whole force: we have only one *tenth*, allowing one company of light infantry to ten companies in a regiment. . . . We ought to increase ours, but that increase of light troops should not be sharp-shooters and riflemen only; no, they should be trained to be *marksmen*, but should also be as *well disciplined* as any *regular battalion* of the line . . . Corps that can *perform every duty that is required of British soldiers*, from the grenadier to the irregular marksman . . . Then they may be used *in any and every way* the commanding general shall judge proper.[69]

Similarly, in 1807, Lieutenant-Colonel John Macdonald urged that:

> In the British Service, there should be, at least, Six *Battalions of Riflemen*, to afford a proportion for every expedition and Service undertaken. Independent of such a Regular Corps, the whole of every Battalion ought to be trained to such duties of Light Troops, or Chasseurs . . . When a sufficient proportion of the Rifle-Corps might not be present, the *whole* of an army would be, then, qualified to act as such.[70]

The Army's high command did make attempts to respond to such suggestions.
A circular order, issued in 1798 to senior officers, explained that:

> The Regulations . . . do not forbid the Practice of the Exercise peculiarly adapted to Light Troops, which Practice is on the contrary particularly recommended, to enable any Corps to act independently when circumstances may require it . . .[71]

The problems attached to deploying troops in regular formations in difficult terrain were also recognised[72] and an 1803 training manual observed that:

> In a country such as Britain, much intersected with inclosures and covered in many parts with extensive woods, it is necessary that all corps of infantry should become acquainted with the mode of warfare generally practised by light troops.[73]

However, such attempts to introduce a greater degree of flexibility into the line infantry's tactics enjoyed little success. As had happened to a lesser degree in the Prussian and Austrian Armies, the British high command effectively stifled the development of line troops that were trained in open-order tactics and marksmanship by imposing restrictive regulations and codes of procedure. Convinced that such light infantry practices as 'running like a Lamplighter' would lead to confusion and 'unsteadiness' in the ranks,[74] the Commander-in-Chief's office decreed that 'Occasional deviations from the system detailed in the *Regulations* can be required only where the whole or any part of a corps is obliged, from the nature of the country, to act in the manner of light troops.'[75] Even the 1798 circular, whilst giving permission for the occasional practice of the 'Exercise peculiarly adapted to Light Troops', criticized some regiments for failing to follow official drill procedures and concluded with the uncompromising statement, 'It must . . . be clearly understood that all troops when brought into the Line are precisely to govern themselves by the principles laid down in His Majesty's Regulations'.[76]

Thus, line troops encouraged to improve their capabilities as skirmishers were simultaneously subjected to pressure from the Army's high command to comply with restrictive, official doctrines. Inevitably, this had a stifling effect and left open-order tactics and marksmanship as the preserve of a few specialist light infantry corps; a situation that was deplored by many senior officers who continued to argue, with little success, for more versatility in the tactical capabilities of the infantry as a whole. Sir Thomas Graham, for example, wrote to the Adjutant-General in 1811, attacking the notion that light infantry training undermined discipline and led to 'unsteadiness' in line troops. 'We have', he observed,

> Battalions called Lt. Infantry that know no more of the matter than my gallant friends of the Guards here, & who consequently expose themselves . . . unnecessarily to be knocked in the head when they might & ought to be under cover. The material consequence of this must be *to occasion a useless Sacrifice of Lives, if not, thereby, to produce confusion.* . . . Now I am inclined to believe that officers & men of every description should be prepar'd for whatever they may meet with on service – A Battalion or Brigade may find itself attack'd alone, without any proportion of light troops, or at least a very inadequate one & in such broken & rough ground as to make *close order* & the *touch of the Elbow* quite impossible during the action. Will not such troops under such circumstances, experience much less loss – be much less apt to be unsteady, & much more likely to get well out of a scrape – if both officers and men have been taught how to act in loose order – how to understand, & take advantage of, all the inequalities of the ground, how to skirmish & support each other either in advancing or retreating, & how to form rapidly as circumstances may require – than if condemn'd by ignorance to remain almost immovable & expos'd, in the closest order the situation will allow of (which they are afraid from want of practice to quit) down to their shoes to the galling of fire of the Enemies (sic) Tirailleurs, not one of whom can be

seen or hurt by a volley of such a Corps?[77]

In addition to the belief that light infantry practice weakened a unit's discipline and led to 'unsteadiness' on the battlefield, there were also political and social factors that served to restrict the introduction of light troops into many regular armies during this period. Generally, the armies of the various states – like many other formal institutions – were reflections of the class-structure of their societies. The European monarchs largely enjoyed autocratic powers, but their position was dependent on the constant support of the next tier in the social hierarchy: the aristocracy. Thus, a relationship developed between the various monarchs and their respective nobilities whereby, in return for unswerving loyalty, the aristocrats had their privileged social and political position guaranteed by the crown.

Besides social standing, wealth – even on a relatively modest scale – could also secure advancement in some armies, and the British and French officer corps in particular were dominated by rich bourgeoisie, landed gentry and aristrocrats. Likewise, in the Habsburg and Russian Empires the nobility played a leading role in providing army officers; but here again the system was fairly flexible and large numbers of men with middle-class backgrounds were also able to enter the service.[78]

But, above all, it was in the Prussian service – which since the days of Frederick the Great had been regarded as the finest in Europe, and which was emulated in many ways by the armies of other states – that the nobility reigned supreme. The Prussian officer corps was almost exclusively composed of aristocrats – *Junker* – many of whom had very little wealth at all.[79] The *Junker*, whilst reluctantly acknowledging that light troops did have an important, military role to play, were, like many of the *noblesse* in other European forces, disdainful of the light service. To such socially minded institutions as the Prussian and Austrian Armies, skirmishers had a decidedly plebeian aura. Even the finest of them – the *élite Jäger* and *chasseurs* – had their origins amongst huntsmen and gamekeepers, and the rest had nothing whatsoever to recommend them: invariably raised purely for the duration of any war, they ranged from little bands of Swiss and German soldiers of fortune – the eighteenth-century equivalents of World War II irregular units such as 'Popski's Private Army'[80] – to militia and borderguards pressed into regular service.

Such 'irregulars' were held in complete contempt by many soldiers of the Frederickian school of thought. Von Ewald described them as 'deserters and ruffians', 'the scum of the human race',[81] whilst Frederick himself dismissed them as 'Adventurers, deserters and vagabonds who were distinguished from the regular infantry only by the lack of what made the infantry strong, namely, discipline.'[82] Similarly, in attacking the suggestion that some Tyrolean sharpshooters should be given regular commissions, Colonel Mayer von Heldenfeld, a senior adviser to the Austrian high command, described the proposal as one that would destroy 'all military concepts of honour, and *esprit de corps*, and thus become the grave of the regular army'.[83]

Likewise, Guibert, in his *General Essay on Tactics*, expressed a preference for doing away with light infantry altogether[84] and dismissed the service as being an unsuitable training school for officers. 'This infatuation', he commented with more than a hint of 'old school' contempt, may 'form commanders of advanced guards, perhaps some good lieutenant-generals, but most certainly never of the first rate ones, like a Turenne or Luxembourg'. 'Uniformed people', he continued, his disdain evidently getting the better of his usually sound military judgement,

> have ever been ignorant to say, that these harassing corps destroyed our armies in Bohemia and Bavaria . . . Absurd reasoners have remonstrated, that we should have opposed them with a similar body of troops.[85]

Similarly, one British officer serving in the American War of Independence described light infantry as being

> for the most part young and insolent puppies, whose worthlessness was apparently their recommendation to a service which placed them in the post of danger, and in the way of becoming food for powder, their most appropriate destination next to that of the gallows.[86]

Other military thinkers, however, took a radically different view of the light infantry service. Captain T.H. Barber of the British Army, for example, insisted that 'The service of light troops . . . demands qualities of a superior order',[87] whilst De Jeney, a Swiss theorist and veteran of twenty-four campaigns, also saw it as requiring men of an extremely high calibre. 'The service of this Corps', he wrote, 'though perhaps the least regarded, is the most fatiguing, the most dangerous and the most extensive'.[88] An officer commanding light troops should, he maintained, be

> Blessed with an imagination fruitful in Projects, Stratagems and Resources: A penetrating Mind, capable of combining, instantly, every circumstance of an action; a Heart that cannot shrink at the appearance of Danger; a Countenance so steadfast and assured, as not to discover the least sign of Confusion or Disquietude; a Memory so happy as never to mistake the Names of Persons or Things; a Dispositon so indefatigable and alert as to give life to every Part, and to every Action: an Eye so quick and strong as to perceive in a moment every Defect, Advantage, Obstacle, or Danger that may arise: such Sentiments as to inspire Respect, Confidence, and Attachment throughout his whole Corps. Besides all this, that he may be able to converse with People of all Nations, he should understand Latin, German and French. He should moreover be perfectly acquainted with the Service, particularly that of light Troops, both of the army to which he belongs, and of the Enemy. Without these Qualifications it will be impossible for him to succeed in his art.[89]

Scharnhorst also realized the importance of light troops and was to play a leading role in incorporating more of them into the Prussian

Army after 1806. In direct contrast to Guibert, for example, he took the view that the service offered the

> greatest opportunity for the training of good and useful officers: daily actions accustom them to danger and by being left to rely more on their own judgement they are taught how to release themselves from the machine like process of their profession. All previous instruction is as useless as it is inapplicable, and therefore the bravery, judgement and independence of the officers grow almost daily. Turn back to history and my claims will be supported by the distinguished examples of Laudon, Trench, Zieten, Seydlitz, Kleist and Lafayette. The military talents of all these men were developed in the light service.[90]

Indeed, there were many theorists and soldiers – particularly Frenchmen – who felt that the 'qualities of a superior order' required of light troops were largely naturally inherited talents and skills. It followed, therefore, that skirmishing was not something to be regulated, but simply left to nature. The soldiers could be told generally what to do, but not how it should be done. 'The Business of a Partisan', noted De Jeney, 'has been generally thought so extreamely [sic] irregular, that the *French* writers upon military Subjects, have never attempted to reduce it to any kind of System'.[91]

Similar ideas, however, did emerge in other armies. General John Money, for instance, of the British service commented that:

> . . . A Chasseur ought to be like an Indian in every respect but scalping. I have seen Indians in Fire, and am persuaded that fifty of them would kill or take two hundred men of any high-dressed regiment in Europe, who had fifty miles to march in a woody or extremely inclosed country. . . . Chasseurs are to be brought as near the Indian as possible, and have nothing to carry when action is expected, but a powder-horn and a bag of loose balls; they ought to be able to run twelve miles in two hours, which any well-made young athletic man could easily be brought to in a fortnight . . . There are not in Europe men whose manners and dispositions are better adapted to the formation of Irregulars than the English . . . But, of all men, the Highlanders . . . make the best Irregulars, if well trained for the occasion, as they are a hardy, nimble, and an intelligent people.[92]

Indeed, the belief that Irish and Scottish troops had outstanding natural talents which suited them for light infantry duties was shared by many British officers[93], and it is interesting to note that the majority of Britain's first light regiments were composed of men drawn from these nations.

In the continental armies too, the concept of the natural light infantryman was one that was taken seriously. Scharnhorst noted in 1811 that:

> A lively regard for honour, for competition and distinctions, the ability to learn quickly and to adapt easily to changing conditions and circumstances make French soldiers better skirmishers than those of any other nation.[94]

Similarly, de Jeney observed in his work *The Partisan* that 'The [light] Infantry may be composed of Men of all Nations; but the . . . French . . . deserve the Preference on account of their natural inclination.'[95]

Indeed, this peculiar quality of the French infantry seems to have been one they exhibited throughout the Napoleonic Wars and beyond. During the Danube campaign of 1809, for instance, it soon became clear that 'In close, wooded country the superior intelligence and individuality of the French carried everything before them'[96] – a consideration which greatly influenced the Archduke Charles in his selection of the battle position at Wagram where he sought to avoid 'broken and wooded ground, in which the French infantry had already demonstrated their superiority . . .'[97] Likewise, in his 1912 study of the Leipzig campaign, F.L. Petre remarked that

> In one department especially, the attack or defence of localities, of woods or villages, the French infantry ever displayed that capacity which, in the French soldier, seems to be an inborn instinct.[98]

As to the other continental armies, Duhesme wrote of the Russians that whilst 'they possess *Jäger*, we can assert that they have no true light infantry; their soldiers do not have sufficient aptitude for this service'.[99] This view was evidently shared by General Radetzky of the Austrian service who, in the 1813 Leipzig campaign, was to issue a general order that 'fighting *en tirailleur* should be done only in a very restricted fashion because neither the Russians nor we have mastered the *manière de tirailleur*'.[100]

Indeed, in view of the success of their light troops in former years, this issue had troubled the Habsburg forces ever since 1792, when General Klein had been puzzled by the fact that the untrained *Grenzer* of the Seven Years' War had proved 'far better light infantry than the present regulated and drilled *Grenzer*'.[101] This led one German officer to deduce that 'too much drill' had made the Austrians poor skirmishers.[102] General Radetzky, however, remained persuaded that they simply did not 'understand this kind of fighting',[103] whilst the Austrian Army's official history of the period concluded that 'It was not realised that the soldier, unless possessing a natural aptitude for skirmishing, must be carefully trained for independent action'.[104]

As we have seen the Austrians eventually tried to secure the results they sought through the imposition of formal drills and procedures of the kind that regulated the movements of their heavy infantry. This, of course, was the opposite approach to the reliance on unrestricted, natural instincts favoured by the French and proved to be quite inappropriate for the production of free-moving, free-firing light troops, capable of independent action guided by the individual soldier's initiative and experience. In the case of the rear rank skirmishers introduced into the line infantry, it was to have particularly damaging consequences and, as Radetzky and others noted, greatly reduced their effectiveness on the battlefield.

But this whole methodical approach to the question of skirmishing was symptomatic of the conservative view of war that prevailed in European military circles. The Frederickian doctrines that formed the basis of infantry training in so many armies at this time sought 'to educate the soldier only in a machine-like manner, to do nothing in accordance with his likes, [and] to regard soldiers as automata that have no thought but only physical movements'.[105] Indeed, as late as 1811, Scharnhorst was to complain that:

> The German tacticians still cannot rid themselves of the evolutions of Frederick the Great's autumn manoeuvres. They made us forget war: everyone, even the English and French tacticians (not those natural soldiers who led armies in 1793 and 1794, and later) regarded them as the basis of higher tactics. Several competent men – Tempelhoff and others – continued to respect these tactics–turned–into–formalities when they commanded in the field. It was generally believed that the mechanics of evolutions alone secured victory. Since people busied themselves primarily with the mathematical principles of fundamental tactics, these in turn became the basis of operations.[106]

Providing a specific example from the theoretical writings of General Georg von Tempelhoff, who was commandant of the Prussian Artillery Academy from 1791 to 1806, Scharnhorst continued:

> Tempelhoff wrote an essay in which – beginning from a given number of bread and supply wagons – he listed all the movements that in his opinion an army could undertake. He took supply as the centripetal and operations as the centrifugal force; they balanced at a radius of fifteen miles. This pretty equation made people forget a thousand contradictory experiences. The disease was so infectious that the soundest heads were affected.[107]

As Scharnhorst observed, such 'pretty equations' were also to be found in the doctrines of other European armies at this time, particularly regarding the functions and training of light infantry. *The Fundamentals of the Higher Art of War*, for example, which were issued to Austrian Generals in 1806, spoke of immutable rules of war 'which shall always remain the same because they are founded on irrefutable mathematical verities'.[108] The proliferation of 'irregular' warfare seen in America and Central Europe over the previous decades had not, it was maintained, altered the fundamental rules of combat. Skirmishing was dismissed as merely a new but subordinate element of battlefield tactics which did not influence the outcome of actions. 'Decision' still rested entirely on the operations of heavy infantry, deployed in the traditional, close-order formations.[109]

This was an extremely conservative theory and it was put forward repeatedly in the drill manuals of the Germanic powers especially. In 1796, for instance, the Archduke Charles issued a series of instructions to his generals in which he criticized their growing tendency to deploy entire units in skirmish order in broken terrain. Even light infantry units were not to be employed in this manner, he insisted, because it weakened the 'impetus of the attack'. Skirmishers, he asserted,

> lacked strength . . . unless supported by a formed body of troops giving them drive, persistence and steadiness. Regular, trained and solid infantry, courageously advancing with closed ranks at a rapid pace, supported by its artillery, cannot be impeded by scattered skirmishers . . . It should close with the enemy as swiftly and in as good order as is possible, overthrow him and decide the battle.[110]

Similarly, four years later, General Melas' Chief-of-Staff issued orders for the Austrian forces in Italy which directed that:

> In action troops must remember not to lose time with firing. Only a few tirailleurs are necessary to screen the front. If these are followed by troops advancing courageously in close-order, with bands playing, and keeping their formation, such an advance cannot be repulsed by an enemy fighting in open order.[111]

Likewise in the *Fundamentals of the Higher Art of War* published in 1806, the views put forward by Archduke Charles some ten years before were restated and officers were directed that 'One must always observe the principle that only a small portion of the troops may be employed as skirmishers while the main body remains as a reserve in close-order to decide the issue.'[112]

In other countries, too, social, political and traditional considerations were combined with objections on tactical, disciplinarian and organizational grounds to resist what many 'old school' officers saw as the unwelcome expansion of the light service with its peculiar dress and practices. In Prussia, prejudice against light troops persisted long after the Jena *débâcle* of 1806, despite official attempts to stamp it out. In an 1810 set of instructions for skirmishers serving with line infantry, for example, one finds the clause:

> If a skirmisher makes an error in close-order drill, he ought not to be disgraced or scolded with expressions that betray contempt for the light service. The commanding officers must strictly see to it that such things do not happen.[113]

Likewise, there were those in the British forces who regarded the light service with a certain amount of disdain. But here the objections levelled against light infantry were usually based on tactical and organizational grounds, rather than on the social factors that were so influential in Prussia and Austria. We have already seen how some senior members of the British officer corps believed that light infantry practice weakened a unit's discipline and led to 'unsteadiness' in action. And there were others, trained in the Frederickian school, who blamed the infantry's continuing adherence to the new – and, they argued, false – tactical doctrines evolved in America on the exaggerated importance acquired there by light troops.[114]

The most prominent critic of the 'new military modes, brought into fashion by the light infantry' was Colonel David Dundas. Born in Scotland in 1735, he first joined the Army in 1754 as a lieutenant fireworker in the Royal Artillery. In 1756 he became a lieutenant in the 56th Foot and saw extensive service in the Seven Years' War, fighting on the French coast, in Germany and the West Indies. Following the end of the conflict, Dundas began a detailed study of military thought and, over the next 25 years, made repeated visits to the great annual manoeuvres held by the Prussians. Supplementing ideas he gathered there with material based on his own combat experience, he devised a system of drill and manoeuvres for use by the British forces and, in 1788, had the work published.[115]

This manual was, as will be explained in more detail in the next chapter, to form the basis of the British infantry's drill throughout the period we are concerned with, and it secured its author a leading position in the Army's hierarchy. A colonel since 1781, Dundas now enjoyed rapid promotion; being made adjutant-general in 1789 and a major-general in the following year. When war broke out with France in 1793, he was sent on active service and, after fighting with commendable skill in Flanders, Toulon, Corsica and Germany, returned to England in 1796. Promoted to lieutenant-general, he served as adjutant-general for a time before taking part in the 1799 expedition to the Helder. Once again he distinguished himself, and returned to receive further honours and appointments, notably the rank of general in 1802. Three years after this he retired, but returned as Sir David to serve as Commander-in-Chief from 1809 to 1811. He died in 1820.

Dundas's main aim in producing his *Principles of Military Movements* was to furnish the British infantry with a comprehensive system of manoeuvres based on Frederickian principles that, he hoped, would be imposed throughout the service in place of the great variety of drills that, as we shall see, were in use in 1788.[116] He was particularly critical of the looser, more open tactical systems that had once been the preserve of light infantry and which, in the wake of the American campaigns, had remained popular with many line regiments. Because of these 'new military modes brought into fashion by the light infantry', Dundas complained,

> There is a great danger in an *irregular system*, becoming the established one of a British army; and the most fatal consequence may one day ensue, if we do not return to a due sense of the necessity of solidity, effort, and mutual dependence, which it is the great business of discipline to inculcate and regulate.[112]

Thus, Dundas called for a return to the traditional principles of the Frederickian school of battlefield tactics and, like the Germanic theorists whose thinking he emulated, he saw light infantry as being only a subsidiary element of the Army with limited tactical roles: 'Their great province', he wrote, is to form advanced and rear guards; to patrol, to gain intelligence, to occupy the out-posts, to keep up communications, and by their vigilance and activity to cover the front, and ensure the tranquility of the army – they decide not, nor are they chiefly relied upon in battle, although on many such occasions they perform regular and eminent service.[118]

'But', continued 'Old Pivot' as he became known because of his fetish for Prussian concepts, 'instead of being considered as an accessory to the battalion, they have become the principal feature of our army, and have almost put grenadiers out of fashion.' 'The showy exercise, the airy dress', he added with more than a hint of derision,

have caught the minds of young officers, and made them imagine that these ought to be general and exclusive. The battalions . . . have been taught to undervalue themselves, almost to forget, that on their steadiness and efforts, the decision of events depends; and that light infantry – yagers, marksmen, riflemen etc., vanish before the solid movements of the line . . .[119]

'There seems no reason', Dundas continued, why the light infantry

should not conform to the same principles of order and movement, as the battalion. The frequent dispersion and peculiarities which they are taught, should be considered as occasional exceptions. By their present open order and independent ideas, they are under very little control of their officers; and their practice seems founded on a supposition of the spirit and exertion of each individual, more than on the real feelings by which the multitude are actuated.[120]

In this last paragraph, Dundas effectively summarized the conflict between the conservative, methodical thinkers of the Frederickian school who saw the ideal infantry as 'moving batteries', and the growing belief that, instead, they should be thinking, free-moving and firing men, guided by a loose tactical system which was indeed founded on the 'spirit and exertion of each individual'. To the likes of 'Old Pivot', these new concepts were heresy which had to be suppressed[121], and, although battlefield experience – culminating in the collapse of the Prussian war machine at Jena – eventually provoked major changes in military thought and practice, many years were to pass before Germanic tacticians had, as Scharnhorst remarked, 'rid themselves of the evolutions of Frederick the Great's autumn manoeuvres'.[122]

In the British service, too, where Prussian doctrines had been embraced, the influence of the 'old school' continued to be felt throughout our period. In 1799, for example, General John Money, in calling for the introduction of large numbers of riflemen and other 'Irregulars' to combat those raised by the French, complained of the 'cheapness' with which such troops were regarded in Britain and of

Old jack-boot prejudices, which no argument, I fear, or example will remove . . . Till this new system of . . . Chasseurs be adopted by Austria or Prussia, whom we copy in most things, and have done for a century past, we shall remain just as we are.[123]

Similarly, as late as October 1809, one finds Major Davy of the Fifth Battalion of the 60th Regiment – a rifle unit – complaining that:

> The service of these corps has been so imperfectly understood in England . . . that they have, generally speaking, been modelled upon the systems of regiments of the Line, which is . . . inapplicable to them; and manifold inconveniences and difficulties have resulted from hence.[124]

Although, as we have seen, there had been intermittent surges of interest in light troops ever since the 1740s, it was not until the 1790s and the outbreak of the French Revolutionary Wars that the importance of such soldiers and their impact on tactics began to be fully appreciated. As Scharnhorst observed, prior to this period:

> Such troops were regarded as a species that could only be used for the protection of the army, to screen its wings and – in broken grounds – its front, not as an integral part of every order of battle. However, this defect was not really felt in major battles as most of them were fought on plains or around fortified positions, and because none of the armies possessed regular units for dispersed fighting. People therefore retained the forms that had been brought about by accident.[125]

The 1790s, however, witnessed a dramatic change in this situation. Since the Seven Years' War, large tracts of the European countryside had been transformed by a process of enclosure and, in the Polish insurrection of 1794 and throughout the 1790s, troops of the Frederickian school became steadily more aware of the limitations of their traditional close-order tactics. One Prussian officer, for example, alarmed by his men's inability to match opponents who had been dismissed as 'irregulars', commented:

> In the woods where the soldier breaks ranks and has no movements to carry out, but only to fire under cover of the trees, they are not only equal but superior to us; our men, accustomed to fighting shoulder to shoulder in the open field, found it difficult to adopt that seeming disorder which was yet necessary if they were not to be targets for the enemy.[126]

Indeed, the 1792 campaigns against the French in France and Belgium saw Austrian and Prussian soldiers struggling to perform their complex evolutions in wooded and enclosed terrain, against an enemy who had largely abandoned the tactical doctrines of the *ancien régime* and who employed substantial numbers of light troops as integral parts of their battlefield forces.[127] Over the previous months, largely by making a virtue of necessity, the French had adopted a more flexible tactical system. The Revolutionary government had removed scores of Royalist, regular officers and the loyalty of those that remained, like that of their regiments, was questionable. The consequent shortage of trained, disciplined troops, capable of performing the elaborate drills practised under the old order, coincided with the influx into the service of thousands of raw volunteers. The net result was a highly effective fusion of professional soldiers with barely trained men, inspired with national-ism and revolutionary fervour.[128] With the departure of hundreds of *ancien régime* officers, many subalterns, NCOs and ordinary regular privates who remained in the Army found themselves open to advancement in a way that had been generally impossible under the Bourbons – particularly in the light infantry and other sections of the service that had been shunned by the fashionable officers of the *ancien régime*.[129] These professional troops helped to shape the new Army by stiffening the masses of volunteers and providing the expertise needed in the technical branches of the service such as the engineers and artillery. Indeed, it was to the regular gunners of the old royalist forces who fired the cannonade at Valmy in 1792, that the revolution principally owed its survival.[130]

However, the masses of inexperienced volunteers also came to play an increasing role in the Republic's victories. Seeing themselves as free men, fighting in the defence of liberty, they seized on Rousseau's concept of the 'natural man' and rejected the discipline of the old order, turning, like the American woodsmen in the War of Independence, to independent skirmishing as their natural mode of combat. Indeed, there was little else they could have done under the circumstances. Denied sufficient time to receive anything but the most rudimentary military instruction before being flung into action, they were incapable of performing any kind of complex manoeuvres. Skirmishing and charges in simple columns were the realistic boundaries of their tactical capabilities.

As time passed, however, the volunteers and, later, conscripts of the French Army became seasoned soldiers[132] – earning the admiration of, amongst others, Arthur Wellesley, later duke of Wellington.[133] The *Règlements* of 1791 which formed the formal doctrine of the Revolution-ary forces were largely based on Guibert's *Essai de Tactique*, which had first appeared some 20 years before. Guibert's system permitted great tactical flexibility. Columns and lines were employed according to need, supported by large numbers of light infantry who screened the close-order formations and harassed those of the enemy. Such versatile co-ordination of close and open order units *on* the battlefield was very much a new development: light troops had ceased to be just an auxiliary arm and were playing an increasingly important role in major actions.

There are few better accounts of this co-operation between skir-mishers and troops deployed in regular formations than that left us by the celebrated French soldier Maximilian Foy. Although it is a general description rather than an account of one particular battle and is marred a little by romanticism, it remains none the less a vivid, eye-witness account of how the armies of the Republic conducted their early battles:

> The action would be opened by a cloud of sharpshooters, some mounted, some on foot, who were sent forward to carry out a general rather than a minutely-regulated mission; they proceeded to harass the enemy, escaping

from his superior numbers by their mobility, from the effect of his artillery by their dispersal. They were constantly relieved to ensure that the fire did not slacken, and they also received considerable reinforcements to increase their overall effect. It was rare for any army to have placed its flanks in impregnable positions; in any case every position presents natural loopholes which favour an attacker. Against such points the sharpshooters would concentrate their efforts, and *élan* and inspiration were not often lacking at such times amongst such troops. Once the chink in the foe's armour had been revealed, it became the focal point for the main effort. The horse artillery would gallop up and open fire from close range with canister. Meanwhile, the attacking force would be moved up in the indicated direction, the infantry advancing in column (for it had little fire to offer), the cavalry in regiments and squadrons, ready to make its presence felt anywhere or everywhere as required. Then, when the hail of enemy bullets or cannon shot began to slacken, an officer, common soldier, or, often a Representative of the People, would start to chant the 'Victory Hymn'. . . . The soldiers would begin to move forward as the drums beat the charge; . . . the sky would ring to a thousand battle-cries constantly repeated: '*En avant! En avant! Vive la République!*[134]

This system of tactics revolved around the employment of large numbers of light infantry who functioned independently on the battlefield as well as around its fringes, and it was to their efforts that the French chiefly owed their successes. As the armies of the *ancien régime* crumbled in Flanders before the Republican onslaught of 1793–4, Scharnhorst noted:

Probably never before has a greater number of light troops appeared on the battlefield than among the ranks of the present French army, nor has military history ever been given more irrefutable examples of the essential value of such troops than during this war. If the campaigns are studied, one may be tempted to maintain that, at least on the French side, this is entirely a war of light troops: the Republic certainly owes most of her victories to her light infantry.[135]

Later, in an 1811 essay on infantry tactics, Scharnhorst was to return to this subject and concluded that

. . . The French armies, compelled by the situation in which they found themselves and aided by their natural genius, had devised a system of tactics that permitted them to fight on open or broken ground, in open or close order, but this *without their being aware of their system*. In the Battle of Hondschoote, the actions at Dunkirk, Wervick, Tourcoing, the Battles of Mouscron and Wassigny, the attacks on the Weissenburg Line – everywhere in the autumn of 1793 they won because of their open order and *tirailleurs*. In the spring of 1794, the Battles of Courtrai, Mouveaux and Fleurus, were won in the same manner. Decisive actions fought in close order were rare, though not unheard of – they occurred only when it was impossible to gain the objective through skirmishers.[136]

This was certainly the case and over the following years the more versatile tactical system of the French helped them to secure a series of victories over the forces of the old order that culminated, in 1806, in the total destruction of the once mighty Prussian Army. The role played in the Battles of Jena and Auerstädt by the French light troops was identified by many military thinkers – like the Prussians Scharnhorst and Gneisenau, and the Austrian Archduke Charles – as being the prime reason for the Prussians' defeat.[137] Thereafter, they devoted themselves to reforming their respective forces to comply more with the French model,[138] and, as we have seen, the Austrian drill manual of 1807 and the Prussian *Reglement* of 1812 both introduced a generally more flexible system of tactics and earmarked the third rank of infantry regiments for training as skirmishers.

In Britain, too, the rise of the French *chasseurs* and their new system of waging war was to cause mounting concern throughout the 1790s and early 1800s. Founded on the Prussian inspired principles of David Dundas, the drill and tactics of the British infantry were just as Frederickian as those of the Germanic powers and, furthermore, the influence of the Prussian school of thought had left the service almost devoid of adequately trained light troops.

Given the trends in warfare taking place on the continent at this time, this state of affairs was exceedingly dangerous. 'I contend, (and shall, till I *am childish*)', wrote one astute British general in 1799, 'that we must be reorganized to fight the enemy on equal terms'.[139] Similarly, two years later, another officer commented with still more perception that:

> The French, since the Revolution, have so successfully introduced such a new military system, that it becomes impossible to oppose them effectually, by any other mode than adopting one founded on similar principles. They send a number of riflemen in front of their line to annoy their adversary, and conceal behind them the different movements of their columns: nothing can be effected against this disposition, but by opposing light troops to light troops.[140]

However, as was the case with the Austrian and Prussian Armies, it was to take several military disasters to sweep away the cobwebs of years of Frederickian influence and reveal to the British the need for tactical adaptability and innovation. The creation and training of light infantry corps capable of countering the French *chasseurs* and *tirailleurs* was to prove a long and difficult process.

CHAPTER II

The British Army and the shortage of light infantry, *c.* 1790–1799

Throughout our period, the general administration of the British Army was carried out by a remarkably complex piece of bureaucratic machinery. The regular Army's supreme headquarters was located at an office at the Horse Guards in Whitehall. The senior, permanent officers of the service, the Quartermaster-General and the Adjutant-General, were to be found here, along with the Secretary at War and a small, civilian staff.

The Quartermaster-General and the Adjutant-General both had extensive though ill-defined responsibilities in the fields of general discipline and administration, while the civilian Secretary at War was primarily concerned with the financial aspects of the service. The engineers and artillery were not, however, directly responsible to any of these officials, but were instead placed under the jurisdiction of the Master General of the Ordnance. This officer had, in addition, responsibilities relating to the dispensing of ammunition and weapons, and to the administration of the Royal Wagon Train. The actual movement of men and *matériel* was, however, mostly covered by the Secretary at War, except when the units were being shipped abroad. In this case, a Transport Board took control of affairs.

This irrational division of responsibility did not end there. Regimental colonels largely controlled the purchase of uniforms and other necessaries, whilst rations and animal fodder were issued by a civilian official, the Commissary General, who was, in turn, controlled by the Treasury.[1] Furthermore, the disposition of forces and the general formulating of strategy involved still more officials in what was already a hopelessly cumbersome administration. With responsibility for the militia and volunteers, the Home Secretary took a major role in planning the defence of the kingdom at a time when the danger of a French invasion loomed repeatedly. Moreover, in the absence of a civil police force, he constantly called on the regular Army for assistance in the maintenance of public order during a period of considerable economic, social and political upheaval. Consequently, thousands of soldiers were scattered throughout the British Isles in tiny detachments to support the authority of local magistrates.[2] Not only did this significantly reduce the number of troops available for other duties and thus weaken the Army's capability for effective intervention on the continent, it also had serious repercussions for the service's tactical efficiency: any attempts to bring together large formations of men for training purposes were drastically crippled; the standardization of drill and tactics became almost impossible and, further, British officers were deprived of any opportunity to practise the manoeuvring of substantial bodies of troops.[3]

At the beginning of the 1790s, two other ministers also vied with one another for the services of Britain's land forces. These were the Secretary of State for Foreign Affairs, who was supposed to oversee campaigns in Europe, and the Colonial Secretary who supervised military operations in the colonies. In 1794, however, a Secretary of State for War was appointed and he assumed responsibility for the direction of strategy in every part of the globe. His department and that of the Colonial Secretary were merged around the turn of the century and the office of Secretary for War and the Colonies was created, a post that continued in being for more than five decades. Nevertheless, although the reforms of 1794 removed the Foreign Secretary's Parliamentary responsibility for the formulation of strategy, his ineluctable interest in his country's military policy remained, as did that of his colleague the Home Secretary.[4] Consequently, rivalry between ministers for a say in the use of the armed forces continued, leading to a tendency towards compromises which were not always based on sound military reasoning and the involvement of yet more officials in the control of an army whose administration was already excessively complex.

The monarchy also exhibited considerable interest in matters relating to the armed forces. As recently as 1743, at the Battle of Dettingen, King George II had assumed personal control of the army, and George III was to exert appreciable influence on military policy during his reign, particularly after the appointment of his son Frederick, Duke of York, as Commander-in-Chief.[5] The holder of this post, which was only filled in times of war, was the principal military adviser to the crown. Although he did enjoy far-reaching powers and served as a source of the overall guidance that the service sorely needed, he did not have the complete control over the Army that his title suggested. The artillery and commissariat, for example, remained completely out of his jurisdiction and the division of the service's administration as outlined above was quite unaffected by the appointment of a Commander-in-Chief. Indeed, in many senses, he was just one more cog in a complicated machine.

Furthermore, that cog itself did not always function as efficiently as it might have. The office being one that was left vacant except in times of open war, from the departure of General Conway at the conclusion of the American War of Independence in 1783 until the outbreak of the conflict with Republican France ten years later there was no Commander-in-Chief of the British Army at all. Moreover, the eventual appointment of Jeffrey, Lord Amherst to the post did little to improve on the former state of affairs. Although Lord Amherst had exhibited reasonable competence, particularly during the Canadian campaigns of 1758 in which he played a leading role, he was, nevertheless, anything but equal to the demands of his new position. When he dutifully took office in February, 1793, the unfortunate man, seriously weakened by ill health, was in many respects even older than his 76 years. Hardly surprisingly, therefore, he carried out his heavy responsibilities with a decided lack of energy, neglecting many of them entirely, whilst leaving still more of them to the civilian Henry Dundas, the Secretary for War, and his colleague William Windham, the Secretary at War.

Although the Adjutant-General, William Fawcett, struggled to make up for the deficiencies stemming from Amherst's impotence, he lacked the authority to govern many important aspects of the Army's administration. The upholding of general discipline, the regulation and inspection of the training of the cavalry and infantry, and the appointment and promotion of officers were all supposed to be supervised by the Commander-in-Chief. If, however, through absence or neglect, that officer failed to carry out these crucial duties, they mostly passed under the control of the civil authorities.

This did little to maintain the military efficiency of the Army, and, furthermore, made it susceptible to excessive, political interference. Ever since 1688 when the crown had shown signs of intending to use the military to extend its powers, Parliament had viewed a standing Army as a necessary evil for which, on an annual basis, they grudgingly provided finances.[6] Blackstone, the pre-eminent eighteenth-century legal commentator, saw such regular forces as nothing more than 'temporary excrescences bred out of the distemper of the State, and not as any part of the permanent and perpetual laws of the Kingdom',[7] whilst the historian Hume described them as '. . . A mortal distemper in the British Constitution'.[8]

As a consequence of such attitudes, the Army was deliberately restricted to a minimum size and was scattered across the colonies and homeland in scores of detachments. Whenever, as in 1793, war erupted and the service needed to be enlarged, new regiments were hurriedly raised under the careful scrutiny of a suspicious Parliament.[9] On the return of peace, they were promptly disbanded again. Against such a background of mistrust and legal restraints, the expansion and improvement of the Army to meet the threat posed by Republican France was to be a slow and painful process.

Reform was to be opposed, too, from within the service. Even today the British Army is a collection of independently minded regiments rather than a unified, fighting force. At the end of the eighteenth century, however, this problem was a still more noticeable feature of the service. The Army largely mirrored the class structure of British society and, although its ultimate allegiance rested with the monarch, the aristocracy and landed gentry retained an effective control over the force: the regimental basis of the services's organization, coupled with the selling of commissions, generally prevented men from middle-class and poorer backgrounds from entering the officer corps; while the rank and file were recruited, largely on a bounty system, from the lower strata of society. Wealth, even of relatively modest dimensions, and social position were, therefore, the key factors in determining a man's suitability for service as an officer.

Consequently, the Army was effectively governed by a body of rich, upper-class individuals, each of whom saw his particular regiment as his own personal property and guarded it with jealous pride. Trying to control such a mass of factions was a difficult and often unsuccessful process at the best of times, but the inherent weaknesses in the Army's system of administration and the necessity to disperse the force in garrisons throughout Britain and her overseas possessions exacerbated the problem enormously. Scattered in innumerable contingents from the bogs of rebellious Ireland to the insurgent-ridden jungles of the West Indies, the Army, unsubjected to the guiding hand of a resolute Commander-in-Chief, and governed from a distance by a divided and feeble bureaucracy, rapidly deteriorated into a multitude of separate little entities. Each battalion adopted its own particular form of drill and manoeuvres, while such matters as standing orders and general discipline were invariably left to the whims of each regimental colonel, or his subordinates.

The foreign policy followed by the British government for much of the 1790s also contributed to the steady deterioration in the quality of the country's available land forces. 'The truth is', King George III told Henry Dundas, 'we attempt too many objects at the same time'.[10] Certainly, a series of ill-advised, overseas adventures, notably to the West Indies in 1794, led to the Army sustaining frightful losses of irreplaceable seasoned troops, mostly from disease. The cost in lives involved in maintaining substantial garrisons in other unhealthy parts of the globe such as India, together with losses due to outbreaks of violent domestic disorder, notably in Ireland in 1798,[11] served to push this figure still higher. 'In the year 1794', recorded one authority, 'there were "killed or dead in the service" 18,596 soldiers. And that in the two succeeding years there were discharged "on account of wounds or infirmity" no less than 40,639 men.'[12]

For a relatively small force like the British Army – it numbered less than 40,000 men in 1793, when war broke out with France[13] – this constituted a vast loss of manpower and, in view of the long period of intensive instruction required to train troops at this time, it could only lead to a serious decline in the quality of the soldiery. Furthermore, such instruction was itself proving more and more difficult to organize effectively. With approximately half of the Army's line regiments deployed in foreign parts at this time,[14] and most of the remainder dispersed throughout Britain – guarding coastlines, giving assistance to the civil authorities or simply maintaining a police presence – opportunities to bring several regiments together for advanced training were relatively rare. Unlike the French and Prussian Armies, for example, the British forces had no annual camps to exercise troops in elaborate manoeuvres and to give senior officers experience in the handling of large formations of men. Moreover, even if such camps could have been organized, the disintegration of the Army into a collection of dissimilar units greatly reduced the scope for useful training. As Captain T. Reide explained in his *Treatise on the Duty of Infantry Officers*:

> . . . We never had any general system of discipline, ordered by authority to be implicitly complied with; on the contrary, (a few review regulations excepted) every Commander-in-Chief or officer commanding a corps, adopted or invented such manoeuvres as were thought proper. Neither was the manual exercise the same in all regiments, nor marching in slow or quick time properly regulated. The consequences of which were, that when 2 or 3 regiments met in the same garrison or camp, they could not act in brigade or line, till the general officer commanding established a temporary uniform system.[15]

Thus, the decade of bad management and general neglect that the British Army suffered after 1783 joined with the inherent evils of dispersion to reduce the force to a lamentably poor condition. As Sir Henry Bunbury was later to write:

> . . . Men of the present generation can hardly form an idea of what the military forces of England really were when the great war broke out in 1793. Our army was lax in its discipline, entirely without system, and very weak in numbers. Each colonel of a regiment managed it according to his own notions, or neglected it altogether. There was no uniformity of drill or movement, professional pride was rare; professional knowledge still more so.[16]

The inept administration of Lord Amherst, however, did nothing to improve this state of affairs. Indeed, his two-year office as Commander-in-Chief only served to deepen the wretched muddle into which the British Army had sunk: basic discipline almost collapsed, the training procedures of the cavalry and infantry remained unsupervised and unregulated, and the overwhelming majority of officer appointments were based on nepotic or financial considerations rather than on military merit. As Henry Dundas later commented, 'Lord Amherst was a worthy and respectable old man, . . . but the mischief he did in a few years will not be repaired but by the unremitting attention of many.'[17]

With the retirement of the ailing Lord Amherst in February 1795, the reconstruction of the British Army as an effective fighting force was begun. The principal architect of the recovery was Amherst's successor as Commander-in-Chief, Frederick, Duke of York.[18] Born in 1763, the second son of George III, he had led the British Hanoverian forces in the Flanders campaign of 1793. Filled with youthful energy yet experienced and perceptive, the duke was ideally suited to the Herculean task that lay before him and in which he was to achieve very considerable success. So much success indeed, that Sir John Fortescue was later to cite him as the person who 'did more for the Army than any one man has done for it in the whole of its history'.[19]

At the suggestion of his father, York's programme of reforms was carried out at a slow but steady pace. John Watkins, the duke's personal secretary, recorded that:

> Error and abuse had for so many years prevailed, and been increasing in every part of the military administration: so that while a general reform was rendered absolutely necessary, it became extremely difficult to determine where the salutary work should begin . . . The King, who, ever since his accession, had paid particular attention to the constitution and management of the army, saw and lamented the corruptions which prevailed, but . . . he was unable to overcome the inveterate prejudices and habitual indolence of the persons in whom he was obliged to confide . . . His Majesty, however, was too prudent a man to recommend any sudden innovations of great magnitude . . . It was his opinion, that the important work of reorganising such a complicated machine . . . should be carried on progressively, to avoid raising the passions of the people against measures, the beneficial tendency of which they could neither perceive nor understand. To this sage principle . . . the Duke of York cordially acceded . . .[20]

The duke's Army reforms ultimately affected virtually every aspect of the service, ranging from recruitment to rations.[21] But here we are primarily interested in the changes York wrought in two main areas: the training and drilling of the regular infantry; and the composition of the officer corps. With regard to the latter of these two issues, we have already noted how from the outset the obtaining of a commission in the British Army was essentially dependent on a person's wealth and social standing. Subsequent promotion, too, largely rested on one's ability to purchase higher ranks and the amount of influence that the officer in question enjoyed over those in authority. This system did enable a few talented, young, rich subalterns like Arthur Wellesley – later the duke of Wellington – to secure rapid promotion. Indeed, as one colonel pointed out, 'An officer who had money could purchase up to the rank of lieutenant-colonel in three weeks or a month.'[22]

On the whole, however, the practice had an extremely detrimental effect on the quality of the Army's officers. '. . . Regulating military advancement solely by a scale of prices', wrote John Watkins,

> . . . was carried to such an excess of absurdity, that sometimes boys on the lower forms at school, and even infants in the nursery, were gazetted as lieutenant-colonels of regiments, to the detriment of veterans grown grey in the service of their king and country, and to the palpable deterioration of the profession itself.[23]

The deterioration of the officer corps was, indeed, palpable. By 1794 the purchase system had got completely out of hand. The government, compelled to raise a large army for the conflict with France, had, on the outbreak of war in 1793, set about creating new regiments on the usual *ad hoc* basis. Plenty of recruits were available and more than 30 new infantry regiments subsequently appeared, together with a number of odd companies and battalions.[24] But the policy of allowing any man, no matter how unsuitable, a permanent rank in the service in proportion to the number of recruits he raised soon proved disastrous. In a situation where simply securing a fixed number of recruits could turn an ensign into a lieutenant, a lieutenant into a captain and so on, wealthy men alone were able to pay the huge bounties necessary to secure the required quotas and gain commands.

Predictably, this did terrible damage to the Army's officer corps. Scores of men who neither knew nor cared about their responsibilities secured control of units to the detriment of professional, veteran officers of more modest financial means. The result was, as Colonel – later General Sir – John Moore told his father in a letter from the West Indies in 1796,

> . . .a total want of discipline and interior economy in the Regiments. . . .
> The Military spirit is now, I think, gone. The officers wish to be advanced, to get more pay and have less duty. . . . Little can be expected from men formed and led by such officers. They neither look up to them as officers, nor do they respect them as gentlemen.[25]

A few days later, in a report to his commander, General Abercromby, Moore elaborated on these views. Warning that the army was utterly demoralized, he continued:

> I fear the same fate will attend whatever troops are sent out, unless serious attention is paid, to get proper officers to put at the head of Regiments who re-establish discipline and inspire those under them, with some of the zeal and ardor [sic] which I am not too young to have seen – but which you must recollect so much better – to have existed in the Service. Such officers, I am sure, still exist in the British Army, tho' they are not to be found exclusively amongst those who have most money or most political interest.[26]

Again, six years after he wrote this letter, when he was busy searching for suitable officers to command the new light infantry regiments he had helped to establish, Moore advised the Commander-in-Chief that:

> . . . To have a tolerable army, it will be necessary . . . to take some strong measures. Some commanding officers, the state of whose regiments justify it, must be told to retire from the service, the duties of which they are unequal to. The command must not be allowed to devolve upon their majors, who may be equally incapable, but be given to officers of approved talents. One or two measures of this sort generally known would excite an exertion which at present is much wanted.[27]

There were others besides Moore who also noted the professional ignorance of many British officers who had gained their commands through political influence, wealth or intrigue, rather than by genuine military ability and good conduct. Sergeants on parade, for example, would often have to whisper the various words of instruction to their captains who 'would have been ashamed to have known [them] without prompting'.[28] Indeed, to many contemporary observers, the lack of skills of the Army's officer corps became a tragic joke. One satirical writer urged officers called on to exercise their regiment to

> get the adjutant or sergeant-major to write out on a small card the words of command in the proper order; and if you cannot retain the manoeuvres in your head, you may at least keep them in your hat, which will answer the same purpose.

'. . . Dry books of tactics are beneath the notice of a man of genius', he continued, and if

> . . . the major or the adjutant advises you to learn the manual, the salute or other parts of the exercise . . . you may answer, that you do not want to be a Drill-sergeant or corporal – or that you purchased your commission and did not come into the army to be made a machine of.[29]

In an effort to remedy the evils that prevailed in the officer corps, the duke of York introduced a number of important reforms. Firstly, he appointed a Military Secretary to serve as the sole channel of communication between the Commander-in-Chief and the rest of the Army. This helped to ensure that soldiers approached the senior officer of the service directly rather than through the Secretary at War or some other official outside the Army itself. Consequently, interference by politicians and other civilians in matters of discipline and other internal issues steadily subsided.

Secondly, the duke implemented major changes in the purchase and promotion system. The purchasing of commissions could not be abolished completely; it was too sacred a tradition in British military circles and, in a country where the possession of property was of supreme social and political significance, was regarded by many as a basic right. However, York succeeded in increasing the number of free commissions and, furthermore, decreed that no subaltern could be promoted to the rank of captain without having had at least two years' experience. A minimum of six years' service was required for promotion to higher ranks.

To improve the general education and professional knowledge of the officer corps, the new Commander-in-Chief founded a Military College at High Wycombe, around the turn of the century.[30] The first commandant of this college – which grew into the Staff College of later years[31] – was a Frenchman, General François Jarry. He had formerly been the head of the Prussian Army's Military School at Berlin and was destined to play a particularly important role in the training of British light infantry officers. Also established by the duke of York was a school for military cadets between the ages of 13 and 16. After completing a course of general education and professional training lasting four years, the cadets were granted commissions in the regular infantry or cavalry. This school eventually developed into the Royal Military College, Sandhurst.

Thus, the duke of York initiated a programme which was to lead to a substantial improvement in the quality of Britain's Army officers. But progress was gradual: some of the old problems persisted and, as late as 1803, General John Moore had to go to peculiar lengths to ensure that the training of the new light infantry regiments he was forming was entrusted to reliable officers.

The second field in which change was desperately needed and in which the duke of York instigated important reforms was the drilling and manoeuvring of the infantry. As we have seen, at the beginning of the 1790s the British Army had no standardized drill or manual exercise for its foot troops and, consequently, whenever two or three units joined together and attempted to co-ordinate their movements, complete confusion often ensued. This state of affairs largely stemmed from the battle experience the service underwent in the various campaigns on the American continent between 1756 and 1783.

The last major war Britain was involved in prior to the outbreak of hostilities with Revolutionary France in 1793 was the American War of Independence, 1775–1783. This conflict was, in many tactical senses, very different from the type of warfare most European states, including Britain, had grown accustomed to fighting. Thus, a whole new battlefield system had to be evolved for its conduct.

The first point to note about the war was the unusual type of terrain on which it was fought. Colonial America, at this time, predominantly consisted of forests, unchannelled waterways and great networks of agricultural enclosures. This clearly affected the manner in which troops could deploy and fight, and the close-order, linear formations normally utilized by all western armies during the eighteenth century were soon found to be hopelessly inappropriate. Thus, a much more flexible and open deployment was rapidly adopted.

Secondly, the numbers and types of troops involved in the American conflict were, relatively speaking, very limited. If, for example, we take the Battle of Blenheim – fought several decades before, but in Central Europe – we find that some 56,000 Anglo-Allied soldiers engaged 60,000 Franco-Bavarians, out of total available forces in the campaign of 100,000 and 150,000 men respectively.[32] If, however, we turn to the American War of Independence, we find that, for instance, the major clash at Yorktown in 1781 involved only some 34,000 combatants all told,[33] whilst more typical actions such as Princeton (1777), Hobkirk's Hill (1781) and Guildford Court House (1781) all consisted of engagements involving less than 7000 men and, indeed, except for the last one, as few as 3000.[34]

Equipped with only such tiny forces and obliged to operate in very difficult terrain, army commanders tended to spread their available troops out as thinly as possible in an effort to make the most economical use of them. In place of the traditional, three-deep firing line, a formation of only two ranks was adopted. This had first been employed by Generals Amherst and James Wolfe in Canada in 1759 – Amherst reasoning that, in terrain where cavalry could not operate, the thinner formation was perfectly safe for infantry use. 'The enemy have very few regular troops to oppose us', he explained, 'and no yelling of Indians, or fire of Canadians, can possibly withstand two ranks, if the men are silent, attentive, and obedient to their officers.'[35]

The two-deep line was a standard method of deployment for the light infantry of most European armies at this time[36] and its general adoption in America by the British led to other practices of the light infantry service being taken over by ordinary soldiers of the line. Operating on long, broken fronts in little detachments, all foot troops acquired the habit of scurrying about the battlefield in a light infantry style. The regularity and precision that was essential to maintain order and cohesion in substantial bodies of soldiers was rapidly lost, as speed of manoeuvre became all-important. As Colonal David Dundas, one of the greatest critics of this development was later to write: ' . . . The facility of dancing about a small body has deluded many, who if they had large numbers to direct, would have found the necessity of method, and of more order in their operations.'[37]

The practice of dispersion was further encouraged by the almost total absence of artillery and, still more important, cavalry. Under normal circumstances, an infantry battle-line with large gaps between units and the regiments themselves deployed in thin formations with open files would have been a recipe for disaster. In the enclosed country of America however, such tactics were quite feasible and often necessary.

But this colonial experience left a lasting impression on Britain's infantry commanders and long after the American War was over and the principal theatre of operations was once more the relatively open terrain of Central Europe – where massed cavalry could easily assail any pockets of dislocated or disordered infantry – they continued to deploy their men two-deep, in loose, open orders; each battalion adopting its own peculiar style of drill. As Dundas was to comment:

> The very small proportion of cavalry employed in the American Wars, has much tended to introduce the present loose and irregular system of our infantry. Had they seen and been accustomed to the rapid movements of a good cavalry, they would have felt the necessity of more substantial order, of moving with concert and circumspection, and of being at every instant in a situation to form and repel a vigorous attack.[38]

Thus, by the late 1780s, the foot troops of the British Army had fallen into a form of organized, tactical chaos. With their colonial experience fresh in their minds and, doubtlessly, their imaginations caught by the exciting contents of Simcoe's *Journal of the Queen's Rangers* and

Tarleton's *History of the Southern Campaigns* – both of which appeared in 1787 and graphically described the important role of light troops in the struggle for the colonies – they perpetuated the tactical system they had acquired in America: one which was largely inappropriate to the European theatre. Furthermore, the absence of a Commander-in-Chief at this time meant that there was no official guidance on what manoeuvres and drill units were to use. Consequently, regiments were obliged to devise their own, which they did: drawing on foreign manuals, customary practice and devices of their officers' own invention. Thus, in 1789, for example, we find that the 17th Foot, at Chatham, was following its own peculiar system, whilst the 38th Foot at Shrewsbury, drew its repertoire of manoeuvres from a number of number of traditonal practices, none of which were enshrined in any formal regulations.[39]

Against such a background of ill-suited tactical doctrines, diversity and irregularity, a disconsolate Dundas was to note that:

> While the other nations of Europe have endeavoured to copy the lessons of the great masters, most of the alterations that we have made are not for the better; more founded on fancy and caprice than on the uniform, comprehensive and immutable principles which should ever direct the operations of great bodies, and of their component parts. . . . The thin order of formation (bringing more men into action where fire is now so material) has become the fundamental one in preference to that on a greater depth. . . . Most of our battalions are invariably well drilled, but no system regulates or connects their joint exertions. . . . It is only to be regretted that . . . a proper direction was not given . . . and that we concluded . . . leaving everyone in a great measure to follow his own mode and imagination.[40]

'Hence', Dundas concluded,

> our very thin and extended order to make more show, an affected extreme of quickness on all occasions, the running of one movement into another, . . . the different and false composition of columns, which each battalion at present adopts, the chance movement of the line . . . regulated by no fixed principle. The hurry practised by individual regiments becomes improper and impossible when acting in conjunction with others; confusion and inaccuracy follow; and time is consumed in endeavouring in vain to correct those errors which original method would prevent from ever arising. Our ranks are so thin, our files so open, and such intervals permitted between companies of the same battalion when in line, that all idea of solidity seems lost.[41]

Needless to say, this state of affairs caused increasing anxiety amongst the higher echelons of the Army's command structure. When there was no Commander-in-Chief in office, leadership of the service effectively devolved upon the Adjutant-General. However, he and the other military personnel at the Horse Guards had no authority to impose regulations on the force they nominally controlled and, furthermore, the government ministers who shared in the administration of the Army declined to interfere in such essentially professional matters.[42]

In desperation, the Adjutant-General, Sir William Fawcett, eventually appealed to the king himself and, in 1786, the first steps were taken towards restoring order through the issuing, 'By His Majesty's Command', of an official drill manual.

The *1786 Regulations* were a small-scale work, based largely on the Prussian General von Saldern's *Elements of Tacticks* which had first appeared in Dresden two years before and had been translated into English.[43] Von Saldern had served as an Inspector General in the Prussian Army until 1785 and his manual was primarily concerned with establishing basic, technical principles which would serve as a foundation for more complex drills. This was just the kind of work Fawcett was looking for, and the *1786 Regulations* did go some way towards achieving their limited aims, thus paving the way for the easier introduction of a large-scale official manual at a later date.

Such a work, however, was some time in appearing. As early as 1781 Lieutenant-Colonel William Dalrymple of the 2nd Foot had produced a book which he advanced as the basis 'upon which the field discipline of the army might be regulated'.[44] A deeply experienced soldier and an avid student of European military theorists, Dalrymple called for the standardization of the Army's tactics, and proposed a new system of comprehensive training that was largely founded on the 1776 *ordonnances* for the French infantry. Like David Dundas, Dalrymple believed that the American experience had undermined the importance and traditional solidarity of heavy infantry: massed fire and cohesion had been abandoned in favour of speed in manoeuvre; the usual three-deep linear formation had been superseded by only two ranks and those frequently deployed with dangerously open files. Whilst he agreed that such tactics might be applicable to certain colonial theatres, he was convinced they could only lead to disaster on a European battlefield; the enemy's cavalry and heavy infantry would easily overwhelm British forces using such methods.

But although there are traces of the influence of Dalrymple's tactical thinking in the *1786 Regulations*, the work that was to shape British infantry training and manoeuvres until well into the 1820s – and, indeed, beyond – was David Dundas's *Principles of Military Movements*. This book, which first appeared in 1788, was highly critical of the irregularity and diversity that had characterized the infantry's drill for so long and, like Dalrymple's *Tacticks*, highlighted the increasingly widespread influence of the faulty tactical procedures that had stemmed from colonial experience. Most importantly from our point of view, however, was Dundas's attack on what he saw as the exaggerated importance that light infantry – with their 'independent modes' – had acquired because of that experience: '. . . Instead of being considered as an accessory to the battalion', he wrote,

they have become the principal feature in our army, and have almost put grenadiers out of fashion. . . . The [heavy] battalions . . . have been taught to undervalue themselves, almost to forget, that on their steadiness and efforts, the decision of events depends; and that light infantry – yagers, marksmen, rifleman etc., vanish before the solid movements of the line.[45]

It is interesting to note that, in addition to these comments on light troops, Dundas's *Principles* did not include *any* instructions for the specialist training of skirmishers, though he did briefly acknowledge their importance in certain select operations.[46]

We saw in Chapter I how many soldiers educated in traditional schools of thought regarded light troops as irregulars and military misfits that failed to harmonize with the neat tactical evolutions that were carried to such perfection on the drill squares at Potsdam or, indeed, in Dundas's own *Principles*. The colonel's complaint that light troops had 'almost put grenadiers out of fashion'[47] revealed a great deal about his Prussian-based attitudes towards such soldiers and, when linked with his evident belief that they were in no way *élite* formations needing special training, betrayed a weakness in his perception of likely tactical developments in Europe. During the wars of Frederick the Great light troops had acquired major importance and, although their significance had subsided somewhat in the ensuing years of peace, in the 1790s and early 1800s the specialist skirmisher was to bring about a dramatic revolution in battlefield tactics. But Dundas, like the Germanic theorists he emulated, largely failed to foresee the importance that light troops would again take on in the event of a major European war. Whilst criticizing the loose-order tactics applied in the broken terrain of America, he overlooked the changes brought about in many parts of the European countryside by the enclosure movement. Frederickian tactics and drill were perfectly suited to the level heaths at Potsdam and in Silesia where the Prussian Army regularly held its manoeuvres, or to the wide fields of Phoenix Park in Dublin where Dundas's own system was first tested. But they were quite inappropriate to the wooded, enclosed terrain which by the 1790s covered much of Europe and in which, as the first campaigns against Revolutionary France demonstrated, light infantry would be crucially important. Light units, wrote Dundas in 1788, 'decide not, nor are they chiefly relied upon in battle'.[48] It took the sight of massed Prussian grenadiers being decimated by French skirmishers at Jena, in 1806, to shatter such views once and for all.[49]

However, on its publication Dundas's manual had a major impact on the senior officers of the British Army who had long been waiting for a drill book to supersede the relatively scanty, interim regulation of 1786. The comprehensive nature of the colonel's work and its comparative sophistication – it had 18 basic manoeuvres – eventually caught the imagination of the high command at the Horse Guards. With the backing of the king, Fawcett, the duke of York and other notables,[50] Dundas's drill was subsequently tested, slightly modified, and published as the *1792 Regulations*.[51] The most notable alteration made to the

original *Principles* was the addition of several clauses relating specifically
to the instruction of light infantry companies. However, this section of
the work was far from comprehensive. Only ten pages were devoted to
it – a tiny percentage of the whole book – and there was little in them
that could be described as specialist training.

Along with an updated manual and platoon exercise[52], which replaced
the fire-arms drill used by many British foot regiments since 1764, the
1792 Regulations became the back-bone of the infantry's tactical system.
Editions of these works continued to appear throughout the period we
are concerned with and, indeed, much of their content was retained in
official drill manuals until as late as the Crimean War. As well as the
formal publications issued from the Adjutant-General's office, a number
of private writers, notably Dominicus[53] and Smirke,[54] produced
simplified versions of Dundas's 18 manoeuvres. These more concise
explanations of the system proved very popular with trainee subalterns
in particular, for, as Henry Bunbury recalled, the official version was 'ill
written and led the large class of stupid officers into strange blunders'.[55]
Also of importance was a manual compiled by Major James Cunninghame and entitled *The Tactic of the British Army*. This was a large work
which examined each of the 18 manoeuvres in Dundas's system in detail.
The application of the evolutions to entire brigades was explained, and
the work was dotted throughout with useful hints and general
observations on the tactical system and its use on the battlefield.[56]

Thanks to the introduction of Dundas's manual, by the end of 1792
the whole of the Army's foot soldiery was following a standardized drill.
On his coming to office as Commander-in-Chief in 1795, the duke of
York ordered that 'every officer of Infantry shall be provided with a
copy of these Regulations', and this directive was reproduced in every
subsequent edition of the manual. Furthermore, having noticed that
some units were either wilfully deviating from the official drill, or were
misinterpreting it, the duke issued a set of General Orders in 1804,
upholding the *1792 Regulations* and directing that the 'strictest conformi-
ty thereto to be observed in every particular of execution'.[57]

Although Dundas's system had its critics – General John Moore, for
example, once complained about 'those damned eighteen
manoeuvres',[58] whilst Lord Lynedoch recalled the 'reluctance with
which the study of this new system was undertaken by those . . . officers
. . . who considered themselves too old and too wise to go to
school . . .[59]' – the *1792 Regulations* did provide the British infantry with
a comprehensive, uniform drill, and were warmly received by a host of
soldiers and military theorists. Now that all of the Army's regiments
were following one set of manoeuvres, units could come together and
act in unison without difficulty. In 1792, for example, a special camp was
established near Windsor to demonstrate Dundas's battalion drill to
George III.[60] Similarly, the papers of Earl Cathcart reveal that on 12 May
1794, regiments from his command and that of the marquis of Hastings

demonstrated to the prince of Wales the '. . . Brigade Exercises and Movements according the King's new regulations for infantry as prepared by Sir David Dundas'. This was, the earl explained, '. . . the first display of Brigade Movements in England'.[61]

However, as far as Britain's light infantry were concerned, the adoption of Dundas's Prussian-inspired system and, above all, his accompanying attack on the exaggerated importance of 'yagers, marksmen, riflemen etc'., did little to improve what was in fact an already deteriorating situation. Ever since 1771, British battalions of the line had one of their ten companies designated as light troops. In addition to these flank companies, certain whole regiments had, at times, also been called on to serve as light infantry. However, it is clear that the training and creation of such units was a purely haphazard affair. The records of the 90th Foot, for example, show that throughout the second half of the eighteenth century the regiment was raised to serve as light troops on the outbreak of war and was promptly disbanded on the return of peace.[62] British light corps were, during this period, generally regarded as irregular auxiliaries and were rarely kept in being except at times of open hostilities. Indeed, this was a widespread practice in European armies, as was the policy of employing foreign mercenaries, mostly Germans, as skirmishers.

As far as training is concerned, Houlding, in his excellent study of the British Army up to the early 1790s, comments that the specialized drilling of light corps was not begun until 'just beyond the close of [this] period'.[63] We have already noted that the *1792 Regulations* devoted only a few scant pages to the work of such troops and, before then, the last recorded case of substantial numbers of light infantry receiving any kind of practical, detailed instruction occurred at Salisbury in 1774. This was at a camp formed by Major-General William Howe,[64] who had devised a comprehensive set of light infantry tactics based on his immense experience in the north American campaigns. As one corporal who served at the camp recalled, 'The manoeuvres were chiefly intended for woody and intricate districts, with which North America abounds, where an army cannot act in line . . .'[65] Howe's system, with official backing, was practised by several regimental flank companies for some years,[66] but after the American War of Independence it faded into obscurity. The paltry clauses of the *1792 Regulations* were a totally inadequate substitute and, as Reide confirms in his *Treatise*,[67] were based on very different tactical principles from Howe's work.[68] Indeed, Dundas really sought to depress the popularity and exaggerated significance of what he saw as the hallmarks of true light infantry which, since 1783, had become increasingly prevalent in the British Army. There can be little doubt that this hostile atmosphere served to stifle the development of new comprehensive manuals similar to Howe's: apart from the brief study by Emmerich that appeared in 1789, the only book of instruction for specialist light troops that was to appear in England between 1783 and 1800 was, as we shall see, Rottenburg's *Regulations for the Exercise of Riflemen and Light Infantry* – and that was a translation from an original German work.

This lack of authoritative writings on the training and role of light formations was to contribute to a general neglect of such forces by the British high command at a time when they were about to become crucially important. Dundas makes it clear in his *Principles* – on which the Army's *1792 Regulations* were based – that he did not regard light units as being *élite* in any sense and did not believe that they needed instruction that was in any meaningful way different from that given to the rest of the Army's foot soldiers. This attitude was, however, based on misconceptions and the prejudices that many soldiers of the traditional Prussian school held against light troops in general. A true light infantry unit was not distinguished as Dundas evidently believed, simply by its use of open formations, a 'showy exercise', or the wearing of 'airy dress'.[69] Many British line regiments had, after the American War of Independence, assumed the trappings of light troops, but this was essentially a cosmetic change. In the absence of any models on which to form themselves and the lack of specialist drills and instruction to direct their efforts, they could in no sense be described as genuine light infantry. What Dundas saw as their peculiar and irregular movements were primarily symptoms of the general chaos that prevailed in the whole Army's training until after 1792.

Indeed, the preoccupation with the modes followed by light troops that Dundas referred to and criticized in his *Principles* was essentially more apparent than real. The British foot at the start of the 1790s was suffering from a total shortage of trained, specialist light infantry. As L. Butler concluded, 'At this period, the Light Infantry spirit and tradition, combining the individual action of the scout with the skill of the marksman, had practically died out in the British Army.'[70] It was not until Britain had been plunged into war with France and the inadequacies of her light infantry had been painfully demonstrated that efforts to revive that spirit slowly began.

The war of 1793 did indeed prove a bitter affair for the slowly reforming British Army, though not all the lessons it provided were to be grasped until several more years had passed. The duke of York's ill fated campaign in Flanders quickly revealed that the light infantry, far from being too numerous as Dundas had maintained, were both dangerously weak in numbers and remarkably inept at their trade when compared with the skilful French *voltigeurs*, *chasseurs* and *tirailleurs*. The functions of these French troops were described in the *Règlements* of April, 1792:

> While battle lines are being formed and batteries placed, the commanding officers order the light infantry to advance ahead of the line, so as to discover the positions of the enemy's guns and to diminish their effect. The light troops are placed in small thickets, behind hedges, ditches or small rises

according to the nature of the terrain. They are commanded to fire at the enemy batteries and to try to kill the gunners. These men do not form in troops so as not to draw artillery fire, but separate, benefitting from any feature that may afford them cover, and remain attentive so that they can quickly regroup at the firt signal of their officers.[71]

Just like the Prussian Army they had emulated – and which was to suffer the same fate, only on an infinitely greater scale, in 1806 – the British troops proved quite incapable of matching these skirmishers, and they and their various allies suffered heavily at their hands in the fighting of 1793. The Austrians, however, later argued that:

The war in Flanders, fought on terrain that was usually so irregular that it was not possible to attack in closed lines, had the unfortunate consequence of upsetting the ideas on the true method of attacking the enemy . . . Even by the line infantry, attack *en tirailleur* was almost the only method used . . . This misuse must be opposed, because it weakens the impetus of the attack . . . Regular, trained and solid infantry, if it advances rapidly in closed ranks, supported by its artillery, cannot be held up by scattered skirmishers. It should, therefore, refuse to waste time by skirmishing . . . It should close with the enemy as rapidly and orderly as possible . . . This is the method that saves lives; firing and skirmishing costs casualties and decides nothing.[72]

However, faith in such traditional beliefs had been severely shaken by the battle experience of many Allied troops. At the Battle of Hondschoote in 1793, for example, one formation of the duke of York's army, deployed in the usual three-deep lines, had suddenly come under attack from numerous '*Tirailleur-haufen*' who, using hedges and ditches for shelter, poured a lethal fire into the exposed, serried ranks of their adversaries. In keeping with the principles outlined above, the Hanoverian general in command of the Allied corps ordered his troops to advance with the bayonet. This they did, only to see their opponents retire, firing all the time, to a second line of covered positions. Eventually, the decimated Allies retreated to their original position, at which the French skirmishers moved forward to harass them once more. This pattern of events was repeated several times until the Allied contingent finally retreated altogether. The French *tirailleurs* sustained very few casualties in the action; the allies' total loss, on the other hand, was some 2650 rank and file, 100 officers and three cannon.[73]

The effectiveness of the French skirmishing tactics in the enclosed country of Flanders was thus clearly demonstrated, as was the Allies' inability to counter them. For their part in the campaign the British, who were totally lacking in specialist light corps, were compelled to rely on a handful of poorly trained flank companies and hastily improvised bodies of foreign riflemen.[74] As one British military theorist was to observe: '. . . From accounts given me by officers, . . . the greater part of the loss we have sustained was occasioned by the want of chasseurs. We shall certainly see, sooner or later, regiments of chasseurs on the permanent establishment of the British Army.'[75]

However, under the weak administration that was running the Army in the early 1790s, the lessons of the duke of York's campaign in Flanders were ignored and, evidently, forgotten. There does not seem to have been any effort to improve the training of the British light infantry, or even to augment its strength, until 1794 at the very earliest. This was the year of General Sir Charles Grey's expedition against the French possessions in the West Indies, whose seizure, it was hoped, would weaken France economically and simultaneously provide Britain with additional revenues to finance her European war effort. Grey arrived in Barbados in January and, after a brilliant campaign, secured control of Martinique, St Lucia and Guadaloupe.

However, matters soon began to go awry for Sir Charles. Slavery, an institution the British had yet to abolish, posed an immediate threat to the indigenous negro population of the islands and, supported by substantial French reinforcements, they turned on the invaders. Ravaged by a very unhealthy climate, the small British forces found themselves locked in a desperate struggle with hundreds of insurgents, backed by French regular forces. By the end of the year Guadaloupe had been lost, and only a constant stream of British reinforcements prevented a complete disaster and stabilized the situation. Nevertheless, the fever-ridden West Indies continued to prove a major drain on Britain's armed forces and thousands of irreplaceable troops were to perish there in the last years of the eighteenth century.

In his *History of the British Army*, Sir John Fortescue maintains that Grey, influenced by his previous experience in America, gave his regimental light companies a course of special instruction on their arrival at Barbados in 1794.[76] Butler, too, in his *Annals of the King's Royal Rifle Corps*, puts forward this theory and actually cites a quotation from an unnoted source that states that Grey sought to recreate the 'perfection of light infantry that was attained during the American War'.[77] It is possible, of course, that such a school did exist at some time in the West Indian campaigns. However, no reference to it occurs in any of the orginal sources consulted in compiling this work, including the correspondence and papers of Sir Charles Grey himself. Furthermore, given the serious state of affairs that prevailed in the West Indies – disease alone cutting down hundreds of men every week – it would seem very unlikely that Sir Charles could afford to indulge in activities which would best be conducted in a peacetime encampment rather than in an active theatre of war where every able-bodied man was desperately needed. Finally, it should also be noted that if this 'school' did exist it was probably little more than a short-term camp, giving a very quick, basic training in light infantry procedures. Any other considerations apart, the officer who supposedly had control of the school died, like many of his men, very early in the campaign on Guadaloupe – not in Barbados.[78]

With the exception of this school – which most probably never existed

– there were no moves to improve the light infantry of the Army until 1797 when the duke of York, in his new capacity as Commander-in-Chief, recalled his experience in Flanders four years before and issued a series of directives on the training of light troops. In addition to several copies of the *1792 Regulations* relating to light infantry companies being dispatched to every foot regiment, a circular to senior officers directed that:

> His Royal Highness thinking it highly expedient at the present juncture, that the Light Infantry Companies . . . throughout the whole Army should be diligently exercised, and prepared as much as possible in those movements and manoeuvres, which are more peculiarly adapted to them, than to the Heavy Infantry, is therefore pleased to direct, that you should give immediate orders for all the Light Companies, attached to the several battalions in the District under your command, to be frequently taken out, in separate bodies, and practised in firing ball at a mark and in such other different exercises as they are principally formed and intended for, when opposed to an enemy . . .[79]

By increasing the amount of light infantry training taking place, this directive could only lead to an improvement on the former situation. But as the *1792 Regulations* only contained a few brief clauses relating to the training of light infantry, the tactical capabilities of the flank companies inevitably remained limited. A detailed manual of instruction for light corps was still sorely needed.

Furthermore, there was no measure adopted to bring about a substantial increase in the numbers of light troops available to British Commanders. Many senior officers, particulary those entrusted with the defence of the south coast of England against French invasion, were deeply concerned about this shortage. The enclosures of Flanders had proved ideal terrain for the numerous French *chasseurs* and *tirailleurs* to operate on, and much of the south of England consisted of countryside that was essentially the same. The limitations of the rigid, linear drills of Prussian-inspired theorists like David Dundas had been all too clearly demonstrated in the 1793 campaign, and the painful lessons of a dozen actions like Hondschoote had been grasped by more than a few British generals and military thinkers. Referring to the war in Flanders, one such theorist wrote:

> Our operations were then carried, in the spring of 1794, into an open country near Cambray; the enemy then felt the superiority of our cavalry, and saw that their Irregulars, with which their army abounded, were useless, and would continue so, unless they could force us to make war in an inclosed country; and this they effected, by obliging us to return into Flanders to protect our magazines, and cover our communication with them: here the country is much inclosed, and here all their Irregulars could act. From that hour we were constantly losing ground . . . and in the short space of a few weeks, it may be said in a few days, those armies which had been acting offensively, were actually obliged to act defensively . . . From the moment

we commenced our sad retreat from Tournay, . . . nothing was to be seen but the enemy's Irregular Troops: this was owing to our having only small bodies of Irregulars to meet large ones, and to the countries being inclosed, which favoured their operations. To this cause, and no other, may be ascribed all our disasters in West Flanders, viz. a deficiency in Light Troops, and of that particular description called by the French *Chasseurs à pied*, and *Chasseurs à cheval*.[80]

By the spring of 1798, the British high command was engulfed by the fear that the fate that had befallen the army in Flanders four years before was likely to overtake the forces defending southern England should the French invade. '. . . The system of David Dundas, and the total want of light infantry, sit heavy on my mind', wrote Lord Cornwallis, 'and point out the advantages which the activity of the French will have in a country which is for the most part enclosed'.[81] Similarly, on 11 April, William Windham, the Secretary at War, had a meeting with General Clinton and 'talked about the state of defence of the country'. Clinton, Windham records in his diary, was 'full of apprehensions; deeply impressed with the deficiency of our force in every respect, particularly in the total want of Light Infantry'.[82] Such apprehensions were also shared by, amongst others, Sir William Howe and General John Moore. Howe wrote to General Cornwallis that '. . . A large body of infantry with a considerable corps of light infantry, are, I think, essentially necessary for the defence of Essex . . .',[83] whilst Moore commented: 'To prevent the progress of an enemy marching to Colchester when landed would require a great superiority of light troops . . . The country . . . is much enclosed and flat.'[84]

At this time, however, apart from the company that was attached to each battalion of the line, the British home forces contained no regular light infantry formations. Moreover, as the Flanders campaign had demonstrated, the flank companies themselves, being inadequately trained and weak in numbers, were a poor match for the powerful units of French *chasseurs* and *tirailleurs*. Indeed, the only unit in the entire British Army which at this time even approached being a specialist light corps on the French model was the Fifth Battalion of the 60th Regiment. As we shall see in the next chapter, this battalion was formed in the spring of 1798 by the amalgamation of several small, German units in British pay. Baron Francis de Rottenburg was appointed colonel of the new formation and under his expert guidance this corps of German *Jäger* ultimately became one of the finest units in the service. However, in 1798 the battalion was still in its infancy and barely ready for action. Furthermore, the terms of its commission dictated that it could only be employed on service outside the British mainland. Consequently it was of no use for the defence of southern England, although it did play a small role in the suppression of the Irish rebellion of 1798.

Throughout that year pressure steadily mounted on the British cabinet to strengthen radically the Army's light formations. But there was opposition to this idea from certain government ministers. On 11 May, the Secretary at War noted in his diary that it was 'Clear now that there is no general plan settled', and spoke of a 'Notion that we did not want light troops, because our troops upon the Continent had been victorious, whenever they had been tried against the enemy by themselves'.[85] Windham unfortunately does not identify whose peculiar notion this was, but it was clearly that of an influential senior official and was probably put forward by Henry Dundas, the Secretary for War.

As the minister most concerned with the armed forces, Dundas seems to have been remarkably slow to see the need for, and then to initiate, any improvements or augmentations in the Army's light forces, and was thus at odds with most of the service's senior officers. In October 1798, Sir John Sinclair, supported by no less a figure than General Sir Ralph Abercromby, put forward to Dundas a plan which amongst other things proposed a major set of reforms regarding light troops. The solitary designated company out of the ten was, in Sinclair's view, far too small a proportion. The establishment of every battalion of foot in the service was, therefore, to be altered, so that each had at least four companies of light infantry; the remaining six companies comprising grenadiers and 'battalion men'. In other words, under the colonel's proposals, no less than 40 per cent of a regiment would be composed of trained light infantry.[86] Moreover, Sir John thought that 'It would be also advisable to have some corps, particularly Highland ones, who are naturally active, to consist entirely (the Flank Companies excepted) of Light Infantry . . .'.[87]

These measures, Sinclair argued, were essential. Like Lord Cornwallis, he identified the success of the French armies as being due to their 'activity' and he felt that unless Britain made her own forces more 'active' by introducing large numbers of light troops on the French pattern, it would prove impossible to defeat the French on land.[88] The German powers would never alter their military system, Sinclair believed, and so Britain should 'show them the example, and prove its superior excellency'.[89]

At around the same time that Sinclair was penning his ideas to Henry Dundas, the Secretary at War also received a letter from General John Money on the subject of light troops. Money was an old soldier who ironically enough had concluded his distinguished military career fighting in the Army of the nascent French Republic. Retiring to England in 1793, he had been deeply impressed by the French light regiments and, like Sinclair, saw the success of the Republic's forces in Flanders and elsewhere as being largely due to the excellence and numbers of her *chasseurs*. Appalled by the relative weakness of Britain's skirmishers, he set his criticisms out in an open letter to Windham entitled *On a Partial Reorganization of the British Army*. The open letter was subsequently produced as a booklet in early 1799.

Money was deeply concerned by the ignorance of many British

officers regarding the nature and function of the French *chasseurs* – troops he himself had seen in action at close quarters. 'It is much to be lamented', he wrote to Windham,

> that officers of high rank in the British service, have not seen the great effect of Chasseurs . . . in the inclosed part of Flanders, and indeed wherever the British troops have been employed . . . I refer such officers to the accounts written by the French Generals, of the great use they derived from their Chasseurs, in every action of consequence that has been fought in this War, as also to officers in the British Army, who have served on out-posts. What was termed in this country the advancing *en masse*, by the French, was nothing more than very large bodies of Irregulars, which covered the country, in the front of their Armies, like an inundation. To their Irregulars, and to their Light Artillery, are the French indebted for most of the victories they gained. . . . The troops styled in France Chasseurs, are, more or less, to be met with in every service in Europe, except the British. The Austrians have many Regiments of them; the Prussians have them attached in a certain proportion to each corps; but the French, seeing the good effect of these Irregulars, have brought them more into the field than all of the Combined Powers together.[90]

Once on the battlefield, the *chasseurs* peformed a crucial tactical role. Should the French succeed in landing in England in force, Money warned, they would advance along the turnpike roads 'preceded and flanked by three or four thousand Chasseurs, and *Infanterie Legere*.' In time, they would encounter the British forces in a defensive position somewhere and then, Money continued,

> Their column would . . . halt; cannon would then be brought forward, and the Light Troops instantly commence a fire upon our out-posts; should we order our men not to fire but to charge with their bayonets? If so, great numbers of our men would be killed in the first attack; and the Irregulars of the enemy would fall back on their second line; that is the next hedge row: by this time our men would be so exhausted, so breathless, that they would be shot as fast as they came up and attempted to form.[91]

To illustrate the point further, Money gave an example from his own experience in the American War of Independence:

> In the action of Freeman's Farm, the 62nd regiment charged four times . . . quitting their position each time: the conflict was grievous to behold; the contest was unequal; the rebels fled at every charge deeper still into the woods; but when the British troops returned to their position, they were slowly followed, and those who had been the most forward in the pursuit were the first to fall.[92]

This, as we have seen, was precisely the tactical system employed by the French skirmishers in Flanders in 1793.

The alternative to attempting to drive away the swarms of galling light troops with the bayonet was for the defending force to draw in its advanced posts and 'trust in its cannon and position'. 'The enemy in that case', Money continued, would examine our weak points; and the weak points are where we have most wood and small inclosures in our front; for there the enemy's *Tirailleurs* could approach within musket-shot of our men formed in battalion, and with impunity; that is, if we have no troops of the same description to oppose them, *and to fight them in their own way*.[93]

In this paragraph, Money revealed the two vital strands in his thinking of the French skirmishers' tactical system and how it might be effectively countered: the importance that enclosures and other forms of cover played in the *chasseurs'* operations; and the need for a substantial body of British light troops trained to fight them in their own style and to keep them from harassing defensive lines or units forming up to mount an attack.

Like most other theorists, Money recognized that dispersed foot troops, operating in open country, were in constant danger of annihilation by enemy cavalry. Since 1700, however, more and more of the European countryside had been enclosed and the scope for effective cavalry action had, in many areas, contracted severely. 'The face of Europe is much changed within the last century', wrote Money,

which has changed the mode of making war. All that can be said is, that the French have perceived it first. . . . With respect to England we are infinitely more strongly inclosed than Flanders, where the Combined Armies met all their disasters; and we have above 40,000 cavalry in this country . . .

'Is there between London and Harwich, or Ipswich', he continued,

any ground on which three squadrons of horse can form, without being in reach of musketry from the hedge-rows in [their] front and flanks? Of what use then, in God's name, is Cavalry, where they cannot form to charge, for if they cannot form they cannot charge. Will any Officer of Cavalry tell me he can enter a field of ten or twelve acres . . . when the opposite hedge-rows are lined with Infantry? No matter whether Chasseurs or any other Infantry: he certainly could not . . .[94]

Turning his attention to specific areas of Britain, Money observed that:

. . . the part in which the enemy was most likely to land was most favourable to their Light Troops, and was where . . . Cavalry could not act, or be of much use. . . . In a country similar to Kent, the army supported best by Irregulars, properly armed and cloathed, will carry their point whatever it may be.[95]

With regard to the British forces deployed for the defence of Kent, Money urged that:

. . . One fifth ought to be trained, armed, cloathed, and disciplined as Chasseurs; that is, one fifth of this army ought to be Irregulars. The hop-grounds are every year rendering these corps more and more requisite; and it is but too true that the country is daily increasing in impediments to Cavalry. This country is as much against them as any other in England,

owing to the smallness of the inclosures, the thickness of woods, the strength
of hedgerows, and, lastly, though not the least impediment, the hop-
grounds. It is true that there are many large inclosures in this country, where
Cavalry could act in partial attacks; but it is not likely that the enemy will be
such idiots as to come upon ground so evidently disadvantageous, expressly
to give . . . an opportunity of charging them.[96]

The general concluded, therefore, that:

Not less than 3000 Chasseurs are wanted in Kent to meet troops of that
description, which the enemy will undoubtedly bring over, if they come; and
as many are wanted in Essex, which is equally as inclosed.[97]

But many British officers believed that the battalion light companies
were virtual replicas of the French *chasseur* units and, therefore, whilst
some agreed that more troops of this description might be required, they
saw no need to give them any training above and beyond that which
they already received, or to equip and organize them in a new way.
Money, however, strongly disagreed: 'Chasseurs are troops indispensable with a great army', he had warned as early as 1794,

. . . particularly in an enclosed country, of which nevertheless some of our
generals have not the smallest conception. They tell me that our light infantry
answers every purpose of chasseurs, but officers lately from the continent
think with me, that there is no comparison between them.[98]

'British Light Infantry', he explained in his letter to Windham,

are not, in every instance, equal to the service performed by Light Troops,
distinguished as they are by the appellations of Chasseurs, Tirailleurs,
Tyroliens, Yagers, Sharp-Shooters, etc. Irregulars, in most services in
Europe, are furnished with a rifle . . . with which they are taught to fire with
great exactness . . . Will any British Officer, who knows the use of fire-arms,
say, that, with one of the muskets used by our Light Infantry, he could fire as
accurately at a mark, as with a park-keeper's rifle? . . . Chasseurs in foreign
service are taught never to waste a shot, and whenever they do fire, it rarely
happens but a man is killed or wounded: they are taught to conceal
themselves as much as possible; to creep from bush to bush, and if pressed to
run off, for retrograde motions are not deemed disgraceful to Chasseurs: in
short, a true Irregular is, or ought to be, in every respect an Indian, except in
scalping. A Light Infantry Man fires where he sees smoke, and continues
firing till he has wasted all his ammunition. This is nine times out of ten the
case. All of this proceeds from his not being trained as a marksman . . . When
a Light Infantry Man hears a ball pass him, which he has the good luck of
having escaped, he turns . . . and fires at random; instead of concealing
himself as a Rifleman would do, and looking for the man that fired at him.[99]

As well as these crucial tactical distinctions, Money also pointed out
other major differences between British light troops and the 'irregulars'
of continental armies. In the case of the latter, he wrote,

The officers are trained to know their duty, and the particular service
required of them; they look for promotion solely in their own corps, like our

artillery or marines. With our Light Infantry, no sooner has an officer learned a little of his duty, than he is removed to one of the battalion companies or grenadiers.[100]

On the question of clothing and camouflage, too, Money made some important observations:

> . . . A brave man will . . . fight well in any coat. No doubt of it; but the plain question is, whether . . . men, who are to be exposed to the enemy's experienced marksmen, should be cloathed in a colour so conspicuous, as to render every movement . . . obvious to an enemy? Or, whether any other colour would better tend to conceal . . . movements, and to save . . . men? A sentry becomes in a scarlet coat, a complete target to Riflemen. A grand guard, or advanced post in scarlet, are easily distinguished, and their numbers nearly ascertained at a great distance, even if they are posted in a wood. If they are cloathed in green, or dark brown, they are not discernible, but at a very short distance. . . . Not only the scarlet coat, which is the cloathing of our Light Infantry, but their white accoutrements, may be objected to for the same reason; they ought to be black. Their arms should not be bright, nor any glittering ornaments, no plumes or feathers, should appear on men . . . employed on the advanced posts of an Army, particularly in an inclosed country. The Austrians are in dark grey; the French mostly in green; the *Infanterie Legere* in grey or mixed colour. In Canada, during the American War, we had two companies of Woodsmen in dark brown, nearly the colour of the bark of trees . . .[101]

Having explained what he saw as the comparative strengths and weaknesses of the British and continental light infantry arms, Money came to the most crucial point of his work and analysed how the tactical system of the French *chasseurs*, when operated in enclosed terrain, could best be countered. Massed volley-fire at such dispersed and sheltered targets was completely ineffective and so, as we have seen, the remedy advocated by many officers of the Frederickian school was to drive off the hostile skirmishers with a determined bayonet charge in the traditional, three-deep linear formation. To employ such tactics was, however, to play right into the hands of the opposing light troops and the futility of such stratagems was repeatedly demonstrated until the Jena *débâcle* of 1806. Money himself had no illusions as to the ineffectiveness of such shock-tactics when pitted against firepower, and warned of their likely outcome: 'Before half your men are entered to form and charge', he wrote,

> those who were not killed or wounded, would either rush forward with fixed bayonets, or rush backwards; if the former the field would soon be strewed with dead men, it would be another Bunker's Hill. What then is to be done, may be asked, since you will not allow that . . . Cavalry can act in such [a] case, nor . . . Infantry charge with a prospect of success? Nothing, Sir, so plain; nothing so evident; meet them as you ought with men armed and trained, to dispute hedge-row after hedge-row; then whichever army has the best Chasseurs (supposing numbers equal) will prevail of course; those who have the most, will not fail of succeeding, judiciously disposed of.[102]

To provide the substantial bodies of light troops that he saw as so necessary, Money proposed a series of sweeping reforms in the organization of the British Army. Firstly, one fifth of the infantry of the line were to be formed into regiments of *chasseurs* on the French pattern. Men unfit for such service were to be drafted out of these units and replaced by soldiers drawn from the light companies of other battalions. Any vacancies created in the flank companies in this manner would, in turn, be filled by volunteers from the light infantry forces of the militia.[103]

Secondly, the general proposed that one quarter of the militia were also to be 'armed, cloathed and trained as Chasseurs'.[104] Furthermore, the Army's cavalry – largely useless as cavalry in enclosed terrain – would also have to undergo considerable reform. Money wished to make half of the light dragoons and the whole of the yeomanry cavalry into true dragoons, capable of fighting on foot, armed with short, accurate muskets and dressed in dark colours. They would then be grouped into 'Legions', consisting of some 600 dismountable dragoons, 200 foot *chasseurs* and some pieces of light artillery.[105] 'When all this is done', Money concluded,

> . . . you need not fear an invasion, or meeting the enemy in any part of Europe. . . . If, on the contrary, the Combined Powers adhere to the old system of fighting, and do not bring more light troops into the field, the enemy will penetrate into what country they can get a footing in . . .[106]

'Our want of well trained Irregulars will soon be seen and felt', he continued,

> though too late to remedy the evil.[107] . . . These are not . . . giddy, hasty, undigested reflections; they are not the productions of a young man, but one who has been 40 years a soldier. . . . I know that it is to this new system of bringing more Irregulars into the field than their opponents, that the French owe chiefly their success . . . Let us learn to fight them by land in the manner they have found out and adopted; never let us be above or ashamed following the example even of an enemy, when we see it is a good one.[108]

The system of countering the French skirmishers with troops of their own description was seen by Money as 'so evident' and, indeed, over the next few years other military theorists joined Sir John Sinclair in broadly supporting the general's views. General Jarry, for example, observed that:

> In such country as England, the greatest utility will be derived from a numerous, active and skilful light infantry, covering the positions and movements of the troops of the line, harassing the enemy's flanks and rear, attacking his detachments and convoys.

'If the French', he continued,

> attempt a landing in this country, they will, no doubt, endeavour to disembark a considerable body of troops of this description and, indeed, all

their troops are accustomed to fight *en tirailleur*. Their army will be constantly covered by sharp-shooters, concealed behind enclosures, hedges, trees, bushes, walls, houses, inequalities of the ground; they must be dislodged by a chain of English sharp-shooters, advancing under the same sort of cover . . .[109]

Similarly, John Macdonald, in his *Instructions for the Conduct of Infantry*, criticized the inadequate clauses of the *1792 Regulations* relating to the training of light infantry and pointed out that:

The Services of Light Infantry of all descriptions, such as Rifle-Corps, Tirailleurs, selected Marksmen, Sharp-Shoots, Hussars and Chasseurs, etc. now influence, so very considerably, the events and operations of a Campaign, that the formation, increase, and training of troops who act so decided and conspicuous a part on the theatre of war, are objects with which the security of the State is materially connected. This active and effectual force has been organised by the Enemy, on systematic principles of discipline, to an unprecedented extent; and the very essential services they have, in every instance, derived from these light troops have been fully adequate to expectations.[110]

'. . . Previous to general Action', Macdonald continued,

the fire of *Tirailleurs*, and *Chasseurs*, or *Marksmen* is of the *greatest importance*. The French have derived *prodigious advantages* from these descriptions, by *unsteadying* Columns and Lines, when deploying, previous to an action. These troops thrown out, cover and mask movements, while they annoy the Enemy beyond all calculation.[111]

However, despite the efforts of people like Money and Sinclair, it was not until a second series of battlefield reverses had demonstrated the growing importance of skirmishers that the Secretary for War began to take the calls for reform particularly seriously. When Sinclair first put his proposals forward, Henry Dundas did not even deign to reply.[112] When Sir John persisted, the minister eventually sent him a rather indignant letter, in which he denied that he had any responsibility for such matters and bluntly refused to bring the issue before Parliament, commenting that 'It would in my opinion be a strange place to discuss what ought to be the training or constitution of all or any part of His Majesty's troops', and advising Sinclair and his supporter, Sir Ralph Abercromby, to submit their views 'to the Commander-in-Chief in whose Department it properly is'.[113] Apart from any other considerations, this document illustrates the type of problems arising from the divided nature of the Army's administration during this period and the attendant confused allocation of responsibility.

Unlike his civilian colleague, the Commander-in-Chief was, however, anxious to respond to the calls for reforms and strengthen the Army's light infantry arm. The inadequacies of the drill for light troops contained in the *1792 Regulations* had been repeatedly attacked and the issuing of drill manuals to the service was one of the few fields of administration in which York had unbridled authority.

Determined to act on this important issue, York authorized the preparation of a manual devoted exclusively to the work of light troops, and in August 1798 the new drill book was published. Actually written in German earlier that year by Rottenburg for his newly formed Fifth Battalion of the 60th Foot, the *Regulations for the Exercise of Riflemen and Light Infantry* had been translated by William Fawcett, the Adjutant-General, into English. This work, which we will examine in more detail later, formed the basis of British light infantry tactical training for the rest of the period we are concerned with.

Furthermore, at York's instigation tentative measures were now being taken to try to increase the numbers of light troops available for home defence. Pressed by the military staff at the Horse Guards and the writings of theorists like Money, the Secretary for War slowly came to see the need for improving and strengthening the Army's light infantry forces. Finally, in April, 1799, a circular was issued from Whitehall to senior officers, containing 'copies of a letter from W. Secretary Dundas and its enclosures relative to forming, and keeping embodied in this Kingdom, distinct corps of . . . light infantry'.[114]

This was the first attempt made to create permanent bodies of troops composed exclusively of light infantry intended for use on the British mainland. Having called repeatedly for the formation of such regiments, many of Britain's military theorists and generals were relieved that steps were finally being taken towards this aim. However, the project soon ran into difficulties as the details of Dundas's proposals emerged.

In the first instance, the Secretary for War envisaged the new units being formed by the simple amalgamation of light infantry companies drawn from individual militia battalions. Certainly, this would have been a relatively quick and inexpensive method of achieving the objective. Unfortunately the legal complexities that governed the terms of service for militia men rendered the whole proposal quite unlawful and, after lengthy verbal and written altercations with the Committee of Lord Lieutenants of Counties, Dundas was obliged to abandon the scheme[115] and the units were disbanded.

Nevertheless, the Lord Lieutenants believed that:

. . . The object which seemed principally aimed at might be attained by training a given number of entire Regt's. . . . of militia, to the exercise of Light Infantry under their respective officers, and that . . . this might be done without any necessary breach of the constitutional principles of the militia . . .[116]

Again, however, the plan was undermined by legal complications, for only regular officers of the rank of general could lawfully court-martial members of militia regiments serving in the field, and this would clearly have led to major difficulties as far as the commanding and controlling of the units was concerned. Furthermore, General Sir Charles Grey, who had commanded the expedition to the West Indies in 1794 and was now serving as head of the Southern Military District, voiced a still more serious set of objections to Dundas's revised proposals: 'In short', he told York, by the annihilation of the Flank Battalions their great strength will be lost in the mass of the militia, and weaken the service very much indeed. Nor can it ever be made up by substituting entire Militia Corps – the proposition is impossible from my knowledge of the general discipline of the Militia, having had a good deal of experience of them – and I am sorry to declare . . . that, some Regiments excepted, the Militia are feeble in the extreme . . .[117]

In a second letter to the Commander-in-Chief, Grey expanded his views on the proposal to form light infantry corps by converting whole regiments of militia: 'As to the training of entire corps to the exercise of Light Infantry', he wrote,

I conceive it to be more feasible in idea than in practice, particularly in that active and fatiguing service, which British Light Infantry have so uniformly and honourably sustained. . . . I beg leave to ask where is the single corps in His Majesty's Service (even the best militia included) that can as a body sustain the exertion . . . to be trained as Light Infantry.[118]

Demonstrating the ignorance that, as Money observed, many British generals had regarding the nature of foreign light troops, Sir Charles then proceeded to attack the 'corps of chasseurs taken indiscriminately (as to the form of their men)' found in continental armies. If formed from militia units, he maintained, the new regiments would prove incapable of performing 'the active services and fatiguing long marches such as the British Lt. Infantry have been repeatedly known to undergo in wonderfull [sic] short space of time'. The light troops of foreign armies were, as far as Grey knew, unable to fulfil such demanding tasks and, if the new British regiments were to be formed and trained in the same manner as he believed *chasseurs* to be, then, he confidently predicted, '. . . Not one half of them would ever be up for service, at the moment of exertion'.[119]

Whilst Sir Charles' views on the nature of foreign *chasseurs* were largely based on ignorance and were open to question, his detailed knowledge of the state of the British militia was beyond doubt. Troops that were 'feeble in the extreme' were not, as he rightly observed, suitable candidates for light infantry training, and Grey's reasonings on the matter 'entirely coincided with those of His Royal Highness . . .' the duke of York.[120] The Commander-in-Chief subsequently informed the Secretary for War of the impracticalities attached to his scheme and the notion of converting militia corps to light infantry was abandoned.

But the project did have some significant repercussions. The experiment having failed with reservist units, regular battalions of the line were likely to be used in any similar scheme tried in the future and, as we shall see, this is precisely what was done; the 52nd Foot being the first line corps to be converted to light infantry. York and Grey also argued that flank companies from infantry units should continue to be brought together, to act as an *élite* battalion when necessary. Indeed, the previous year, the duke had seen such a step as an 'essential measure' and had had 'frequent communications with Ministers urging the adoption of it'.[121] As early as 1796 orders had been issued for the provisional establishment of such bodies, including flank corps composed of militia companies,[122] and during 1798 interest in forming light corps by such means had revived and grown. Henry Dundas, however, in the wake of the collapse of his project to convert militia units into light regiments and in view of the passage through Parliament of a bill which would permit regular corps to expand by recruiting directly from the militia, gave directions that all extemporized light battalions that were not composed of regular infantry were to be disbanded.[123] As such formations constituted the bulk of the available light infantry in Britain, the Secretary for War's directive provoked a storm of protest from senior Army officers and it was a measure that York himself 'acquiesced in with considerable reluctance'.[124] Indeed, over the next few weeks, the Commander-in-Chief made frantic efforts to create other improvised light infantry corps to take the place of the disembodied militia formations. Light infantry companies from regular infantry battalions were hastily grouped together; York's secretary directing Earl Grey, for example, that

> The Duke . . . is anxious that no time should be lost on forming the Flank Companies of the Regt's. comprising the 1st, 2nd and 3rd Brigades into two Battalions and desires that you will be pleased to give directions to that purpose forthwith.[125]

The habit of amalgamating flank companies into unified battalions was a long-standing practice in the British Army.[126] Officers favoured the system because it gave them a body of picked troops to call on, and it was particularly popular with 'old school' generals like Amherst, Grey and Howe, though it was still in use during the Peninsular War. On the whole, however, the practice had undesirable effects which manifested themselves in two principal ways.

Firstly, the very need to amalgamate light companies to provide commanders with substantial bodies of trained skirmishers was itself symptomatic of the Army's shortage of genuine light infantry corps, armed, equipped and instructed as such. The temporary expedient of grouping together detachments of what were often poorly trained skirmishers did not correct this deficiency. Indeed, as we have seen, many officers erroneously saw such units as the equivalent of the continental *chasseurs* and consequently failed to recognize the need for more specialist light troops in the British service.

Secondly, the practice severely weakened the battalions of the line that were called on to donate their flank companies to form these makeshift units. The grenadiers and light infantry were the *élite* sections of any battalion, and without them the parent formation was clearly enfeebled in terms of morale, experience and numbers. Moreover, denied the services of these specialist troops, the remaining centre companies were at a decided tactical disadvantage when pitted against a more comprehensive formation of skirmishers, grenadiers and ordinary line troops.

Probably the worst case of the detaching of flank companies occurred in 1794, when over 20 such units were removed from their regiments in Europe and sent to the West Indies as part of Sir Charles Grey's expeditionary force. Not only were most of these detachments themselves materially destroyed in the ensuing campaign, but their absence also served to cripple their parent battalions for several years to come.[127]

With no regiments of skirmishers available for duty in Britain having yet been raised and with Rottenburg's drill manual only just coming into common use, the light infantry of the British Army were barely more numerous or better instructed in the summer of 1799 than they had been some six years before. When the duke of York led an expeditionary force into action in north Holland in August, 1799, it soon became painfully clear that progress in the growth and development of the light infantry arm had been minimal. Other than a few inadequately trained flank companies, the only other corps of skirmishers available for service was the Sixth Battalion of the 60th Foot. Even this unit, however, promised to be of little use. Raised in July[128] – only weeks before sailing for Holland – it was inevitably weak in numbers and totally lacking in training.

Pitted against their old opponents, the French *chasseurs* and *tirailleurs*, this battalion – raised on the traditional *ad hoc* basis – and the other British skirmishers proved exceptionally inept on the battlefield and, as several diarists recorded, the consequences were appalling. At the Helder landing, for example, Sir Henry Bunbury recalled that:

> The enemy from the crests of the sand-dunes kept up a constant and destructive fire, while he was himself sheltered by their folds from the guns of the British . . . The loss of the enemy in killed or wounded was probably small: but the disadvantages under which the invaders fought necessarily exposed the three brigades . . . engaged to a serious loss of men; and a large proportion of the superior officers of the staff fell under the aim of the . . . riflemen. Two Lieut.-Colonels and about fifty men were killed on the spot: and Lieut.-General Sir James Pulteney, five field officers and nearly 400 others were wounded.[129]

Similarly, at the Battle of Bergen, fought on 19 September, William Surtees, for example, who was serving in a 'flank' battalion consisting of eleven regimental light companies grouped together, recalled that:

> . . . We soon got into a smart fire from the enemy's riflemen, which we found was the only description of troops, except a few artillery, that we had to contend with . . . They had greatly the advantage over us in point of shooting, their balls doing much more execution than ours; indeed it cannot be wondered at, for they were all riflemen trained to fire with precision . . .[130]

Amongst those officers cut down at the Battle of Bergen was the marquis of Huntley, who was 'struck with a rifle-shot in the shoulder, whilst animating his men to the charge'. Likewise, in the fighting around Egmont on 2 October, General John Moore was hit in the thigh and face by French sniper fire.[131] Ironically enough, he was destined to play an important role in the later formation of British light infantry corps to match those of the French.

However, by far the most perceptive eye-witness account of the operation of the French light infantry in the 1799 Holland campaign was left us by John Watkins, York's private secretary. He observed that the fighting took place on terrain that was

> most favourable to the French mode of making war . . . Our system . . . and favourite weapon were now of little use. The movement of solid lines, and the imposing aspect of a charge of bayonets, could not be injurious to troops scattered over an immense surface, and frequently acting in small detached bodies, which alternatively occupied and abandoned the eminences, and were always protected by the long and mischievous shots of lurking riflemen. The principle of the latter was only to fire, hide, or run, as self-preservation, assisted by skill and enterprise, dictated.[132]

In comparison, one officer of the 92nd Foot noted that the British light troops seemed to be 'perfectly unacquainted with the system of sharp-shooting (and it is impossible not to lament the want of that species of warfare in our army)',[133] while Sir Henry Bunbury remarked that '. . . The French were more practised soldiers, and more alert and intelligent in turning to account every little wave on this great sand sea . . .'[134]

Thus, as in 1793, the weaknesses of Britain's light infantry were again forcibly demonstrated to the duke of York, as was the effectiveness of the French skirmishers. 'Observing the superiority of the French system', Watkins recorded,

> . . . [York] resolved to introduce . . . the rifle practice into the British service. This establishment accordingly took place after the conclusion of the . . . expedition . . . The new rifle corps was placed under Colonel Coote Manningham of the 41st . . . and Colonel Stewart of the 67th Regiment . . .[135]

As we shall see in the next chapter, this experimental corps of riflemen was to be the first of several light infantry regiments that the duke of York was to introduce into the British service. Like General Money, he had come to the conclusion that the only way to combat the French *chasseurs* effectively was by opposing them with large numbers of trained British light troops. A few weeks after establishing the new rifle corps, he issued a booklet of information and instructions to the Army's senior officers in which he stressed that:

> There cannot be too many light infantry established, either in companies or battalions. They are essential in the country we are to preserve, and when intelligently and well led, they will by their spirit, perseverance and exertion soon attain an ascendant over those of the enemy . . .[136]

CHAPTER III

The light infantry units of the British Army, c. 1790–1815

The 1799 campaign of north Holland having underlined yet again the need for better-trained and more numerous light troops to counter the French *voltigeurs*, the duke of York quickly redoubled his efforts to that end. Indeed, the closing weeks of the eighteenth century witnessed the initial steps of a programme which, over the next four years, was to lead to the creation of Britain's first permanent regiments of specialist light infantry.

In 1799, Britain's land forces had at their disposal a number of battalions which could be loosely described as light infantry; although none of them actually appeared under that title in the *Army List*. Practically all of these units, however, were unavailable for use in any European theatre as they were predominantly colonial regiments, formed specifically for duty in the region in which they were raised.

The most substantial concentration of these troops was located in the West Indies. Here, during the campaigns of 1794, the British – fighting in an exceedingly hostile climate, amongst dense tropical forests and across mountainous uplands – quickly came to realize the value of swiftly moving columns of light troops, capable of withstanding the rigours of both the climate and the terrain. No such European forces – other than a handful of poorly prepared, battalion flank companies – being available, slaves were withdrawn from the plantations, organised into units with European commanders and employed as light infantry on their respective home islands. In many senses, these regiments were classical examples of eighteenth-century light infantry forces. Given such titles as 'Drualt's Guadaloupe Rangers', the 'Carolina Rangers' and 'Malcolm's Rangers', they did not appear on the official *Army List*, were raised solely for the duration of hostilities and were, in general, regarded very much as temporary, irregular battalions. By October 1794, there were no less than 3600 mulattoes and blacks employed as skirmishers[1] and, by the end of the following year, this figure had risen to around 9000 men.

The ranger corps were formed exclusively for use on the respective West Indian islands on which they were raised and they soon proved to be amongst the most effective troops available to the British commanders in the Caribbean theatre. 'The Black troops', General John Moore told his father, 'are the only troops equal to scour the woods – the British are unequal to such service.'[2] Similarly, Henry Dundas, the Secretary for War, commented to one general:

> The English troops are inadequate for any length of time to the fatigue of long marches and other duties of the field, destructive to European constitutions in the West Indies . . . Whilst on the other hand, the native troops are better adapted to this mode of Warfare than for garrison service; the only duty on which the English . . . can be employed with advantage.[3]

Joining with detachments of light cavalry – and, sometimes, artillery – the rangers were frequently grouped into 'legions' of between 700 and 800 men.[4] These legions were, like those that had appeared in the American War of Independence, combined forces of all three arms and were perfectly suited to the independent, small-scale operations that characterized *la petite guerre*. They were also similar to the self-contained divisions which, largely at the suggestion of General Pierre Bourcet, were being introduced into the French service at this time. These were soon to form the organizational basis of all major European armies and, as they allowed for more flexibility in manoeuvre and greater speed of movement, led to a radical change in the conduct of campaigns.

The legions played a leading role in the war in the West Indies. 'I have had the honour to mention to you the great utility the British Legions have been to us', wrote Major-General Williamson to Henry Dundas in August 1794.

> Indeed, I may in a great measure attribute our success to them. It is impossible that regular troops can ever follow the Brigands into the mountains: they must have people somewhat of their own description to engage them.[6]

However, the situation in the West Indies steadily deteriorated and in April, 1795 the British supplemented the existing four ranger units with two new regiments of native troops.[7] These were raised as regular battalions, added to the *Army List*, and entitled the First and Second West Indian Regiments. The expansion programme continued at a rapid pace, with another six units – based on *cadres* from the existing ranger formations – being added in as many months.[8] Finally, the four original ranger corps were incorporated into the regular Army and entitled the Ninth, Tenth, Eleventh and Twelfth West Indian Regiments.

Whilst none of the West Indian regiments were ever officially dubbed 'light infantry', their functions during the insurgent period of the conflict on the islands was indisputably that of light troops. Indeed, there were even some attempts made to introduce rifles – almost exclusively light infantry weapons – into the corps[9], and this factor alone is strong evidence for the belief that these battalions were light regiments in all but name. Certainly, they performed their allotted role of skirmishers with considerable success and they can, with some justice, claim to have been amongst the first regular light corps of the British Army.[10] It is also interesting to note that such officers as John Moore and Coote Manningham – both of whom were subsequently to play prominent parts in the augmentation and education of Britain's light infantry arm – saw extensive service in the West Indies and, in the case of the former officer in particular, the experience gained alongside the rangers was to exert an appreciable influence on their later work.

In addition to the West Indian regiments, at the end of the eighteenth century the British Army had a number of other infantry corps which, broadly speaking, were light battalions; though, as in the case of the rangers raised for service on the Caribbean islands, most of them never enjoyed War Office recognition – either as light infantrymen or, indeed, as troops deserving to be placed on the published *Army List*.

This last point reveals a good deal about the nature of these corps and the manner in which they were regarded in British military circles. Firstly, all of them were composed of foreign nationals. The employment of provincials or outsiders as light troops was a fairly common eighteenth-century practice amongst European armies; notably the Austrian, whose *Grenz* infantry became, as we saw in Chapter I, a model for the first French and Prussian light regiments. German *Jäger*, particularly those from Hessen and Weimar, were regarded as some of the finest skirmishers in the world and were greatly sought after,[11] whilst Hungarian hussars enjoyed an outstanding reputation as light horsemen.

The British, in incorporating larger numbers of light troops into their armed forces had, as we have seen, lagged behind France and other European powers – most of whom had, at least, designated regiments as skirmishers even if, as in the case of Prussia, the distinction between light units and common line troops was only a superficial one.[12] But the practice of using foreign soldiers as skirmishers had extended to Britain – notably the use of Hessians and other Germans in the American War of Independence[13] – and, indeed, was to continue until beyond the end of the Napoleonic Wars. The great bulk of the light corps that fought in Wellington's Peninsular army, for example, consisted of Germans and other foreign nationals. Only a dozen or so battalions actually consisted of British troops and virtually all of these units had been created since 1800.

Thus, the light infantry units available to the British Army at the very end of the 1790s were almost exclusively composed of foreign troops and, indeed, several of them – like the West Indian regiments – were permanently based in one of the colonies, having been raised there. Frequently named after their colonels, who often had to pay for their upkeep, these small units were not dissimilar to the little bands of soldiers of fortune who, in earlier times, had wandered about Europe tendering their services to whatever king, prince or duke needed them and could offer them suitable material rewards.[14]

Indeed, a large number of the units in being at this time could be almost perfectly described in this manner. These included the 'York Fusiliers', 'Waldstein's *Chasseurs*', 'Löwenstein's Fusiliers', 'Hompesch's *Chasseurs*', the 'York Rangers', the 'York *Chasseurs*' and Bentinck's Corps of Dutch Riflemen. All but the last of these formations consisted of German troops and were amongst the 'corps of foreign riflemen' raised, rather hastily, by the Allies in the midst of the 1793 campaign in Flanders.[15] After the failure of that campaign, they returned with the British forces to England, though most of them were never added to the official *Army List*. Weak in numbers to begin with they were further reduced in size by gruelling service in the Caribbean, where they joined with the West Indian ranger battalions to form some of the legions described above.[16] On their return to England, all of them save the 'York *Chasseurs*' – who were renamed the 'Royal African Corps' and posted to Africa where, in 1807, they became the 'Royal York Rangers' – were banded together in 1798 to form the Fifth Battalion of the 60th Foot. However, due to the weakness of the various units that merged to create it, this corps still came to little more than a thousand troops.[17]

The remaining unit mentioned, the Corps of Dutch Riflemen, dated from November 1799. Following the duke of York's abortive expedition to Holland during that year and the subsequent Convention of Alkmaar, a substantial number of disaffected Dutch light troops returned to England with York's command. The recent campaign having highlighted the deficiencies of the British light infantry arm, a Mr John Bentinck grasped what he doubtlessly saw as a golden opportunity to form these Dutch *émigrés* into a body of riflemen and to offer their services to the crown.[18] By the end of November 1799, Bentinck had, at his own expense, assembled over three hundred *Jäger* and the new regiment was rapidly taking shape.

Regrettably for Bentinck, however, matters did not go quite as he had envisaged. The cost of recruiting, paying, equipping and feeding an entire battalion soon proved far too much for his limited resources and, contrary to his expectations, the government was not interested in contributing any significant sums towards the maintenance of the Dutch corps. Indeed, far from wishing to enlist new formations, the Secretary at War was, at this time, busy amalgamating the existing foreign units in British pay – such as those of Löwenstein and Hompesch – in order 'to reduce within the narrowest limits the amount of the Army Expenditure . . .'[19] The signing of the Treaty of Amiens in March 1802 led to further – and more drastic – cuts in military spending which extinguished Bentinck's last hopes of securing any significant governmental support for his unit. Having sunk deeper and deeper into debt over the previous two years, he finally went bankrupt and his rifle corps – which had flourished under the leadership of a Colonel Hyde – was disbanded, never to be reconstituted.

Despite its short life, however, Bentinck's battalion of Dutch riflemen did make a valuable contribution to the future development of Britain's light infantry arm. Having seen the corps on exercise in October 1800, the duke of York, greatly impressed, contacted Colonel Coote Manningham who, as we shall see, was at this time engaged in the assembly and training of an experimental unit of British riflemen. York directed Manningham and his senior subordinates to pay a visit to the Dutch corps, 'so that,' his secretary wrote, 'you may make yourself acquainted with the system that Colonel Hyde has acted upon, with a view of the same being observed in the formation and exercise of the corps under your command.'[20] Thus, Bentinck's *Jäger* served as something of a model for the later British 95th Rifles, and this raises the second important point that should be made regarding the employment by the British Army of foreign auxiliaries or mercenaries as light troops.

In the eyes of a great many British officers, the professional light infantry units that appeared increasingly in European armies after 1740 were, quite simply, something alien. Light infantry work – especially that of riflemen, as we shall see – was, therefore, regarded as the preserve of foreigners who had a better understanding of such matters and who had always served Britain well in this capacity in the past.[21] And, it may be added, to what better use could the motley collection of oddly dressed foreign troops that Britain had gathered from all over the western hemisphere be put? Little wonder then that prior to 1800 there was but a handful of units in the British Army that were capable of functioning as true light infantry and every single one of them was composed of foreign soldiers, stationed abroad.

Consequently, when the painful experiences of the 1799 campaign in Holland had underlined the need for more skirmishers, and Britain – increasingly isolated from her traditional recruitment areas for such troops by an ever more hostile international situation – was obliged to employ more British soldiers for such tasks, the shortage of suitable models on which to mould the new units, and the related lack of the expertise that was required for their proper training, were both acutely felt. General John Money, writing to the Secretary at War in 1798, had stressed the danger posed by the powerful French skirmisher forces in the event of an invasion of England and had called for the formation of corps of British *chasseurs* to combat them. '. . . Bills', he wrote a year later,

> had just passed both Houses of Parliament, to give almost an indiscriminate liberty for the people to arm; it was the moment I thought the most favourable to have organized corps of Irregulars such as would have been capable . . . to have held the enemy's Chasseurs in check on the instant of their landing. But alas! Sir, I reckoned without my host; for was it likely that country gentlemen, who knew no more of battles than what they read in the newspapers, would have adopted my plan, and formed their tenants into corps of Irregulars, of the use of which they had not the most distant idea? What is a Chasseur? they ask; what is his duty? If they had been called Irregulars or Riflemen, the same question would have been asked . . . It cetainly was not likely, when there is not a single model for them to have

been formed upon.[22]

Thus, the officer corps's lack of professional knowledge regarding the work of light troops and a shortage of suitable existing formations to use as blueprints for new units helped to retard the development of a truly British light infantry arm and perpetuated a traditional but, by now, dangerous reliance on a dwindling number of foreign auxiliaries. The painful lessons the British Army received on the battlefields of Holland during 1799 taught that this state of affairs had to be altered, and the Commander-in-Chief promptly attempted to rectify the problem by introducing more skirmisher battalions into the service. The opportune appearance of Bentinck's Dutch rifle battalion provided a timely example for the new units – beginning with Manningham's Experimental Rifle Corps – to follow and, as more fresh regiments were created, York placed each of them under the supervision of officers who had acquired the skills of the light infantry soldier through foreign service. These were to include Manningham and Moore, who had fought alongside the rangers in the West Indies; Stewart, who had observed the French and Austrian light corps fighting in Italy; Rottenburg, a German *Jäger* with a long and distinguished record of service in Europe and America; and Jarry, a Frenchman, who had presided over the Prussian Military Academy. Furthermore, the light infantry training manuals written by these last two officers and based on their service with the troops of other nations were translated into English,[23] thus becoming the first books of instruction on the subject to appear in that language since Emmerich had published his rather limited study in 1789.

In addition to the units examined so far, there were four other formations of foreign light troops serving with the British Army at the end of the 1790s and more were to be added over the next four years. The regiment of *Chasseurs Britanniques* was raised in 1794, when the British high command – finding itself encumbered with a mixed body of French *émigré* soldiers with which nobody seems to have known quite what to do – eventually decided to bolster Britain's dangerously weak light infantry arm by forming the refugee Frenchmen into a corps of *chasseurs*. In the face of the prevailing international situation, the unit inevitably suffered from a chronic shortage of suitable recruits and, whereas at this time a typical line battalion would number around one thousand bayonets, a report of June 1803 reveals that the corps mustered a total of only 524 men.[24] Indeed, had they been Germans rather than Frenchmen, it is probable that the *chasseurs* would, like the Hessian regiments of Hompesch, Waldstein, York and Löwenstein, have been amalgamated into the Fifth Battalion of the 60th Foot when that force was created in 1798.[25]

Over the next four years the formation shrank in size still further until, at the outbreak of the Peninsular War, most of its remaining men were descendants of the *chasseurs* who had originally founded the battalion.[26]

Bolstered by the ill-considered addition of French and Italian prisoners-of-war, the regiment was subsequently sent to the Peninsula where it was constantly ravaged by mass desertions and serious indiscipline.[27] Throughout its history the value of the force – except, perhaps, as a token, political gesture to the exiled Bourbon king of France and his followers – remained dubious. Indeed, in sharp contrast to the generally good service records of the Army's other light battalions, this corps seems to have been distinguished primarily by a chronic lack of training and good discipline.

The first of the three remaining foreign units in British service prior to York's expansion of the light infantry arm in 1800 – and that will be dealt with at this particular point – was, perhaps, the most bizarre of them all. When the British occupied Cape Colony in the September of 1795, they followed their usual colonial practice of enlisting men from the indigenous population to serve as light infantry. In this case, the corps raised was a formation of Hottentots who, having 'perfectly acquired the habit of soldiers and being excellent marksmen,' wrote Major-General Dundas, 'are qualified to render important service as light troops'.[28] The Hottentots were duly issued with the same green uniforms and other equipment that were already in use with Manningham's Experimental Rifle Corps.[29] Like most of the units we have discussed, however, they were never added to the official *Army List*.[30]

This was not the case with the last foreign unit that was in British service before 1800 and which we will examine here. As we saw in Chapter I, the 'Queen's Rangers' had first achieved fame as a formation of loyalist light troops, fighting under the leadership of Colonel John Simcoe in the American War of Independence. After the 1793 campaign in Flanders had illustrated the weaknesses of the British light forces, Simcoe's regiment was revived and placed on the *Army List* as a regular formation in 1794.[31] As in earlier times, however, it was a corps of foreign troops primarily intended for duty abroad, and after seeing mundane service in the western colonies the 'Queen's Rangers' were finally dissolved at the beginning of the nineteenth century as part of the Army reductions following the Treaty of Amiens.

Having examined the foreign light infantry units that were serving with the British Army before 1800, we will now turn to those foreign corps that were taken into the service after that date. The first of these was a body of Corsican soldiers who – much like the *Chasseurs Britanniques* or Hompesch's regiment – found their way into the British Army when their homeland fell under the control of their mutual enemy, France. When the British garrison evacuated Corsica at the end of 1796, a number of Corsican troops left with them. These were formed into a body of skirmishers by the then Captain Lowe – later to be Sir Hudson Lowe, governor of St Helena and custodian of the captive Napoleon. The unit served with General John Moore in the Egyptian campaign of 1801, but more or less disappeared with the signing of the

Treaty of Amiens. In July, 1802, Moore – observing Britain's steady slide back into war with France and disturbed by the acute shortage of trained light troops – drew the duke of York's attention to the Corsicans' suitability as skirmishers, and warned that in the event of renewed hostilities they could provide the best corps of light troops Britain would be able to field.[32] Nevertheless, it was not before the actual outbreak of war in 1803 that the Corsicans were added to the *Army List* and even then they appeared only as a skeleton, temporary unit entitled, quite simply, 'A Regiment of Infantry'.[33] In the October of 1804, however, they were rechristened the 'Royal Corsican Rangers' and under this title gave solid, if unglamorous service abroad until well beyond the end of the Napoleonic Wars.[34]

Another corps that spent much of its time on garrison duty abroad was the 'York Light Infantry'. Few documents relating to this force having survived, virtually all that is known about it is that it was a small battalion formed in England from French deserters early in 1803. Then, either to try to satisfy the Caribbean theatre's incessant demand for light infantry or, more likely, because of the unit's dubious loyalty, it was posted to the distant West Indies a few weeks before the Peace of Amiens collapsed. There the combined effects of desertion and Yellow Fever apparently led to its extinction within a few months.[35]

Two other foreign skirmisher regiments raised after 1800 were the light battalions of the King's German Legion. The origins of the legion date from 1803, when the French invaded the Electorate of Hanover and disbanded her armed forces. The duke of Cambridge who, in the name of his father, King George III, administered the electorate, persuaded the Commander-in-Chief to issue a warrant for the formation of a contingent of Hanoverians to serve with the British Army. The duke of York agreed to the proposal and by November the new corps had enlisted over a thousand former Hanoverian soldiers. Extending its field of recruitment to men of all European nationalities except citizens of France, Spain and Italy, the legion continued to grow in size, until, by 1806, when the Prussians marched into Hanover and prevented any further enlistments there, the corps numbered some 14,000 men.[36] Predictably, however, the formation was very much another body of foreign troops in British pay. Indeed, British subjects were not even permitted to join it except as officers and, despite the fact that the usual purchase fee was not required for commissions in the legion, only a handful of British citizens actually enlisted. Largely composed of mercenaries, deserters and impressed prisoners-of-war, the legion had a decidedly plebeian aura which did little to recommend it to the many socially minded members of the British officer corps.[37]

A mixed force of foot, horse and artillery – like the West Indian legions – the King's German Legion included several battalions of infantry, two of which were designated as light troops. Virtual replicas of the British 95th Regiment – which we will discuss in more detail later

– these skirmisher battalions had the same organization, equipment and weaponry. In addition to them, the light companies of the legion's ordinary line battalions formed another body of specialist skirmishers; being armed with rifles and given instruction as sharpshooters. Together, these forces proved to be some of the best light troops in the British Army and, in the Peninsular and Waterloo campaigns, were to acquire service records which were second to none.

The last foreign light corps to be absorbed into the British service during our period was the Brunswick *Oëls Jäger*. In 1809, Frederick William, the duke of Brunswick and a nephew of George III, raised a force in his duchy with a view to overthrowing the French administration in Westphalia while Napoleon's armies were preoccupied with the war against Austria. However, the project was a complete failure and, assisted by the Royal Navy, Brunswick and the remnants of his little army fled to England. Here, two regiments, one of them a light infantry unit, were formed.

Dressed in black uniforms, the Brunswick *Oëls Jäger* initially consisted of north Germans, officered by Prussians. However, because recruits could not be obtained from Germany a large proportion of the corps was subsequently composed of other nationalities, including French, Polish and Italian volunteers from prisoner-of-war camps. Needless to say, these men were prone to desert to their old colleagues at the earliest opportunity and, indeed, during the Peninsular War the regiment could not be deployed on outpost duty because of this recurrent problem. Nevertheless, the battalion did contain a nucleus of good quality *Jäger* and, throughout Wellington's campaigns in Portugal and Spain, made a useful contribution to his available light infantry force, frequently being separated into single companies and scattered amongst the divisions of the army to strengthen the brigade skirmishing lines.[38]

With the exception of the 60th Foot – which in many respects was a special case and which will be examined later – these units constituted all the foreign light infantry regiments that took service with the British forces at various times between 1790 and 1815. It should be noted here, however, that as well as directly employing many hundreds of Germans and other aliens as skirmishers, the British Army, rather than expand its own light infantry arm still further, frequently looked to its close allies to furnish sufficient numbers of such troops for its formations. This practice first rose to prominence in the War of the Austrian Succession, but it was still very much in evidence during the Peninsular War some 60 years later. In this – the largest and most protracted struggle undertaken by Britain's land forces during the period we are concerned with – the Portuguese Army's twelve *cacadore* battalions, each one thousand men strong, were constantly used to supplement Britain's own light troops; often being merged into brigades which were, in all other respects, British. Even the Light Division – the pride of Wellington's army – contained two of these Portuguese formations.[39] Clothed in brown, armed with rifles and trained on Rottenburg's drill, they proved to be excellent skirmishers and gave invaluable support to their British allies. However, by preferring to rely on the soldiers of another power as skirmishers instead of training troops of their own to perform such tasks, the British both extended and perpetuated what was already a dangerous dependence on foreign light corps.

It is now time to examine in more detail a regiment that dated from before 1800 and that has been mentioned several times in the preceding pages. This was the 60th Foot, the Royal American Regiment, which was created by a special act of Parliament in 1755. The formation consisted of colonial and other foreign recruits and was primarily intended solely for service in America; though its legal sphere of operations was later extended to cover any territory outside the British mainland. After distinguished service, the regiment rapidly increased in strength until in 1763 it had four battalions. Halved in size at the end of the Seven Years' War, it was transferred to the West Indies in 1775. Once here, two new battalions were added to the establishment but were promptly disbanded again at the conclusion of the American War of Independence. Four years later, the regiment was returned to full strength and, thereafter, its four battalions served constantly in the West Indies and Canada.[40]

In the spring of 1798, a fifth battalion was added to the regiment. The new formation was, like its sister battalions, intended for duty in America and was to be 'composed of Germans (both officers and men) to be incorporated from the several foreign regiments now in the pay of Great Britain, but which are to be forthwith reduced from the day of their incorporation respectively'.[41] The foreign corps alluded to were principally Löwenstein's regiment of fusiliers and Hompesch's unit of *chasseurs*. Some 30 officers and 600 men were provided by the first of these two regiments, 17 officers and 300 men by the latter.[42] In all, the new battalion totalled a little over 1000 rank and file, with the rest of the troops being furnished by the tiny units known as the 'York Rangers', 'Waldstein's *Chasseurs* and the 'York Fusiliers'.[43] The 5/60th was placed under the command of Lieutenant-Colonel Baron Francis de Rottenburg who, as we have seen, was the author of one of the Army's official light infantry manuals and was destined to be the trainer of several of the skirmisher formations added to the service by the duke of York.

Like its sister battalions, the 5/60th was raised specifically for duty overseas, and after a brief period in Ireland and the West Indies was based on the American continent until 1806 when it was recalled to Europe. Dressed in bottle-green, cut-away coats with scarlet facings, blue trousers, black leather helmets and black belts, the unit had become accomplished skirmishers under Rottenburg's expert guidance and was to give long and distinguished service in the Peninsular War. Like the battalion of Brunswick *Jäger*, it was invariably dispersed through the army in its separate companies to give additional strength to the skirmishing lines of the various brigades.

Whilst in most respects the Fifth Battalion of the 60th was an exact replica of the other component parts of the regiment, there was, however, one major distinction that was to set the battalion apart from the others and secure it a special place in the history of the British Army. As Henry Dundas instructed York: 'It is further His Majesty's intention that no difference should be established between this Battalion [sic] and the other four, except in what may arise from the manner of arming them with Rifles instead of common musquetes'.[44] It thus became the first regular battalion of the British Army to be equipped with rifled weapons and this marks an important step in the development of the service's skirmisher arm. For, in addition to the lack of importance that, as we have seen many of the more conservative minded British officers attached to expanding the light infantry in general, riflemen and their weapons were faced by a number of other economic, technical and tactical objections that severely restricted their entry to the service.

The first of these was based on the limited experience and technical expertise that eighteenth-century British gunmakers had in the production of military rifles. Captain T.H. Barber – who commanded a formation of militia marksmen and compiled a manual of instruction for the use of other such corps – commented in 1804 that:

> The Rifle Guns of America and Germany were formerly considered superior to those of any other country; and it must be admitted, that the long rifles of the Americans throw a ball 100 or 150 yards with more truth, than the military rifles of this country, notwithstanding their superior workmanship.[45]

Similarly, as late as 1808, the author of another authoritative work on the use of rifled weapons noted that:

> It is but within these few years that the rifle has been *generally* known in this country, although in Germany, Switzerland, and most parts of the continent, it was in common use. The consequence was that their manufacture was but little understood among us, and probably hence arose that predilection for foreign rifles, which even now has not subsided.[46]

Before we continue with the examination of these factors, some discussion of the weapons themselves might prove worthwhile. The standard muskets used by British infantry throughout this period were the 'Brown Bess' flintlock and a slightly different model of the same musket known as the 'India Pattern'. Both of these weapons had barrels of around forty inches in length, with a calibre of .75, and were fitted with a 17-inch, triangular-section, socket bayonet. The ammunition consisted of lead shot, weighing around three-quarters of an ounce, which were individually packed with a quantity of gun-powder in thick paper cartridges.

To fire one of these weapons, the musketeer took a cartridge from his hip pouch, bit off the end containing the shot, poured a small amount of powder into the flash-pan and emptied the rest down the barrel. He then inserted the shot and, using a ram-rod that was stored within the fore-stock of the musket, rammed it down the barrel with the empty paper cartridge on top to serve as wadding. When the trigger was pulled the small amount of powder in the flash-pan was ignited by a sparking flint and this, in turn, detonated the main charge in the barrel. A skilled musketeer might fire between two and three shots per minute under good conditions, but the loose-fitting bullets and other deficiences made the weapon extremely inaccurate. Consequently, the effective range of the musket was only around 50 yards.

The majority of units in the British Army that carried rifles were equipped with a pattern produced by Ezekiel Baker of Whitechapel. This model was selected for use after York had a number of British rifles tested at Woolwich Arsenal in February 1800. It had a 30-inch barrel of .615 calibre and, in place of the usual triangular bayonet, took a 24-inch flat sword, the grip of which fitted on to a spring-loaded clip on the side of the barrel.

The firing process for these muzzle-loading rifles was much the same as that of the smoothbore musket but, instead of using cartridges, two powder-horns were employed, together with loose bullets. One of these horns contained a special, fine-grain gunpowder that was used exclusively for priming the flash-pan. Whilst the ammunition itself fitted loosely into the barrel, it was used in conjunction with a greased, leather patch that gave the bullet a firm grip on the rifling. This rendered the fit very tight, and often small mallets had to be used to propel the ramrod with the bullet and patch down the barrel. Needless to say, this made loading a slow and awkward process, though the rifle's single shot per minute could be placed with much greater accuracy than the more rapid discharges of an ordinary musket. Indeed, some riflemen became extraordinarily good marksmen. William Surtees, for example, who was a veteran sharpshooter himself, recalls two of his colleagues in the 95th Regiment who, when practising, held 'the target for each other at the distance of 150 yards, while the other fired at it, so steady and accurate was both their shooting'.[48] It is unlikely, however, that, under combat conditions, many snipers could achieve quite such high standards of marksmanship.[49]

As well as the normal method of firing described above, in emergencies a rifle could be treated like a smoothbore musket to speed up the rate of fire and, for such eventualities, riflemen did carry a few ordinary musket cartridges amongst their usual ammunition. However, they were never used if it could be avoided, for the wadding and crude powder swiftly clogged the delicate rifle turnings in the barrel and, as a rifle at least, the weapon was rendered useless until somebody had performed the difficult and tedious task of cleaning the blocked grooves.

All of this helps to explain why rifled weapons were unusual at this time. When compared with the ordinary muskets used by most foot troops, such weapons were complex to manufacture and difficult to maintain in good working order. Quite sophisticated, breech-loading rifles, for example, had been developed in Britain as early as the 1740s.[50] The breech was formed by a number of converging plates that screwed open to allow the bullets to be inserted, and this mechanism enabled the rifle to be fired as many as seven times a minute, the need for the time consuming task of ramming the shot down the barrel having been eliminated. Captain Patrick Ferguson of the 70th Foot had devised such a gun in 1776 and had issued it to the small corps of sharpshooters he commanded in the American War of Independence.[51] However, whilst highly effective when in good working order, these rifles proved unsuited to the prolonged use and rough treatment they inevitably received on active service. Ferguson's gun was withdrawn from use after a few months on campaign, and although later gunmakers attempted to perfect their own models of the screw-locking breach for use in military rifles they were all thwarted by the practical difficulties involved. Ezekiel Baker, for instance, commented that

> I have tried various ways of loading rifles at the breech, by means of screws placed in different positions; but after a few rounds firing, the screws have become so clogged by the filth of the powder working round them as to be very difficult to move, and will in time be eaten away with rust, which will render them dangerous to use.[52]

The difficulties attached to maintaining rifles in a sound condition when on active service were not, of course, confined to those rifled weapons used by the British Army alone. For instance, in 1780 a Bartholomew Girandoni invented a remarkably sophisticated weapon that was quickly taken into service by the Austrian Army. This was the deadly *Repetierwindbüchse*. Drawing its power from a flask of compressed air that fitted ingeniously into the stock, this air-rifle was remarkably advanced for its time. Extremely accurate, almost silent and with an effective range that was comparable with that of the traditional flintlock rifles, it was even equipped with a magazine – containing no less than 20 rounds of ammunition – which made possible a rate of fire hitherto undreamt of. Indeed, the magazine could be emptied at a target in a little over a minute.

Employed in the 1790s by the Austrians, the *Repetierwindbüchse*, however, did not prove quite as successful as one might have expected. To compress the air in the flasks – and a new flask of air was needed every time the magazine was reloaded – a portable air pump had to be employed. However, the technology of the day proved incapable of furnishing a compressor of sufficient power that was, at the same time, small enough to be truly portable. Consequently, the device used was of heavy metal, six feet tall and far from ideal for accompanying fast-moving troops over difficult terrain. Furthermore, the complex rifles required all too frequent maintenance work and, in the face of these tactical and technical problems, the Austrians finally withdrew the gun from service in 1800.[53] Although it had been manufactured for around 20 years, the intricacy of the design had prevented any real attempt at mass-production. Indeed, only some 1100 were actually made – one of which, along with an example of the compressor, can now be seen in the *Heeresgeschichtliches Museum*, Vienna.

Thus, in Britain as in other countries, the relative complexity of rifles, coupled with the lack of the expertise needed to produce and maintain them, effectively prevented their introduction on a large scale. Generally, rifles remained the preserve of a few specialist, sniper battalions. Indeed, during the French Wars, several proposals to equip more British troops with rifled weapons were put forward, only to be abandoned because of the inability of the Army's ordnance department to supply the guns. Thus, in January 1804 for instance, the Adjutant-General had to advise one correspondent that

> . . . Even in the event of H.R.H. approving of the formation of Rifle Companies . . . there is little possibility that such arrangements could at this time be effected, as in a recent instance of a similar nature, it has been found impossible to obtain . . . the supply of Rifled Arms'.[54]

Similarly, whilst the duke of York was even prepared to approve the issue of such weapons to the light companies of some militia regiments, he was compelled to stipulate that the project be undertaken only if the guns could be 'conveniently furnished from the ordnance stores'.[55]

Indeed, the problem of obtaining adequate numbers of suitable arms to equip the Army's few rifle corps persisted for much of the Napoleonic Wars. Consequently, substantial numbers of men in existing regiments that were officially rifle units had to be issued with ordinary muskets,[56] whilst plans to create new rifle regiments were largely undermined by the shortage of appropriate weapons. This, for example, proved the case with the Sixth Battalion of the 60th Foot – the last light infantry unit the British Army formed before the close of the eighteenth century. Although intended as a replica of the Fifth Battalion, apparently only part of this formation was equipped with rifled guns.[57] Raised for foreign service in July 1799,[58] it saw action with York in Holland later that year before being posted to America with the rest of the regiment.[59] Along with all but the First and Third Battalions of the corps, it was finally dissolved in 1815.

However, even if the weapons were available from the ordnance department, the equipping of a unit with rifles was, for a very cost-conscious administration, an unusual step. Rifled weapons were considerably more expensive than the smoothbore guns employed by most troops. The German rifle used by the Fifth Battalion of the 60th, for instance – a model known as the 'Hompesch', an example of which can currently be seen alongside the Baker Rifle in the Light Division's museum at Winchester – cost the battalion between 32 shillings and two pounds each, and Baker's gun was still more expensive. For the same amount of money, two or three soldiers could be equipped with ordinary muskets[60] which, incidentally, did not require the leather patches, special powder and other items necessary for the loading and firing of a rifle. Clearly, it was a far more economical proposition to field soldiers armed with ordinary muskets.

Furthermore, the Baker Rifles employed by the British tended to consume appreciably more powder than their German or American rivals as they fired a heavier bullet. Typical American rifle ammunition, for example, was very light and as many as 30 or 40 bullets would only weigh one pound. The British shots, on the other hand, weighed nearly an ounce each and only 20 such rounds would weigh a pound.

This considerably greater consumption of metal and powder involved in the firing of each shot not only reduced the cost effectiveness of the British rifle, it also meant that the rifleman faced a bleak choice between two courses of action, either of which would, in differing ways, compromise his tactical flexibility and, possibly, his life. He could either carry sufficient ammunition for only a brief period of action, or be burdened down by several pounds of lead shot that would clearly affect his mobility. Moreover, as Captain T.H. Barber noted in his *Instructions for Sharpshooters*, the large charge of powder necessary to propel the heavy bullets used in the British rifles tended to result in a recoil of such force that the accurate aiming of the gun became somewhat harder.[62]

This brings us to the second and perhaps most important objection to the introduction of more rifles into the British Army. In addition to opposition based on economic and technical issues, many British officers had grave doubts as to the tactical value of troops armed with rifled weapons because of their slow rate of fire. In his work on the use of rifled barrel guns, Henry Beaufoy, for instance, warned that:

> . . . A rifle should begin where a musket ceases to be of use; and unless riflemen are kept at least 250 yards from a line of musketry, the latter will by their greater facility and expedition in loading and firing, drive the former out of the field; the number of balls from a musket being at least double or treble to those fired in equal spaces of time from a rifle.[63]

This inherent weakness of troops armed with flintlock rifles was clearly demonstrated on several occasions in the eighteenth century and noted by later military theorists. Colonel George Hanger, for example, who had spent seven years serving in the American War of Independence with Hessian *Jäger* and American woodsmen, commented that:

> Riflemen, as riflemen *only*, are a very feeble foe, and not to be trusted alone any distance from camp; and at the outposts they must ever be supported by regulars, or they will be constantly beaten in, and compelled to retire on the main army . . .[64]

In addition to providing examples from his personal experience, Hanger also graphically illustrated the point by citing the case of a clash between Colonel Abercrombie's British light infantry, armed with muskets, and Morgan's American riflemen in Pennsylvania. The moment the Americans appeared, wrote Hanger,

. . . [Abercrombie] ordered his troops to charge them with the bayonet; not one man of them, out of four, had time to fire and those that did had not time given them to load again; they did not stand three minutes; the light infantry not only dispersed them intantly, but drove them for miles over the country: they never attacked . . . our light infantry again, without a regular force to support them.[65]

This basic weakness of riflemen when opposed, unsupported, to ordinary musketeers at close quarters had a major impact on the thinking of many senior British Officers. Lord Cornwallis, for example, when asked for his views on the proposal to form an experimental corps of riflemen under Colonel Coote Manningham that was to serve as the prototype for other rifle units, wrote to Major-General Ross that:

The Duke of York has . . . asked my opinion on the formation of a corps of riflemen of 600 or 800 men . . . I have proposed that . . . only a tenth part of the corps should be armed with rifles, and that the others should be trained as light infantry . . . I quoted the instance of Colonel Wormb in America, who solicited that the rifles should be taken from a great proportion of his Yaghers, and that they should receive firelocks instead.[66]

Similarly, in a letter of 11 July 1803, the duke of York's military secretary replied to an officer who had proposed the formation of a body of volunteers 'to act as light troops, and to be armed with rifles', that:

I cannot help thinking that a corps armed with Rifles unless it is always supported, would be exposed in a very short time to be cut to pieces.

The Rifle as a defensive weapon is soon abandoned in the hands of a soldier when forced to retire, and except in *positions*, behind works or intrenchments, I own I am by no means an advocate for this arm *generally*. For this reason it was that the Austrians lost so many of their Tyrolean Chasseurs [in the] last war, when once broken in upon they were gone. In the trenches they were to be dreaded – in the field of very little use. Should it be determined that you should form a corps of . . . 500 men, I should recommend each company to have 5 men armed with rifles which in ten companies would give you a very ample proportion. The best marksmen might be picked out for this service – the rest of the corps to be armed with smooth barrels . . .

Independent to the objection to the Rifle as a defensive weapon, . . . you can fire with the smooth barrel, 3 shots to 1 of the rifle piece. I feel myself so convinced from all that I have heard and . . . seen, that no corps should be entirely composed of Riflemen. . . . I should always advise the proportion to be kept to, and the great reliance to be had on a good musket, reserving the Rifle principally for entrenchments.[67]

The Commander-in-Chief, too, had his doubts about the practice of creating whole battalions of riflemen. Whilst he acknowledged that small numbers of such soldiers 'when being properly armed and being encouraged to practise firing at a mark, might be expected to render the most important Service when called into the Field',[68] he told William Stewart, the lieutenant-colonel of Manningham's Experimental Rifle Corps, later the 95th Regiment, that:

. . . A Rifle Reg., from its composition, must always be subject to serve in Detachments and can seldom if ever act together as a corps. It is on this Principle, that a corps of Chasseurs, with a proportion of Rifle Men has been generally esteemed preferable to a Regt. composed wholly of Rifle Men . . .[69]

Indeed, Stewart himself came to question the notion of forming entire battalions, like his own 95th, of soldiers armed with rifles. In a series of reforms he first proposed in 1805, he wrote that:

. . . The plan of having light troops in whole corps, as is universally the case in foreign armies, should be adopted, as preferable to a company being assigned to each battalion of infantry, at present the case in our service. As riflemen . . . are merely the *élite* of light troops, their post on the right of each light infantry battalion appears to be more appropriate than in whole bodies, as in the 95th Regiment. This service is, however, open to much improvement, and if it were placed on the footing of a corps of science, a very different plan for the disposing of riflemen might be suggested.[70]

Thus, there were serious doubts within British military circles as to both the utility of troops equipped with rifled weapons, and how they should best be organized and deployed. A general study of battles within the Napoleonic period reveals that the companies of rifle units were, in accordance with some of the opinions presented above, invariably spread throughout the Army's brigades, rather than being kept together in a compact, regimental block. Indeed, the only British rifle corps that seems to have deployed battalions in a unified form was the 95th Regiment, which during the Peninsular War usually provided one such body for the famous Light Division. However, the remaining two battalions of the same regiment – like the overwhelming majority of the available riflemen – were invariably scattered in single companies throughout Wellington's army; and the Light Division being, as its name implies, *entirely* composed of light troops, was a very exceptional formation.

As well as these tactical, technical and financial complications that obstructed the introduction of more rifles into the service, there was one other significant factor that retarded the adoption of such guns by more units of the British Army. We have already seen how rifled weapons were largely regarded by the British as alien devices, the manufacture and use of which was barely understood except by the Germans and Americans. This helped to maintain a sincere belief amongst many officers that British troops were not themselves particularly adept in the duties of riflemen and that, wherever possible, Germans or Americans should be employed for such tasks. Colonel George Hanger – a veteran light infantryman himself, who had fought alongside German *Jäger* and had witnessed the marksmanship of the American woodsmen – summarized this view when, in 1808, he wrote to Lord Castlereagh criticising attempts to employ British soldiers as sharpshooters. Pointing out that an essential requirement of a good marksman was an ability to judge distances with great accuracy in order to level the rifle correctly, Hanger wrote

> Now the German *Jäger*, brought up in the forests to shooting at every thing, for the sake of practice, which presents itself, with the rifle from the age of fifteen, is taught all distances by the practice of years: for he can never offer himself to service . . . as a *Jäger*, unless he can produce certificates from the masters of the forests that he has served an apprenticeship of seven years, *and is a perfect shot.*

'A British soldier', Hanger concluded,

> *can never be taught to be a perfect judge of different distances* . . . Jägers from their natural servitude, and great practice, are in no want of being taught distances; the knowledge and precision of judging different distances comes to them naturally from practice, from their early youth.[71]

Thus, not only were there objections to the simple notion of arming any troops with rifles, there was also particular opposition to the equipping of *British* soldiers with such guns. German *Jäger*, although aliens and difficult to procure, were seen as naturally more professional and were, therefore, preferred to bodies of the nations's indigenous soldiers who had received relatively little instruction in the work of riflemen. This attitude was, of course, related to the belief held by many theorists that aspects of the work of light infantry could not actually be taught: some people, because of their professional, social and cultural backgrounds, were *naturally* more adept as light troops than others. 'What a host of military marksmen might we turn out in our sportsmen and gamekeepers', noted one British officer ruefully, 'were the practice of accurate ball firing encouraged, even without the ordinary military training.'[72] Indeed, as we saw in Chapter I, it was precisely to such social groups as gamekeepers that the Germans and French looked for the *élite* light infantry units of appropriately-called *chasseurs* and *Jäger*, adapting the natural skills of these huntsmen to military purposes.

If the composition of units is taken as an indicator, then the view that Germans made better light infantry, especially riflemen, than any other troops prevailed in the British service. Virtually all of the formations armed with rifles – the Brunswick *Jäger*, the Fifth Battalion of the 60th Foot and the light battalions of the King's German Legion – were composed of Germans and the majority of the Army's light troops in general were not actually British. Despite the addition of more British skirmisher formations to the *Army List* after 1800, this dependence on foreigners was to persist, particularly so far as riflemen were concerned. The reliance on Portuguese *cacadores* in the Peninsular War has already been noted and, indeed, the only truly British rifle unit to appear throughout the whole of this period was the 95th Regiment which, as we shall see, grew out of an 'Experimental Corps', initially intended to do no more than introduce British troops to the rifle and its role on the battlefield.[73]

We now come to the light infantry units that were added to the Army by the duke of York after his 1799 campaign in Holland had highlighted the weaknesses of Britain's skirmisher forces. The first of these new corps was a body of *élite* riflemen. The idea of forming such a battalion was initially put to the Commander-in-Chief in December 1799, after Colonel William Stewart had written to the Secretary at War outlining a plan for the creation and training of a body of skilled marksmen, armed with rifled weapons.[74] Originally from Scotland, Stewart had risen to the rank of colonel in the 67th Foot. As an observer attached to the Austrian forces in Italy in 1799, he had witnessed at first hand the fighting with the French there and had been deeply impressed by the growing importance of light troops, notably riflemen.[75] Well aware of Britain's lack of such marksmen, he proposed that a body of eight hundred men be 'formed from volunteers from infantry battalions and from the undrafted parts of the militia in Ireland.'[76] Like Sir John Sinclair who, in October 1798, had called for the creation of more light infantry units,[77] Stewart believed Scottish Highlanders and Irishmen to be the best indigenous soldiers available for the service in question, as 'being less spoiled and more hardy than [other] British soldiers, [they were] better calculated for active light troops.'[78]

The need to enlarge and improve Britain's light infantry forces being a matter of particular interest to the Commander-in-Chief at this time, Stewart's proposals were warmly received and within days were being circulated to the Army's senior officers for examination.[79] Much of what Stewart put forward was subsequently adopted and it was decided to place Colonel Coote Manningham – a veteran light infantry officer, who had served with distinction in the West Indian campaigns – at the head of an 'Experimental Corps of Riflemen', with Stewart as his assistant.[80] Accordingly, as early as 7 January 1800, the Adjutant-General wrote to Manningham that:

> The Cmd. in Chief proposes assembling a corps under your command . . . for the purpose of instructing them in the use of the Rifle, and in the system of Exercise adopted by soldiers so armed. I shall be very glad to have the pleasure of seeing you on this subject, and for that purpose I beg you to call at the Horse Guards as soon as you conveniently can.[81]

Manningham seems to have responded to this request with the utmost celerity, for, only two days after the duke of York summoned him to London to discuss the project, a circular was dispatched to 14 regiments of the line, calling on each of them to send four non-commissioned officers and thirty privates to a camp at Horsham to receive instruction in the use of the rifle and in the exercises used by troops equipped with such weapons.[82] The 14 regimental colonels were further directed that the detachments were to consist only of 'such men as appear most capable of receiving the above instructions and most competent to the performance of the Duty of Riflemen'.[83]

However, from the very outset the project ran into grave difficulties as the hapless Commander-in-Chief struggled to impose his wishes on jealous and independent-minded colonels. A full month after the original circular was issued, six of the regiments that had been sent the missive had still not complied with its contents and had to be prodded with a further directive before they finally consented to send the requested detachments.[84] Moreover, to many of the 14 colonels approached for contingents, the duke's orders provided an excellent opportunity to unload the 30 worst soldiers in their respective battalions on to some other unfortunate officer. Consequently, when all the detachments had eventually drifted into Horsham, far from having amassed a body of picked men 'most competent to the performance of the Duty of Riflemen', Stewart and Manningham found themselves at the head of what probably constituted the most despicable unit in the service.

On 22 February, York began the time-consuming task of trying to rid rid the new rifle corps of unsuitable soldiers. Letters had to be sent to no fewer than five colonels, advising them that *all* the troops detached from their particular regiment were 'unfit for Service' and were to be replaced immediately by 'good and serviceable men'.[85] Similarly, several more of the 14 regiments involved received complaints that substantial numbers of the troops in their contingents were, likewise, unsatisfactory for light infantry work and that good-quality replacements were required.[86] By means of such efforts, the duke of York eventually secured Stewart the kind of soldiers he was looking for. Nevertheless, April was well advanced before the issue of the new unit's basic equipment could begin.[87]

However, much to Stewart's disappointment, it soon became clear that the rifle corps was regarded very much as a temporary, experimental formation by the Commander-in-Chief and that its future was uncertain. When in a letter of 11 May, the colonel expressed the desire to see the corps permanently established and complained of what he saw as excessive interference in the internal arrangement of his battalion by the Horse Guards, the duke of York's reply was firm and pointed:

> . . . As the corps of riflement was formed of detachments from different Regt's. for diffusing a general knowledge of the Rifle throughout the Army and under the express condition of them rejoining their own Regiments, it is impossible from the Nature of the Establishment that it should be a permanent one, and it will necessarily remain liable to such further changes as His Majesty's Service judges expedient. The Com. in Chief is at a loss to judge on what ground you have founded your expectation of the permanency of the corps formed from detachments, . . . particularly as it was fully explained that the Officers and men continued in every respect to belong to the Regt's. from which they were detached, nor can H.R. Highness approve the terms in which you convey your sentiments on the arrangements which have by His Majesty's command been made relative to the Rifle Corps.[88]

Calvert concluded with the uncompromising remark: 'If under these circumstances, you prefer joining your R'gt. to continuing your services in the Corps of Riflemen, H.R. Highness has commanded me to signify his acquiescence.'[89]

Manningham, too, was anxious to see the rifle corps become the nucleus of a permanent battalion and he also expressed concern to the Commander-in-Chief over the temporary nature of the unit. Giving a basic education in light infantry procedures to a collection of detachments from other regiments was, in his opinion, unlikely to lead to the forging of a specialist formation with any real *esprit de corps*. A unified, permanent body of satisfactory trainees was essential if such a unit was ever to be created.[90]

Nevertheless, York's position remained unchanged, and in a letter to Manningham on 14 May he restated the views he had expressed to Colonel Stewart:

> Detachments are not to be considered as being draughted [sic] from their Regt's. but merely detached for the purpose above recited, viz being instructed in the use of the Rifle, and in the system of Exercise adopted by soldiers so armed.[91]

However, the arguments of Stewart and Manningham appear to have had some impact on the duke of York, for, in another dispatch from this same period, Calvert, the Adjutant-General, informed Colonel Manningham that

> I have laid your letter . . . before the Com. in Chief; H.R.H. agrees perfectly with you on the general principles therein laid down; but reverting to the peculiar Establishment of the corps under your command . . . H.R.H. perceives all the inconveniences you suggest, and your remarks may possibly furnish the groundwork of the Establishment of a corps hereafter; but the present is rather a corps of Experiment and Instruction and I trust its utility, and the progress it cannot fail to make, under your Col. Stewart's superintendance will ensure a similar one being formed on a permanent footing.[92]

Such a permanently established corps was, however, to be some considerable time in coming to fruition. At the beginning of July 1800, only a few months after its inauguration, the Horsham school was broken up and those few detachments that did not return to their parent battalions accompanied Stewart on the ill-fated expedition to Ferrol.[93]

On their return from this venture to England, the notion of an experimental corps of riflemen was revived and a new camp was formed at Blatchington, in Sussex, towards the end of August.[94] Stewart and Manningham were again appointed to superintend the training of the unit. However, the latter officer having now been made an aide to King George III, the amount of time he could devote to the rifle corps diminished appreciably and thus most of the work devolved upon Stewart alone.[95]

Under that officer's guidance, a specialist body of riflemen slowly began to take shape. Towards the end of September, 1800, in answer to his request, the duke of York finally granted Manningham authority to write to the various regiments whose detachments comprised the experimental unit, asking for permission to retain the men concerned on a permanent basis.[96] Most of the colonels involved subsequently consented to the implementation of the proposal. Stewart, meanwhile, busied himself laying the foundations of the new formation's codes of training and discipline: a list of standing orders was produced; regimental decorations for good conduct and valour were instituted; lectures and classes on light infantry procedures and combat drill were organized, including visits to the training sessions of Bentinck's Corps of Dutch Riflemen;[97] and daily target practice was introduced for the rank and file. To encourage a sense of competition and thus raise the overall standards of marksmanship, the riflemen were divided into grades according to ability – the finest sharpshooters receiving much coveted emblems to adorn their dark green uniforms.[98]

Apart from a few brief interruptions, the work continued throughout the coming year and the unit that had begun its existence as a purely experimental corps eventually became a fully fledged battalion of the line, the 95th. In February, 1801, Manningham sought permission from the Horse Guards to begin open recruitment to the new regiment, but the Commander-in-Chief refused his consent.[99] Fourteen months later, however, Calvert advised Colonel Stewart that '. . . The Rifle Corps will be open to recruit in Ireland, . . .' and recommended that an enlisting party be dispatched at once to 'some County Town where the militia are to be disembodied'.[100]

Towards the end of 1802, General John Moore – the officer commanding the forces in the Southern District of England[101] – sent Stewart an order for the movement of the rifle battalion to a new camp which, he told the colonel, he hoped could be 'adapted, both to your Target practice and Field Movements'.[102] The new base, at Shorncliffe, Kent, was, over the next few months, to become the venue for the instruction of several new light infantry units.

By now, Stewart's teaching programme had become quite advanced in its scope. The rifle corps's standing orders – initially compiled at Blatchington and known as the 'Green Book' – were enlarged upon, while, during the spring of 1803, Manningham delivered a series of lectures to the regiment's officers.[103] He also wrote to the duke of York requesting him to suggest a manual his men could study on the 'Scientific part of their profession'. The Commander-in-Chief subsequently recommended a 'Study and Explanation of a small treatise on the Science of Light Troops, which was compiled by General Jarry and published with H.R.H.'s sanction . . .'.[104] Indeed, during 1803 Jarry began giving personal tuition to groups of officers from the 95th at the new Royal Military College,[105] and his book on the science of light troops was to become one of the two principal manuals used by the

Army's light infantry.

Under the guidance of these accomplished instructors the 95th – Britain's first regular unit of indigenous troops to be armed with rifled weapons – steadily took shape and, in March 1803, Calvert, the Adjutant-General, informed Manningham that

> . . . H.R.H. looks with confidence to the Rifle Regiment being speedily brought to that degree of perfection, which is necessary to evince the expediency of adopting on a limited scale the arm by which the corps is distinguished.[106]

Indeed, the 95th Regiment did become a model skirmisher unit and was subsequently regarded by many as the finest corps in the light infantry arm.[107] The introduction of rifled weapons into the British forces, however, never extended beyond the 'limited scale' that Calvert spoke of. Whilst two more battalions, each of ten companies, were added to the 95th Regiment during the Napoleonic Wars, the rifle remained very much the preserve of a few specialist units – mostly German corps incorporated into the British Army more by accident than design.

Following the creation of the 95th Regiment, the next specialist light infantry corps to be formed under the duke of York's expansion programme was the 52nd. At the start of the nineteenth century, this unit was an ordinary regiment of the line, the 'Oxfordshire Regiment of Foot', the colonel of which was General John Moore. When the Commander-in-Chief resolved to augment the numbers of trained skirmishers in the Army, he approached Moore, amongst others, for his opinion as to how it should best be done.[108] The general subsequently replied that:

> . . . The Proportion of our Infantry which is to be made Light, should be calculated . . . upon that part of it only, which is kept in Europe. The service of India does not, I believe, require Lt. Infantry, and as for the West Indies the Black Corps will be found the best Lt. Troops – but until a system of Lt. movements is determined and ready to substitute for the present regular one, it will be advisable to confine the change to one, or to as few Corps as possible.[109]

Previous efforts to convert militia regiments into skirmisher units having failed,[110] Moore suggested that his own regular battalion should be the prototype for the new light corps and, according to the recollections of his brother James, further advised that these regiments 'should be practised as marksmen, with the usual muskets, and instructed both in light infantry manoeuvres and also to act when required as a firm battalion'.[111]

This blending of the light and line services to produce all-purpose infantrymen – the forerunners of the foot troops that constitute the infantry arms of modern armies – was, as we have seen, first suggested in the last quarter of the eighteenth century by theorists like Von Ewald and Guibert. Rottenburg also advocated it in his *Regulations for the Exercise of Riflemen*, directing that:

> . . . Before the soldier is instructed in the manoeuvres of light troops, he must be taught how to hold himself, to march, face, wheel etc. as in regular infantry.[112]

Thus, it was not an original idea that Moore put forward and, indeed, at much the same time that he was seeking to extend the practice to Britain's new light infantry corps, the Austrians and Prussians were already embracing it by designating and training the rear rank of their line regiments as skirmishers.[113]

At the beginning of January 1803, the Commander-in-Chief gave his approval to Moore's project and requested the general to provide 'some detailed plan as to the manner of carrying the measure into execution'.[114] It was eventually agreed that those men in Moore's battalion who were deemed unfit for light infantry work should be transferred to another corps in exchange for soldiers who were better suited to the 52nd's new role. This process was completed before the end of January,[115] and on the eighteenth of that month the regiment was officially retitled as the 52nd Light Infantry.[116] A pattern having now been established, York quickly issued a directive for a second unit of the line to be converted in similar style and, on 12 July 1803, the 43rd 'Monmouthshire' Regiment likewise became light troops.[117]

After some delay – caused by the inability of the Army's ordnance department to produce weapons that were in any way out of the ordinary – both of these units were equipped with short, lightweight fusils,[118] which were better suited to light infantry manoeuvres than the usual long, heavy muskets. However, as they were still considered as being essentially regiments of the line, they retained their traditional scarlet uniforms, no camouflaged dress being introduced as had been in the 95th Regiment. Nevertheless, to distinguish them from ordinary line troops, they were issued with shoulder wings and a tunic of a distinctive pattern.[119] Furthermore, in view of the nature of the service of light troops and 'their mode of acting in small divisions and in large order', a lieutenant, a sergeant and a corporal were added to the official establishment of each company.[120]

Several years after the conversion of the 52nd and the 43rd Britain's light infantry arm was, however, still dangerously weak and it was decided that several more units would have to be added to the existing forces. Accordingly, in September 1808, the Secretary at War informed the colonels of the 68th ('Durham') and 85th ('Buckinghamshire') Regiments that:

> His Majesty having taken into consideration that the proportion of Light Troops was much too small for the extended scale of the British Army, and that the utility of this Description of Force has been most eminently displayed on every occasion when they have been employed, and the whole of that arm

being at this moment embarked or employed on Foreign service . . . His Majesty has been pleased to command that two more battalions of the Line should be formed into Light Troops with all practicable dispatch, and that the 68th and 85th Regiments should be allotted for this purpose, and assimilated with regard to their clothing, arming and Discipline to the 43rd and 52nd Regiments.[121]

The last two line regiments to be redesignated as light troops during this period were the 51st 'Yorkshire' Regiment and the 71st 'Highland' Regiment. Both of these formations took up their new duties during the summer of 1809, following a period of training under Rottenburg.[122] They were subsequently clothed and armed in the same manner as the 52nd and 43rd. The 71st, however, as a Highland regiment, were allowed the distinction of wearing a tartan band around their shakos.

In deciding exactly which regiments of the line should be converted to light infantry, the high command seems to have been influenced by relatively few considerations. The selection of Moore's 52nd Foot as the prototype was an obvious choice. As commander of the troops in the Southern Military District, Moore had a particular interest in correcting the deficiencies in Britain's light infantry forces. The Southern District was the area most likely to be the site of a French landing and contained large tracts of terrain that were ideally suited to the operations of their *tirailleurs*. Consequently, the lack of British light troops to oppose them would be felt more acutely here than in most other regions (a point that was further emphasized by the former French general Dumouriez who, as we shall see, arrived in Britain during 1803, became adviser to the War Office and wrote a major study on defence policy).[124] It was, therefore, almost inevitable that the first of the new skirmisher corps would be established in this area and the choice of the 52nd – its colonel also being an experienced light infantryman, the district commander and a member of the Board of General Officers that advised the Commander-in-Chief on general military policy – undoubtably appeared to be the most logical course of action.

This view is also supported by the fact that the 52nd, prior to its conversion, evidently had no inherent qualities that made it particularly suited to the work of light troops, and the adjustments to the regiment's composition that followed its nomination as a light corps seem to have been based on only one principle. This was suggested by Moore in January 1803, when in answer to the Commander-in-Chief's enquiry as to how the 52nd could best be adapted for light infantry work he replied that:

> The service of light infantry does not so much require men of stature as it requires them to be intelligent, handy, and active, and they should in the first instance be young, or they will neither take to the service nor be easily instructed in it.[125]

In accordance with this principle, Moore was given permission to transfer those men he considered unfit for the 52nd Regiment's new role to another battalion and replace them with more suitable men. However, in an effort to minimize the need for this tiresome process, when it came to converting more regiments into light troops the high command seems to have been careful to select units that already contained a high proportion of young soldiers. A May 1809 inspection return on the newly created 71st Light Infantry, for example, reveals that, out of a total of 859 officers and men in the First Battalion, only 125 were aged over 35.[126] Likewise, in June of the same year the regiment's second battalion mustered 366 men, of whom only 38 were over 35;[127] whilst an inspection return from the same period on the newly-formed 85th Light Infantry shows that, out of a total of 578 officers and men, just 71 were over 35 years old.[128]

While Rottenburg was giving the 51st and 71st their preliminary training as light troops, a colourful corps of light infantry was also being formed in the British Ionian Islands by Major Richard Church. The Greek Light Infantry were raised primarily for local defence. Dressed in traditional Greek costume, the regiment consisted of tribesmen commanded by their own chieftains and a few British officers. In 1813 a second regiment was founded on a *cadre* from the first. Both units, however, saw little action and were disbanded in 1814.

Finally, the case of the 90th Foot merits some discussion here. This regiment had, since its creation in 1760, given intermittent service as a corps of light troops. In accordance with the practice of raising light infantry units whenever war broke out and then disbanding them again on the cessation of hostilities, the regiment was established and disestablished several times between 1760 and the end of the eighteenth century. The last occasion on which it was revived during the period we are concerned with was in 1794, when Colonel Thomas Graham – later Sir Thomas and then Lord Lynedoch – raised the battalion at his own expense as the 'Perthshire Volunteers'.[129]

Graham was very interested in light troops in general and particularly in the traditional function of his own regiment. A regular writer of perceptive comments on the tactical importance of skirmishers, he was also a close friend of Lieutenant-Colonel Kenneth Mackenzie who – as we shall see in the next chapter – played a central role in the training of the light regiments founded by the duke of York and General John Moore. This friendship first began in 1794 when the veteran Mackenzie commenced the training of Graham's newly raised volunteers.[130] Four years later whilst seving in Portugal with Lieutenant-General John Stuart, the 90th and some light companies learnt and performed Rottenburg's new light infantry drill.[131] Amongst those who watched this spectacle was General John Moore, and it would seem likely that it was on this occasion that Moore first laid eyes on the officer he was later to summon to train his own 52nd Regiment as light troops.[132] Certainly, General Stuart was most impressed by Mackenzie's work with the 90th, and was later to recommend him to the Commander-in-Chief as an expert instructor of light troops.[133]

There can be little doubt that from its formation in 1794 until the Peace of Amiens the 90th was a light infantry corps in all but name. According to Graham himself, the unit was 'considered as a light infantry battalion' as early as 1795 and was trained accordingly,[134] whilst the regiment's later practice of Rottenburg's skirmisher drill has already been noted. Similarly in the Egyptian campaign of 1801 we find the regiment serving as the army's vanguard – a duty invariably performed by light formations – where, on at least one occasion, it drove off French cavalry with 'it's well directed fire, in light infantry style'.[135]

After the signing of the Peace of Amiens in 1802, however, the status of the 90th became that of an ordinary regiment of foot. Like 'Campbell's Highlanders' and 'Keith's Highlanders' in 1763, this corps of light infantry volunteers was 'standardized' by being assimilated into the ordinary infantry of the line. Predictably unhappy about this decision and having seen the formation of the 52nd and 43rd Light Infantry Regiments, Graham petitioned Lord Moira in September 1803 to 'recommend to His Royal Highness to restore the 90th to what it originally was, a light infantry battalion . . .'.[136] Moira's reply, Graham told Lord Cathcart, was that:

> . . . The system of making a particular regiment a light infantry battalion was one which he in his own mind had strong objections to, . . . but that as it had been adopted in England in the case of the 52nd, he would certainly recommend the 90th, satisfied that none of his general objections referred to it. He did so accordingly, and in course of post received an answer from Clinton, to say that H.R.H. would take His Majesty's pleasure on it. This is considerably more than two months ago and no further notice has been taken.[137]

Indeed, it would seem that Graham never did receive the answer from the Commander-in-Chief that he hoped for. Certainly, the 90th was never returned to the light infantry arm during the Napoleonic period and, as the official inspection returns confirm, continued to be known quite simply as the 90th Regiment of Foot.[138]

However, despite the demise of the 90th as a skirmisher corps, by the end of 1809 when the Peninsular War was gathering its full momentum the British Army had, for the first time in its history, a number of permanently established light infantry regiments, properly drilled, equipped and clothed as such. Throughout the conflict with Napoleonic France these corps were to give solid service and, indeed, some proved to be amongst the finest battalions ever created. Leaving the inadequacies and disasters of the 1790s far behind them, Britain's skirmishers were to become an adequate match for the once supreme French *tirailleurs* and, as we shall see in Chapter VI, played a crucial role in the battlefield tactics that helped secure the duke of Wellington an almost unbroken series of victories.

CHAPTER IV

The architects and their works

Having traced the origins of the various light infantry regiments that were incorporated into the British Army during this period, we now turn to the respective contributions of the individuals who were pre-eminent in the creation and training of these units.

As the author of the two standard manuals used by the Army's skirmishers from around 1800 until well after 1815, Baron Francis de Rottenburg played a key role in the training of Britain's light infantry arm. Born in Danzig, he joined the French Army in 1782, but left the service on the outbreak of the Revolution. After spending some time in Naples, he fought with Kosciuszko's forces in the 1794 Polish rebellion before joining Hompesch's *Jäger* regiment. Here, he rose to the rank of lieutenant-colonel, seeing extensive service in the Americas.[1] In October 1797, however, it was decreed that Hompesch's corps was to be merged with several other German units to form the Fifth Battalion of the 60th Foot, which was to be dressed, equipped and trained as a rifle regiment under Rottenburg's Command.[2]

At this time, there were, as we have seen, no organized light infantry battalions in the British Army and Rottenburg's makeshift unit was something of an experiment with rather unpromising materials. However, 'a good organiser . . . and disciplinarian', he swiftly turned his hotch-potch of a regiment into a highly efficient force, trained to be 'the eyes of an army' and in the specialized skills of the rifleman.[3]

His simple but effective tactical system quickly drew attention and when the drill was subsequently embodied in a book and published, the duke of York had the Adjutant-General translate it from German into English and approved it as the official light infantry manual.[4] Like its author, who became a leading trainer and inspector of Britain's light troops, it remained pre-eminent for many years after it was first published in 1798 and, as Rigaud was later to observe in his book on the Fifth Battalion of the 60th:

> So good indeed was the system and teaching of this Lt.-Colonel that ten years later he was employed as a Brigadier-General at a camp on the Curragh and at Ashford in Kent, and he was the father of the Light Infantry of the British Army, and such fine regiments as the 68th, 71st and 85th . . . passed through his hands . . . The 5th battalion 60th could not have had a better instructor in its first start in life.[5]

As far as tactical drill is concerned, Rottenburg's system was a relatively uncomplicated one, clearly influenced by the drill manual written by *Oberstleutnant* von Ewald. When acting in line of battle with closed ranks and files, light infantry units were governed by the same regulations as applied to the Army's foot troops in general. Thus, before the soldier was instructed in the manoevres that were peculiar to skirmishes he was 'taught how to hold himself, to march, face, wheel etc. as in regular infantry'.[6]

Next, the novice was instructed in marksmanship which, as the following entry from the order book of the Fifth Battalion of the 60th demonstrates, was regarded as the hall-mark of all good rifle corps:

> The true Rifleman will never fire without being sure of his man . . . And he will recollect that a few well-directed shots, that tell, will occasion greater confusion than thousands fired at random and without effect, which will only make the enemy despise our fire, and inspire him with confidence in proportion as he finds us deficient in skill and enterprise.[7]

For training in this vital work, Rottenburg specified that the target used

> . . . should be at least five feet in diameter; for if it were smaller, the unpractised recruit would be apt to miss so often as to despair of hitting it; and to become expert a man should find encouragement, and even amusement in this practice. Another disadvantage in its being too small would be, that the rifleman could not become acquainted with his rifle, as in missing the target altogether, he could not ascertain whether he had shot too much to the right, or too much to the left; whereas a target of a proper size, and painted in circles, being easily hit, the rifleman sees at once the fault he has made, and learns to correct it . . . He should begin by firing at the distance of fifty yards, and increase it by degrees to three hundred.[8]

Once they were proficient at firing while standing, the riflemen were practised in shooting and loading while kneeling, sitting 'as a tailor' and lying down on both their backs and their fronts. Shooting practice against moving targets was provided by mounting a target 'on a sledge, or a truck upon wheels, [which was] drawn backwards and forwards by a person placed under shelter'.[9]

The recruits now progressed to the execution of the various manoeuvres performed by skirmishers. Formed in a line, two men deep, they were taught to expand their frontage to the right or left, an 'anchor' file at one end of the unit holding fast, whilst the rest of the formation extended themselves in the appropriate direction. Similarly, extension from the centre of a unit could be carried out: the middle file would hold their ground, while the men to their left and right moved outwards.[10]

All of these manoeuvres were executed in a 'quick time' of 120 (30-inch) paces per minute, and '. . . To preserve that control which is requisite, and restrain the dispersion (inherent to light troops, particularly Tirailleurs) which in the field after the firing of the first shot would take place', each skirmisher unit had a larger proportion of officers and

NCOs than a line battalion.[11] At close range, these supervisors could shout their instructions to their men. For communicating over longer distances, however, they carried whistles with which to signal their intentions[12] and, to command a sizeable unit deployed over a still greater frontage, officers utilised the regimental buglers. By the playing of certain distinctive tunes, a whole variety of commands and even pieces of information could be relayed across the battle zone. These included directives for a unit to extend, halt, close ranks, charge, incline to the right or left, open fire, cease fire, retreat, disperse, and form line, column or square. The signals for passing intelligence included calls that indicated that the enemy had been sighted, and whether they were infantry, cavalry or both.[13]

In prolonging the frontage of a unit, the eventual spacings between files could be varied to suit prevailing conditions. They were usually deployed two paces apart, but the regulations laid down that:

> In particular case, when they are required to cover the front of a corps, or mask a manoeuvre, the commanding officer will signify at what distance the files are to form from each other, before he gives the order for them to extend themselves.[14]

There were, however, three specific distances in the manuals: 'loose files', which had six-inch intervals; 'open order', where the files were two feet apart; and 'extended order', where the spacings were six feet across.[15]

As the fate of Colborne's brigade at the Battle of Albuera in 1811, or indeed that of the whole Spanish Army at Medellin in 1809 demonstrate, foot soldiers formed in even relatively solid and deep lines were highly susceptible to sudden enemy assaults.[16] For infantry deployed in only two ranks and in extended formations – particularly if they were armed with rifles which, as we have seen, were slower and more cumbersome to load than an ordinary musket – the dangers from such attacks increased dramatically.[17] Rottenburg, therefore, stressed the basic points in his tactical training. Firstly, that in any file at any given moment, at least one soldier must be ready to fire.[18] Secondly, that '. . . Never more than half a body of riflemen must be sent forward to skirmish, the other half remain formed and ready to support'.[19] It was around these two central points that the rest of his tactical system revolved.

Once they had mastered the art of extending their frontage, light infantry recruits were taught the remaining part of the basic drill; the section that effectively combined shooting with movement. While half of the unit remained in close order in reserve, the skirmishing companies, having deployed in their extended two-deep line, would advance, the reserve keeping some fifty paces to the rear. Once they came within range of the enemy, although the manoeuvre was executed at the usual rapid speed, progress was relatively slow. Both men in each file of the skirmishing line would start off with their rifles loaded. The leading man would take aim and, at his discretion, fire. The man behind him would then run six paces in front of him and slightly to his right. Meanwhile, his colleague, now in the rear rank, would reload and, when he had finished, would call 'ready' to the soldier in front who would then fire. The sequence could be continued for as long as was required and ensured that at least one man of each pair of soldiers had his rifle loaded and ready to fire at any given moment. To execute a retreat, the process was simply reversed and the distances run by each soldier in the movement phases of the sequence increased to twelve paces.[20]

A similar device to the skirmishing line described above was the 'chain'. This was usually used when contact was first made with the enemy. 'The object of this branch of the duty of light troops', Rottenburg's manual explained

> is to scour a tract of the country by means of numerous and detached bodies, clearing the woods and inclosures of the enemy's posts, and in a word, to establish a complete chain of your own troops, by occupying, as far as circumstances will permit, every advantageous spot; taking particular care, however, that your own posts are so stationed as to have easy communication, and the power of mutually supporting each other.[21]

When serving as a chain, three-quarters of the light infantry corps would deploy in a formation similar to their usual battle line; the only difference being that the men would be grouped together in fours – rather than in pairs – and the intervals between each of these 'divisions' would be increased to ten paces. The remaining quarter of the light infantry unit would form a solid reserve and would march some fifty paces behind the line 'in order to give support to any part of the chain that . . . [was] attacked'.[22]

Guidelines for the conduct of vanguards were also laid down so as to minimize the possibility of a corps being surprised when on the march and to make the gathering of intelligence easier. A light infantry vanguard was to consit of several bodies of troops. The first of these – recommended to be half a platoon (about 25 men) strong – kept some five hundred paces directly in front of the main force. (This distance was reduced to 300 paces at times of poor visibility.) Two hundred paces in front of this unit was to be another half platoon, with an NCO and six men scouting a further 100 yards ahead of them. Covering each flank of the advance was yet another half platoon – some three hundred paces to the side of the detachment that was deployed immediately in front of the main force – with an NCO and six men probing another 100 yards forward from them and towards the outer flank.[23] This elaborate arrangement enabled the light infantry to scour the coutryside ahead on a frontage of at least 1000 yards, and greatly reduced the chances of the column they were escorting being surprised or ambushed.

Like the works of Emmerich and Ewald, Rottenburg's manual concluded with detailed sections on the conduct of patrols, sentries and pickets, providing a fairly comprehensive system of operation for light infantry in and between battle zones. What did not feature very much in his manual, however, were his views on how the men were, in general, to be disciplined for their work. The details of this important aspect of his thinking emerge more from various anecdotes about the baron and especially in the papers of his disciple, Major Davy, who succeeded him as commander of the Fifth Battalion of the 60th in 1808.[24]

As we shall see, Rottenburg's attitude to the question of general discipline bore a striking resemblance to that held by several of the other officers who, during this period, were pre-eminent for their work with the light infantry. The key to the baron's policy was that

> . . . He never flogged his men when in command of the 5th battalion of the 60th, but governed them in a patriarchal manner, more as a father would his children, than as commanding officers used to do in those days.[25]

This more enlightened style of discipline was aimed at creating the tremendous *esprit de corps* that Rottenburg regarded as essential for the proper functioning of a light-infantry unit. In their operations, such troops frequently acted in small, isolated detachments, the epitome of which were the separate pairs of soldiers who made up the skirmishing lines on the battlefield. Their efficiency and, indeed, their very survival depended on the skilful execution of their respective tasks, individual initiative and, above all, a strong sense of mutual confidence in each other's abilities and support. All of this required a highly developed team spirit which extended throughout the unit and was encouraged at every level. When functioning in pairs, the soldiers were, as far as possible, allowed to choose their respective colleagues,[26] while the officers were encouraged 'to learn the capacities and characters of their men that they may employ them to the best advantage; this', the officers were advised, 'may be easily done by conversing with them, and hearing their opinion and sentiments on different subjects'.[27]

To complete the atmosphere, an intense awareness of personal, professional and regimental pride was developed. In addition to a general regime of meritocracy, the best marksmen, for example, were permitted to wear various coveted adornments to show their prowess[28] and, indeed, the British Army's first medals – largely one of Colonel William Stewart's innovations – appeared at about this time.[29] To maintain the unit's physical preparedness for action, regular exercise and good hygiene were, as Guibert had first advocated, encouraged to increase 'bodily activity and strength'.[30] Similarly, especially just before hostilities were commenced, regimental proclamations were issued to remind the troops of their proud traditions and generally prepared them psychologically for the impending action. The following order, issued by Major Davy to the officers of his rifle battalion shortly before the unit left for the Peninsula in 1808, was typical:

> The men are to understand that by the maintenance of order and discipline we can alone look forward to a successful operation; . . . they must on every

occasion conform with alacrity to the orders of their officers, and as great fatigue is often connected with the duties of Light Troops, they must cheerfully submit, and bear like men the hardships of a soldier's life.[31]

This then, was the method of drill and instruction pursued by the Rottenburg school and which the majority of Britain's light infantry forces were trained on. In addition to the baron's book, however, there was another manual which, for many aspects of *la petite guerre* was equally important and influential. This book was the *Instruction Concerning the Duties of Light Infantry in the Field*, by General François Jarry. It first appeared in 1801, when it was published by order of the duke of York as a supplement to Rottenburg's work. Within a year it was being used by the newly formed 95th (Rifle) Regiment as their basic text on the science of outpost duties.[32]

Born in France in 1733, Jarry had seen long and varied service on the European continent in Frederick the Great's army, and prior to moving to Britain was head of the Berlin *Kriegsakademie*.[33] In autumn 1798, he moved to England to take up an appointment as commandant of the newly created Military College at High Wycombe, the forerunner of the present-day Staff College.[34]

Jarry's work in no sense attempted to change the actual skirmishing drill laid down by Rottenburg. Indeed, his comments on battlefield operations were primarily grand tactical guidelines and hints for light infantry commanders to apply in specific circumstances. But his observations on these issues were of great importance, and his book also enhanced the instruction available to officers on the outpost and reconnaissance duties of light forces.

From the very outset, Jarry emphasized the forward role of the light infantry in military operations and the need for detailed instructions as to their conduct; especially in enclosed terrain, where, as General Money had noted, the use of cavalry was limited and light infantry became of crucial importance: 'Light troops are', he wrote,

in general entrusted with the out-duties of camps. . . . This kind of service is very extensive, whatever be the nature of the country; but its importance, with regard to light infantry, augments in proportion to the difficulty of employing cavalry. In covered and inclosed countries, the surface of which offers a successive variety of heights and vallies; when the view is interrupted by woods, thickets, scattered trees, and a number of country houses; when the fields are surrounded by high hedges, and when you meet, besides, with ditches, ponds, morasses etc: under such circumstances, almost the whole of the out-duties of camps must be performed by a numerous body of light infantry, and the long details of these duties . . . require a particular body of instruction, to enable light infantry to supply the deficiency of cavalry, where such local circumstances forbid almost entirely the use of that arm.[35]

Because of the peculiar nature of this type of duty, Jarry argued that light infantry, particularly the officers, needed to acquire a whole host of specialist skills:

The duty of light troops being more than any other performed by small detachments, in general commanded by only one officer, instruction is the more necessary to him, because everything that he wants he must find in himself, and, in many perilous situations of that so often insulated service, bravery, united to military knowledge, can alone extricate him with honour. How necessary then for every light infantry officer to study attentively every part of the service, which concerns the safety of an army, either on a march or in camp, either with regard to foraging parties, escorting convoys, raising contributions in kind, and taking prisoners, or hostages etc: especially with regard to reconnoitring the posts and positions occupied by the enemy, and giving notice of the marches or movements which he may undertake, either in totality or by detachments.[36]

In his ensuing examination of the relationship between light infantry officers and their men, Jarry concurred with such authors as De Jeny and Emmerich,[37] and effectively summarized the general system of discipline followed by the Rottenburg school: officers were to teach by example,[38] and were to develop a close personal knowledge of the characters and abilities of the men under their command. This would not only facilitate the efficient conduct of operations by enabling officers to select the soldiers best suited to the task in hand, but would also help to foster the great *esprit de corps* that most theorists[39] believed essential in a light infantry corps:

It is very requisite for an officer of light troops, to obtain a thorough individual knowledge of the men under his command, that he may employ them according to their intelligence and courage . . . One serjeant, corporal or private will answer better for reconnoitring openly the enemy . . . Another will be better employed as a scout, or in watching the enemy's motions without discovering himself; and another will be found useful by his manner of questioning the peasants, and of getting from them the best information . . . Another will be better calculated for an ambuscade, and have the necessary cunning for taking prisoners without compromising himself. Some old soldiers have the genius of resources, and . . . may be able to give a good advice, which ought to be turned to advantage. . . . All these different characters may be easily found out by conversing with them, and chiefly by attending to their reports.[40]

'It is not only necessary', Jarry continued,

for an officer of light troops to obtain of those under him a perfect confidence in his judgement, his courage and skill; but it is likewise important for him to gain their affections. He must know, that he cannot carry everything by his single sword, and that if he is not heartily seconded in a service . . . he will never be able to undertake or perform anything without fear for his reputation. However, the good will of the men is not to be obtained by the sacrifice of discipline, which is more particularly the requisite with light troops, as they have more opportunities of escaping from its strictness. The best manner of gaining the affections of the soldiers, without prejudice to discipline, is by providing carefully for their wants.[41]

The bulk of Jarry's book was devoted to extensive instructions on the outpost duties of light troops and included sections on the posting of sentries, the functions of pickets and intelligence gathering and reconnoitring. All of these *petite guerre* operations were elaborately described and their practice in the field regulated down to the smallest detail. In the section on the procedures to be followed by sentries, for example, Jarry advised that 'When the sentries can be distinctly seen from the principal post, and are not above three hundred paces distant from it,' they should operate in pairs with a chain of 60–80 men being deployed for every mile of front. Each man in each pair of sentries was to position himself so that he faced his colleague and thus could keep a watchful eye on both him and the horizon behind him, including the position of the next soldier in the chain. This meant that each section of the front to be guarded was observed by at least two men from different positions and each of those men could also watch and, if necessary, give covering fire to, the two sentries to his right or left depending on in which direction he was facing.

'But', Jarry continued, should the sentries

> not be clearly seen [by the main post], or be at a greater distance than three hundred paces, it will be better to place on that spot a small detached post of four men and a corporal. This small post will be placed behind a hedge, or on the skirt of a wood, so as to remain concealed, and will plant one sentry at about fifteen or twenty paces in front.

'No light infantry soldier', Jarry concluded,

> is ever, when on sentry at the out-posts, to support or slope his firelock . . . The reason is, that in raising and moving their arms they are more likely to be seen: and every sentinel, placed for the purpose of observation, ought to endeavour, as much as possible, to see without being seen.[42]

Jarry's directions for the conduct of other aspects of *la petite guerre* were similarly detailed. With regard to light infantry acting as pickets, for instance, he noted that their importance increased 'in proportion to the difficulty of employing cavalry'.[43] A light infantry picket, he suggested, should in most cases number between 120 and 160 men, with up to half of them posted as sentries in the manner described above and the remainder kept in reserve. The terrain immediately in front of the picket should be cleared of cover as far as possible, the trees and hedges should be 'cut down to two or three feet, so as to . . . [enable the picket] to fire over them'.[44]

Yet, Jarry explained, '. . . A piquet is not to be considered as a post for [serious] resistance. A piquet is essentially calculated to give timely warning.'[45] Thus, they were, where possible, to centre themselves on villages, woods and other defensible positions to enable them to fight effective delaying actions and thus give the army they were screening 'timely warning' of enemy attacks. In his *Instruction*, Jarry particularly recommended the use of churches as bases for pickets to operate from.

Usually located at the very heart of a settlement at the confluence of the major communication routes, they were generally relatively large, sturdy buildings, surrounded by walls. This made them ideally suited for defence by a comparatively small number of soldiers in the event of an attack and, above all, as the operational base for a unit that was primarily concerned with controlling and observing the local road networks.[46]

Jarry also taught light infantry officers that on taking up a new position they and their senior subordinates should immediately familiarize themselves with the surrounding countryside and make contingency plans for use in the event of an attack. Several reconnaissance patrols each consisting of four men and an NCO officer should be sent out to explore the locality and question the inhabitants, and sketch maps of the terrain should be produced. Such diagrams should include place names and as many other details as the picket was able to secure – particularly information relating to enemy troop movements and dispositions – and copies of them, along with any other reports, should be forwarded without delay to the army's headquarters by light dragoons 'who ought always to attend the piquet to carry messages swiftly'.[47]

The concluding part of Jarry's *Instruction* consisted of an examination of the tactical functions of light infantry units during an engagement. He saw their initial role in an action as being:

> to cover the deployment of the [heavy infantry] columns, by occupying the houses, hedges, hollow ways, and thickets, in front, to the distance of about six or seven hundred paces, according to the proximity of the first batteries of the enemy and the situation of his outposts. In the execution of this duty it sometimes becomes necessary to dislodge the enemy from places where his out-posts have entrenched themselves . . .[48]

Once the battle proper was under way, he continued,

> . . . Light infantry is employed . . . in covering the front of attacks, in connecting them together by occupying intervals, and in protecting their flanks; by gaining the hedges, woods and uneven ground, of which the enemy might avail himself.[49]

In the performance of these roles, Jarry saw the 'first quality' required of light troops as being an ability

> to discern the proper time to advance, to resist, and to retire. . . . Light infantry, acting parallel with the troops of the line, must resist to the utmost. In advancing, it must advance with them, and cover their wings; and if they be forced to lose ground, it must check the enemy at every hedge, wood and passage, occasioning him as much loss as possible.[50]

Although the skirmishers were always to fight in open formations and make use of any cover that presented itself, their operations were not to be without control and direction. 'Disorder and confusion' were to be avoided, as was close-quarter fighting with the enemy: damage was to be inflicted through firepower alone, while the capability to promptly 'execute whatever manoeuvres may be commanded' was always to be preserved. As well as a highly developed team spirit amongst the troops, this, Jarry stressed, would call for special skills on the part of the light infantry commanders; notably an ability to adapt their dispositions and tactics to rapidly changing circumstances as the battle ebbed and flowed. Local conditions were to be kept under constant and careful scrutiny in order that the skirmishers could quickly react to both opportunities and threats. 'The *coup d'oeil* of the officer', commented Jarry, 'ought to be well practised. He ought to be able, at once, to fix upon the road most likely to conduct to success, with least bloodshed'.[51]

That route to success was, Jarry believed, to be secured by a combination of judicious manoeuvre and accurately directed firepower. Simple frontal assaults were often ineffective and led to heavy casualties, and were best reserved for containing operations. The preferred manoeuvre for most attacks was penetration into the enemy's rear by turning the flanks of their positions. This would expose the light troops themselves to the minimum amount of danger and would, simultaneously, present them with opportunities to strike at the opposition's 'soft', rear *échelons*: local chains of command or supply could be disrupted or severed, while fire delivered from the flank or rear could have devastating repercussions for a unit's morale. As Jarry observed: 'An inconsiderable body showing itself in the rear, is sufficient to produce a great effect; and experience proves that retrograde movements are catching'.[52]

Once such a 'retrograde movement' was achieved, the skirmishers were to press and harass the retreating enemy so that 'they would be thrown into complete confusion, and not allowed time to rally at a short distance'.[53] The ground secured by the light troops could, meanwhile, be occupied by their supporting heavy units, who could then consolidate or exploit any advantage that had been gained. But in pursuing a defeated force, light infantry, Jarry urged, were to be kept under the careful control of their officers; for there was always the danger that, in the heat of the chase, they would spill carelessly on to open ground and thus become vulnerable to counter-strokes by enemy cavalry. 'Cavalry, in an open country', he warned, 'is destruction to light infantry, as light infantry is to cavalry in a covered country.'[54]

This observation is hardly less true today than it was in the early nineteenth century. Light infantry caught in the open by armoured regiments – the modern equivalent of the cavalry in Napoleon's time – would still be likely to suffer annihilation. But entrenched around buildings, or in dense woods and enclosures, the foot troops – shielded from fire by a barrier that would also keep their assailants at a safe distance – would have the advantage. As we have seen, in devising his tactical drill Rottenburg had attempted to safeguard skirmishers from cavalry attack. Half of a unit's firepower was, he maintained, to be kept in effective reserve so as to be available to confront any sudden assault.[55] But this, Jarry suggested, was very much a last line of defence and was prone to be ineffective; the firepower of single rank of scattered marksmen was not sufficient to halt a determined cavalry charge in open countryside. 'Musquetry', he explained,

> cannot be advantageously used against cavalry, unless the light infantry fire under the protection of cover, where it can load in safety; for it is evident, that those who are loading . . . cannot, in that instant, defend themselves, nor take the proper position for resisting cavalry . . .

However, he continued, as there was always the danger that foot skirmishers might 'be surprised by cavalry on open ground', their commander must be able to decide

> at the first *coup d'oeil* whether the light infantry can reach the hedges or other cover in time; and if not, they must instantly run . . . to form a round mass. Infantry, armed with bayonets, and formed into a close mass, can always resist a charge of cavalry . . . The cavalry will soon retire beyond the reach of musquetry. The infantry will take the advantage of their retreat to proceed to some cover, without stopping to fire or load again. As from the nature of its duty light infantry is often exposed to be attacked unawares by cavalry, it ought to be practised to form quickly into a round mass, whenever it is threatened by a charge . . . Having repulsed the charge, the commander will cause it to march in close column to the nearest shelter. Forming the square is not a proper manoeuvre for light infantry.[56]

By providing a collection of sound observations on such tactical and grand tactical issues, and by enhancing the existing guidance on outpost duties, Jarry's *Instruction* formed the perfect companion volume to Rottenburg's drill manual, giving the British Army's skirmishers a comprehensive series of methods on every aspect of their work, ranging from combat drill to reconnaissance and other features of *la petite guerre*. These two publications were to form the basis of British light infantry training for the whole of the Napoleonic Wars and many decades beyond. Indeed, as late as 1869, Jarry's writings on outpost duties were produced as a supplement by Major-General W.C.E. Napier to the *Field Exercises and Evolutions of the Infantry*.[57]

Two other officers who also made significant contributions to the formation and training of the British light infantry arm during this period were Colonels William Stewart and Coote Manningham. As we saw in the previous chapter, both of these officers were deeply involved from the very outset in the creation of the 95th (Rifles) Regiment, and in many senses they established the model on which later light infantry units were moulded.

Their work first began in January, 1800, when the Commander-in-Chief, influenced by his experience in Holland the previous year, took up a suggestion made by Stewart as the basis for forming a rifle regiment[58] and appointed the two officers to superintend the training of the new unit which was to be formed by assembling detachments from several regiments of the line.[59] Manningham – a veteran light infantry officer who had served with distinction in Sir Charles Grey's West Indian Campaigns – was appointed colonel of the new formation, with Stewart as his deputy. Originally sited at Horsham, the school subsequently moved to Blatchington and, then, towards the end of 1802, was relocated at Shorncliffe in Kent. Under the later leadership of General Sir John Moore the reputation of this camp grew enormously. Indeed, to this day it remains the most celebrated camp of instruction for light troops in the history of the British Army.

However, long before Moore ventured near Shorncliffe, Manningham and Stewart had established the foundations of the system of training that, later, was to make the camp famous. Clearly influenced by the military thinking of Jarry and Rottenburg, the two officers sought to create a force of light infantry that was based on the models found within the writings of those theorists. The unit's tactical drill was that of Rottenburg – the official skirmishers' manual at this time – while officers from the rifle corps were regularly sent to the Military College at High Wycombe where they received personal instruction from Jarry.[60] His book on the 'Science of light troops'[61] had also been drawn to their attention by the Commander-in-Chief, and within a year of its appearance was being used for the instruction of officers.[62]

It should not be thought, however, that Manningham and Stewart merely regurgitated material that they had absorbed from the books of Jarry and Rottenburg. They were both perceptive men with considerable combat experience of their own and both produced substantial amounts of important written work on military thought, particularly on the training of light infantry. Indeed, Stewart appears to have been primarily responsible for developing the system of general discipline that Rottenburg and Jarry first advocated and which, as we shall see, General Sir John Moore and Colonel Kenneth Mackenzie were to carry to perfection. In his early work with the experimental rifle corps, Stewart produced a collection of standing orders (the so-called 'Green Book'), instituted regimental decorations for valour and good conduct, and, to encourage professional pride and a sense of competition within the unit, divided the riflemen into grades according to their ability as marksmen, the finest shots receiving distinguishing emblems to adorn their uniforms.[63] Some time later, he produced a book entitled *Outlines of a Plan for the General Reform of the British Land Forces*. In this work, he set down his views on how soldiers should, in general, be disciplined and thus left us with a valuable insight into the system he had evolved with Manningham at Horsham, Blatchington and Shorncliffe.

The work was very much a development of the ideas practised by Rottenburg in his training of the Fifth Battalion of the 60th. Stewart believed that the efficiency of regular troops rested on:

cultivation of those moral qualities, which are only to be attained by a long process of careful instruction. . . . An artificial insensibility of mind, the result of a long process of discipline, must be acquired. This discipline of the mind is not to be understood as excluding it from the reception of milder impressions; subordination in an army is rendered most perfect when authority is softened by the feelings of honour and affection, but in order to attain a full degree of vigour, must be incorporated with the better sentiments of the heart. It has invariably been the object of great commanders to mingle authority with lenity, to inspire their troops with confidence in their own capacity, to call forth their enthusiasm, and to create a common feeling between the officer and the soldier. Upon these principles, Frederick, Suvarrov and the great Nelson acted, and we need not cite further examples.[64]

Stewart went on to criticize what he saw as excessive emphasis by many British officers on drilling and other mechanical aspects of training soldiers. Such concerns, Stewart argued, were of secondary importance when set against psychological training and preparations:

It is not so much on mechanical dexterity, as on the acquirement of peculiar moral habitudes that the superiority of regular troops depends; the profession of arms is one of those pursuits in which the mind strongly participates; with regard to our countrymen it is a mistaken view of the subject to consider it as mechanical.[65]

Indeed, Stewart eventually concluded that:

So wide is the difference between the discipline of the mind, and the precision of tactique, that the want of the latter, which is observable in the manoeuvring of any French brigade . . . whose character to discipline is unquestioned, would lead to a conclusion that such a degree of proficiency must have been attained in those qualities which perfect the military character, as actually to supersede the necessity of all that scientific dexterity, upon which, in less disciplined corps, the whole success of the machinery seems to depend.[66]

Stewart's *Outlines* are also interesting from our point of view in that they include proposals for dramatic changes in the manner in which the Army's light infantry were organized. He saw the retention of flank companies as undesirable and preferred that whole battalions should be earmarked as skirmishers. The only exception he made to this was that of the case of riflemen who, 'as the elite of light troops', properly belonged 'on the right of each light battalion', rather than 'in whole bodies, as in the 95th regiment'.[67]

We should also mention here that, although it has failed to survive, Stewart evidently wrote a manuscript in 1803 on the 'Exercise and Movements of Rifle Men of Light Corps'. The document was submitted to the Commander-in-Chief in the December of that year and he duly passed it to the Board of General Officers for consideration.[68] However, they were apparently not over-impressed by Stewart's tactical composition; for, the following January, the duke of York returned the manuscript to him, commenting that he did not propose 'to make any additions to the instructions for the Exercise of Light Troops, which have already received His Majesty's sanction'.[69]

A more successful piece of work was a series of military lectures that were composed by Colonel Manningham and delivered to the officers of the 95th at the beginning of 1803. The first of these stressed the vital reconnaissance work performed by the light troops of an army. Manningham described such units as:

> a light or beacon for the General, which should constantly inform him of the situations, the movements, and nature of the enemy's designs: it is upon the exactness and intelligence of what they report, that he is enabled to regulate the time and manner of executing his own enterprises.
>
> The officer who is deprived of this support, whether it be for want of sufficient numbers, or their want of expertness in this particular branch of the military art, being soon circumvented, ignorant of what his enemy is preparing to execute, his views on every occasion anticipated, and arriving constantly too late to prevent mischief, will experience daily losses, checks without end, and such disheartening circumstances, as may lead eventually to a general defeat.[70]

He eventually concluded that:

> The safety of an army, the justness of those measures which have so direct an influence upon success, depend frequently on the vigilance, the expertness, and the superiority of the light troops compared with those of the enemy.[71]

All of this, Manningham believed, required a skill and knowledge on the part of the light infantry officer that far exceeded what he termed the 'old and practised strategems of a partizan . . .'. To that basic role, he argued, must be added 'an exact method and reflections that are intimately connected with the grand operations of war'. Every officer of light troops, he continued,

> should know how to occupy a post, how to keep it, to support it, to retire from it when requisite. He should be well acquainted with the means and precautions necessary to secure himself upon all marches, how to penetrate the enemies [sic] chain of sentries, to reconnoitre his position, his force, and his movements, the circumstances which favour an attack on those places he may occupy as well as such as are favourable to himself when attacking.[72]

Like Jarry before him, Manningham believed that this extensive knowledge of military science called for the detailed instruction and training of officers in particular, and his *Military Lectures* sought to provide material that went above and beyond that found in the writings of the Military College commandant. The work gives us a useful insight into the breadth of subjects that the officers of the 95th received instruction in whilst at Shorncliffe: there are whole lectures on the duties of patrols (with separate sections covering patrolling by night and by day); pickets; and the conduct of advanced and rear guards. These are supplemented with smaller sections on the specific duties of sentries, and scouts and NCO's leading detachments. There is also a useful collection of general observations.

Whilst Manningham's set of lectures forms, in many senses, nothing other than a more elaborate discussion of the duties of light infantry covered in Jarry's *Instruction*, it also contains a significant amount of new material, much of which bears the hallmark of having stemmed from Manningham's personal combat experience. A colourful characteristic of *la petite guerre* was the frequent use of skilfully prepared ambushes, ingenious small scale manoeuvres, and other tricks and stratagems. Indeed, the *ruse de guerre* forms a prominent feature of much of the literature on the light infantry service:[73] Simcoe's *Journal*, for example, is riddled with such devices; De Jeney's *The Partisan* contains nearly 50 pages of them[74] and, following the tradition, Manningham, too, suggested several ruses for use by the officers of his regiment when in action. If, for example, an encampment should suddenly be attacked, he directed that:

> The patrols and sentries, if pressed by the enemy, should not retire upon the main post, but must, if possible, make a detour, that they may not bring a superior force upon the principal guard.[75]

For his concluding remarks, Manningham made some general observations about the duties of riflemen and their commanders. One point of particular interest is the emphasis that he – like other theorists such as Money – laid on making every shot tell. Good marksmanship was, of course, a great tradition amongst such troops; but the implications of the policy went beyond mere tactical considerations: combat sustainability posed peculiar logistical problems for light units which, strategically, often functioned far from the main body and supply lines of the army and, on the battlefield, were regularly marooned in 'no man's land'. An 1801 circular order had instructed that skirmishers were to be 'taught to be careful and provident of their Ammunition';[76] and, in similar vein, Manningham impressed on his officers that:

> The stock of necessaries to be carried in the field must not be great, and no possible want of ammunition should occur; though at the same time from their being frequently so far detached, and from the difficulty attending the constant supply of that article to an advanced corps, the greatest caution must be observed that the men neither lose their ammunition, nor throw away their shots idly.

Finally, Manningham also touched on matters of general discipline and, in keeping with the principles laid down by Rottenburg and Jarry, advocated that:

> The officers will look well to the diet of their men, and to those things they may occasionally stand in need of; and as far as the service they are upon admits of it, the greatest attention must be paid to their dress and good appearance. However it may be in other services, British troops should never be permitted to get into slovenly habits, which produce both idleness and disease; this may be done without harassing the soldier, and the officers

should set the example by being as attentive to their own dress as circumstances will admit.[77]

By far the most celebrated officer connected with the creation and training of the British light infantry during this period was General Sir John Moore. Born in November, 1761, this son of a Glasgow doctor was commissioned into the Army in 1776 and, after distinguished service in America, Corsica, the West Indies and Ireland, was made a major-general in 1798.

The following year, while fighting at the head of one of York's brigades in the Holland expedition, Moore was seriously injured when a French *tirailleur* shot him in the face during the Battle of Egmont. He survived, however, and went on to play a prominent part in the Egyptian campaign of 1801. Knighted in 1804 and promoted to lieutenant-general the following year, he subsequently led the British expeditionary force into Spain in the early months of the Peninsular War, being mortally wounded in the closing stages of the Battle of Corunna.

Moore's lengthy service in the West Indies – where the light infantry legions played such an important role – gave him a first-rate education in the work of such troops. Indeed, during his tour of duty in Ireland in 1798 and 1799, he devised a set of light infantry movements for the use of a battalion of Irish militia of which he had command. Running to 16 pages of simple drills and evolutions, these 'Instructions' provide an interesting insight into the tactical system used by these troops. Furthermore, this early document also contains elements of Moore's thinking on the role of the light infantry, and in it one can trace the origin of many of the ideas he was later to apply when forming the 52nd into a light corps. The notion, for example, that modern light troops should be 'a mixture of the Yager and the Grenadier' is stressed from the outset in these early *Instructions*,[78] and the all-purpose infantrymen of the 52nd Light Infantry were to constitute just such a fusion of the line and light services.

However, whilst there can be little doubt that Moore made an important contribution to the training and formation of some of Britain's light infantry units during this period, much of the 'traditional' view of that contribution – based on the work of such historians as Sir W.F.P. Napier, J.C. Moore and, more recently, J.F.C. Fuller and Carola Oman – would seem to have been founded on superficial research and evidence. In the foregoing pages we have seen how, prior to 1802, Rottenburg and Jarry had already constructed the theoretical basis on which the new light infantry regiments were to be moulded, and Stewart and Manningham had been steadily adding to those foundations with their written and practical work at Horsham and Blatchington. There is no evidence to suggest that Moore had anything to do with the early stages of this process. His correspondence confirms that when, in early 1800, the Experimental Rifle Corps was first assembled at Horsham and later Blatchington, Moore was actually *en route* to the Mediterranean with Abercromby's expeditionary force; and as Maurice – the editor of his diary – points out there is not so much as an allusion to these camps or their functions in any of Moore's papers.[79]

Indeed, Moore's first connections with the rifle corps arose from his appointment, on 21 May 1802, as commander of the troops in the Southern District of England; although he was attached to the staff there in the previous December.[80] This district had its headquarters fixed at Chatham and included the Shorncliffe camp. Thus, as the general officer commanding the area, it was Moore who wrote to Colonel William Stewart on 2 October, 1802, issuing him with a route for the 'march of the rifle corps under your command' to Shorncliffe, and expressing the hope that he would find the station suitable for both 'target practice and field movements'.[81]

After this simple communication, however, as Maurice again confirms,[82] there is no further mention of the subject in Moore's correspondence until as late as January 1803, when he became involved in a plan to convert several regiments of the line into light infantry. This idea was, according to the recollections of Moore's brother, developed by Moore from a suggestion made to him by the duke of York[83] who, as we have seen, had been promoting various projects to form specialist skirmisher corps for some years. The failure of the 1799 scheme to convert battalions of militia into light troops[84] prompted York to experiment more with regular soldiers and, by the end of that year, he had 'several arrangements . . . in their infancy'.[85] These led to the formation of the Experimental Rifle Corps the following January. But concern over the numerical weakness of the light infantry arm persisted and the decision to train units of the line to act as skirmishers was taken.

Moore's 52nd Foot having been selected as the prototype, it was moved to Shorncliffe early in 1803 and brigaded with the 59th, 4th, 70th and 95th Regiments.[89] The last of these units had been at Shorncliffe since the previous October and, under the guidance of Stewart and Manningham, had already received two years of training as a skirmisher corps. Some of its companies had seen action at Ferrol in 1800 and since then the 95th's reputation as an *élite* light regiment had flourished.

If his own regiment was to attain the same standards as the 95th, Moore believed that officers of Stewart and Manningham's calibre would have to be brought in to lead and train it. However, as we have seen, many of the Army's officers at this time had little to recommend them and, indeed, Moore was highly critical of the indolence and professional ignorance that prevailed in the British officer corps. Anxious to replace the inept lieutenant-colonels of the 52nd with the finest light soldier he knew of, he wrote to York's secretary on the matter in January 1803:

> A most essential point is the choice of an officer to place at the head of such a corps, and fortunately the situation of the present lieutenant-colonels of the 52nd Regiment . . . enables H.R.H. to remove one, or both of them,

without injuring either their interest or their feelings, and of bringing forward officers who, with the necessary talents, have the inclination to dedicate their whole time to their duty. Of this description, Lieutenant-Colonel McKenzie [sic] of the 44th is one; and if H.R.H. chooses I can write to him on the subject – and perhaps it will be best to remove one lieutenant-colonel only at first, reserving the other one in case a fit person presents himself hereafter.[87]

Kenneth Mackenzie, a native of Broughty Ferry, Dundee, first joined the Army in 1780. After seeing long service as a light infantry officer in the West Indies and various parts of Europe, he joined Thomas Graham's newly raised 90th Regiment (the 'Perthshire Light Infantry') in 1794. At its head, he served with Sir Charles Stuart's corps in Portugal in 1796 and, later, on Minorca where he became Stuart's Adjutant-General. Resigning from that post to go to Egypt, he distinguished himself at the (Second) Battle of Aboukir,[88] where he fought under the immediate command of Moore, doubtlessly enhancing that general's already high opinion of him. On his return to Britain, he was transferred to the 44th Foot from where, in early 1803, he was summoned to the 52nd and Shorncliffe, by Moore.[89]

Although Moore himself did nothing to disguise the fact that Mackenzie was the principal architect of the tactical drill taught at Shorncliffe and that he also played a major role in developing the camp's system of general discipline, Mackenzie has enjoyed little recognition for this work in the past. As he himself complained to Thomas Graham in 1809:

> What . . . was done in the 52nd was put down to Sir John Moor's [sic] credit, and of course without him I would be thought of little use in the discipline of a light corps.[90]

Indeed, the notion that Moore was solely responsible for the various innovations in drill, discipline and weaponry that occurred at Shorncliffe has, with little modification, been perpetuated by several generations of historians.[91]

However, this view of the situation requires considerable reappraisal. It largely originated in the writings of Sir William Napier who, in his autobiography and in his biography of his brother Charles, made some generalised references to the Shorncliffe camp and the activities of Sir John Moore; the principal one occurring in his account of Charles's life:

> To awaken the faculties of those under him, inspiring and teaching, was one of Sir John Moore's qualifications for command. At Shorn Cliff camp he divised such improvements in drill, discipline, dress, arms, formations and movements, as would have placed him for military reforms beside the Athenian Iphicrates, if he had not the greater glory of dying like the Spartan Brasidas. His materials were the 43rd, 52nd, and Rifle Regiments, and he so fashioned them that afterwards, as the Light Division under Wellington, they were found to be soldiers unsurpassable: perhaps never equalled.
> . . . Certainly it was a great school, and Moore's teaching is thus well

1   *The Flanders Campaign: a skirmish between French infantry and British dragoons*

2   *Austrian Jäger privates, 1813*

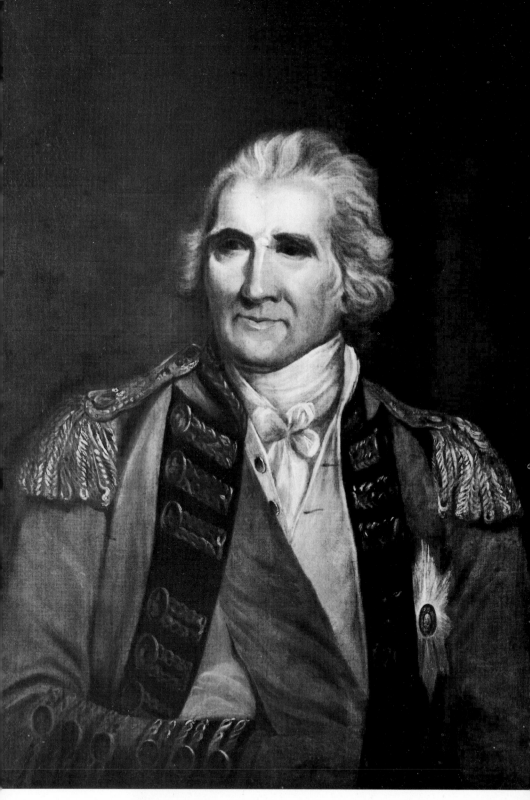

3   General Sir Ralph Abercrombie

4 Frederick, Duke of York

5 British rifle-
men in action,
1814

6 *The counter-attack by the 52nd and 43rd Light Infantry Regiments at Bussaco, 1810*

7 The 71st (Highland) Light Infantry in action at Quatre Bras, 1815. Note the bagpiper

8 General Sir Robert Craufurd, Commander of Wellington's Light Division during the Peninsular War

9   *Lieutenant-General Sir John Moore*

10   *General Sir Thomas Graham (Lord Lynedoch), Colonel of the 90th Foot*

11   *British infantry practising close-order drill*

RIFLE MANUAL EXERCISE IN FIVE PLATES.

Stand at Ease   *Attention*   *Shoulder Arms*   *Carry Arms*

...ished as the Act directs May 14.th 1811 by B.Brookes, at W.WEST'S Circulating Library 13 Exeter Street Strand.

12   *A plate from the* Manual Exercise *for rifleman, c. 1811*

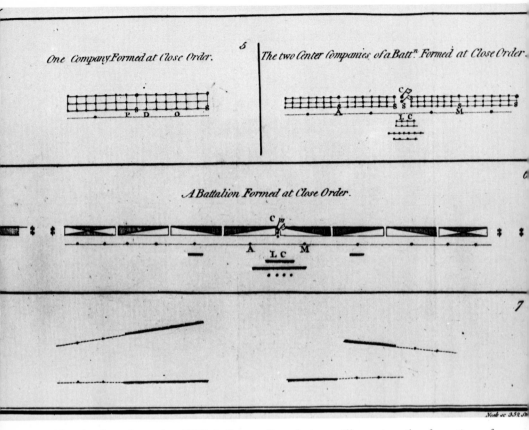

13   A plate from the 1792 Infantry Regulations *illustrating the formation of companies and a battalion in close-order*

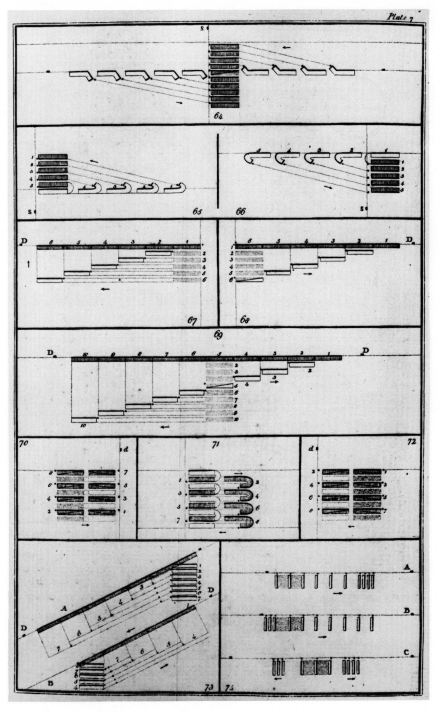

14   *This plate, taken from Dundas's 1792 Regulations, graphically illustrates the complexity of Napoleonic infantry manoeuvres*

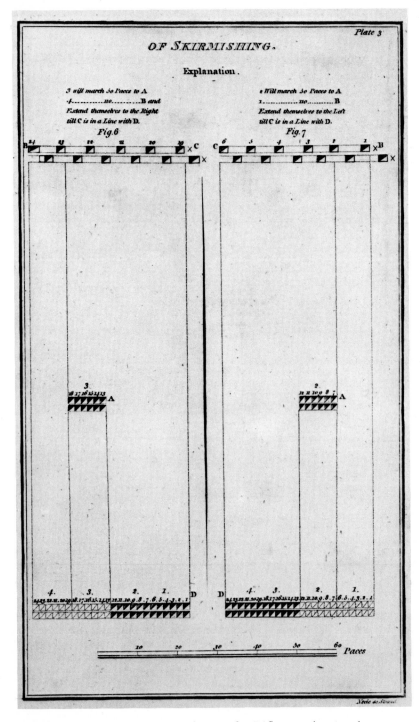

15   *A plate from Rottenburg's* Regulations for Riflemen *showing the movements for the deployment of a skirmisher screen*

16 and 17 (over) *Light infantry bugle calls from Rottenburg's* Regulations for Riflemen

Signals of the Bugle Horn in the Movements of Light Troops.

18　A French short musket (1786). Carbines like this one formed the basic weaponry of most European light infantry units

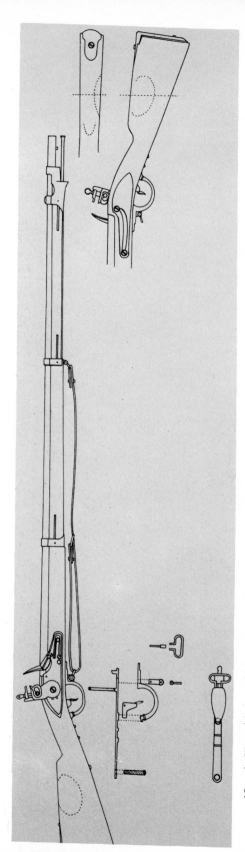

19　A (French) smoothbore musket of the Napoleonic era

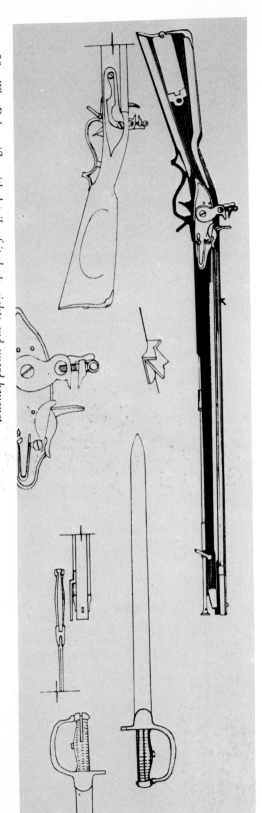

20   The Baker rifle with details of its lock, sights and sword-bayonet

described by one his scholars★ . . . 'It pleases me that you design to notice that real camp of instruction – Shorn Cliff. There officers were formed for command, and soldiers acquired such discipline, as to become an example to the army and proud of their profession. The details of Moore's system, from the setting up of a recruit to the movement of a brigade you are well acquainted with: but though drill was an important part of the instruction, it was not by that alone the soldier was there formed. It was the internal and moral system, the constant superintendance of the officers, the real government and responsibility of the captains, which carried the discipline to such perfection.'[92]

At this point, we need to undertake a brief examination of the connection between the various members of the Napier family and the Shorncliffe camp. The first of the three brothers to go there was Charles. He had joined the rifle corps early in 1801 and moved with his unit to Shorncliffe the following year.[93] Shortly after, he was joined by his brother George who had joined the 52nd Foot, 'which was Sir John Moore's and commanded by Colonel Mackenzie'.[94] Finally, William also joined the 52nd towards the end of 1803, but, the following August, transferred to the 43rd Regiment which had also been redesigned as a light corps and had moved to Shorncliffe for training with the 52nd.[95]

Thus, superficially, William Napier was well qualified to write about both the nature of the training that took place at Shorncliffe and who was responsible for its introduction. He was, after all, an officer in Moore's own regiment for a time and served under Mackenzie. But he has, as we shall see, been demonstrated to be an unreliable witness by a number of historians, and the above passage on Shorncliffe he included in his account of Charles Napier's life is of very questionable value as a piece of sound historical evidence.

In the first instance, this account was produced some 53 years after William Napier left the 52nd, and as a very general description of the work done at Shorncliffe it fails to furnish any real detail as to who was responsible for introducing the various innovations that took place there. One is provided with no more than the sweeping – and rather romanticized – observation that Moore

> devised such improvements in drill, discipline, dress, arms, formations and movements, as would have placed him for military reforms beside the Athenian Iphicrates, if he had not the greater glory of dying like the Spartan Brasidas.

In the section on Shorncliffe in his work *Peninsular Preparation*, Glover dismisses this passage as 'an error sprung from an old man's rosy-tinted reminiscences',[96] and goes on to argue that the improvements in discipline and arms, for example, were largely the responsibility of the duke of York. It was, Glover points out, York who 'selected for the 52nd regiment the improved light infantry pattern of musket', and he

---

★Napier does not identify this officer.

attributes the 'far happier system of discipline' Moore maintained in his brigade to the fact that York authorized him to form his regiments from 'picked officers and men'.[97]

Similarly, the distinguished military historian Sir Charles Oman also found fault with the reliability of Napier's accounts. He noted that, for instance, Napier's *History of the War in the Peninsula* – whilst a remarkable piece of work in many respects – contains numerous, blatant distortions of fact.[98] Indeed, in his account of, for example, the Battle of Albuera – an event he did not actually take part in – Napier indulged in invention and factual distortions paralleled only by Thiers's account of Waterloo. A little knowledge can be a dangerous thing, and Napier's scathing, 'very prejudiced and erroneous'[99] criticisms provoked a lengthy and extremely acrimonious row with Viscount Beresford – who had commanded the Allied forces – and other officers who had served in the campaign. One commented, for example that:

> Style is not the only essential of an historian; and Colonel Napier is most unhappily defective in all the greater qualifications. He wants sound and authentic information – he wants that experience of military affairs, which might enable him to form an opinion of great and extensive operations – he wants an accurate knowledge of the localities in which some of the most important events occurred; and, above all, he wants that calm spirit of impartiality which affords the only guarantee for historical fidelity. With these glaring and radical defects, the author's style – clear, flowing, various and perspicuous as it is – is more an evil than an advantage. It only tends to propagate error, to circulate misrepresentation, and to continue to the nineteenth century the difficulty of discerning where 'fable ends, and history begins;' or rather, indeed, to preserve the belief that 'all history is fable.'
>
> In [Napier's] . . . narrative of the Peninsular war, every reader, whether military or civil, must be struck with the very sparing manner in which he produces his authorities. He cannot . . . have been present in every transaction he discusses; indeed, from his gross and innumerable errors, it might be conceived that he had not been personally engaged in any one of them: and it would be some satisfaction to learn from whom his intelligence was derived. . . . I have taken the trouble of inquiring from many of the Generals, the principal officers of the staff, and others capable of enlightening his ignorance, whether he had . . . communicated with them upon the subject. . . . I have only been able to find one who had been consulted; and from that one . . . he only asked for half the necessary information, and supplied the remainder by a random and most erroneous guess of his own. . . . I do affirm, that with regard to those parts of the Peninsular war which fell under my own observation, and of which I profess to have a full and certain knowledge, there is not a single instance in which I find [Napier] . . . altogether correct, or giving a just, and fair, and accurate relation of the events.[100]

Just how much of this kind of manipulation crept into Napier's autobiography and his study of his brother Charles's life is a matter for speculation. However, there is an aura of excessive egoism about these works too, and many of William Napier's claims are again contradicted by the evidence of other eye-witnesses who were perhaps better qualified to judge these matters and who were, almost certainly, very much more impartial.

We have already noted the general comments William Napier made about the Shorncliffe camp in his account of Charles's career. In addition to these, there are also a few pages on this period in William's autobiography. The only thing that is particularly striking about their content, however, is the absence of any reference to the training work, coupled with the youthful William's child-like reverence for Sir John Moore; a feature observed by H.A. Bruce – the editor of the memoir – who, after only a few pages of the work, comments that, 'The reader may find already in the foregoing pages proof of the warm – it may be said passionate – admiration with which William Napier regarded Sir John Moore.'[101] Indeed, a few lines later, Bruce makes the interesting revelation that Napier primarily wrote his account of the Peninsular War because of 'his burning desire to vindicate the memory of his beloved chieftain [Moore] from the unjust aspersions with which it had been assailed.'[102]

This 'passionate admiration' for Moore marred William Napier's account of life at Shorncliffe camp. In his letters to his family, the 18-year-old subaltern pours scorn on those who find fault in any degree with his beloved general, whilst repeatedly heaping praise on him himself. Indeed, in one missive to his mother, William, when speaking of his idol, even remarks 'Where shall we find such a king?'[103]

In view of this evident bias in favour of Moore and William Napier's all too frequent tendency to misrepresent a situation, one feels that his general comments about the innovations that, he suggests, Moore alone affected at Shorncliffe can, at best, only be accepted with great caution. But there are, furthermore, other objections one could level at Napier's ability to speak with much authority about these matters. The camp's system of instruction had, after all, been established nearly a year before he went there, and whilst he served for a time in Moore's 52nd Regiment he held no post of any importance. Indeed, there were over 40 officers in the unit when he joined it[104] and he was one of the most insignificant amongst them: an 18-year-old freshman who held the most junior of commissioned ranks and, from what is known of the system of instruction at Shorncliffe, must have spent virtually all his little time in the 52nd undergoing basic training with 'other raw recruits'.[105] He was, therefore, more than unlikely to have played any significant part in the instruction of other soldiers in the camp until after August 1804 when, along with several other officers who had been trained in Moore's prototype light regiment, he was moved to the 43rd which had also been converted to light infantry and was to be 'assimilated with regard to . . . clothing, arming and Discipline to the 52nd Regiment.'[106]

Indeed, at the end of March 1804 in a conversation regarding this transfer, Moore had, as William Napier confessed in a letter to a relative, told him that:

. . . I [Napier] must know that from the little time I have been in the 52nd I cannot be of much use in forming a regiment, and therefore he will not say so to the Duke of York; but that, from what he had seen, and from Colonel McKenzie's [sic] report of me, he thinks that I would be if I stayed five or six months longer in the regiment. However, as a Company is not to be had every day, he will write everything to the Duke that he thinks will make him give it me.[107]

Thus, as late as March 1804, Moore himself did not believe that William Napier would be 'of much use in forming a regiment' until he had undergone a further 'five or six months' instruction himself. And, as we shall see, by the end of 1804 both Moore and Mackenzie were devoting increasingly less time to Shorncliffe; for Mackenzie was suffering from ill health and, as he later told Sir Thomas Graham, Moore – who, in any case judging from the dating of his correspondence, seems to have spent much of his time at the Southern District's headquarters at Chatham, over thirty-five miles from Shorncliffe[108] – was 'otherwise occupied' on service abroad.[109]

In view of these considerations, it would seem unlikely that William Napier ever had the opportunity for much contact with either the Shorncliffe brigade's distinguished – and very busy – general, or the other senior officers of the 52nd who, in spring 1803, had been there to witness the initial formulation of the camp's system of instruction. Indeed, Napier makes only passing, mundane reference to Colonel Mackenzie who, as his battalion commander, took an active, daily part in the training work and would have been the one high-ranking officer one would expect this lowly subaltern to have some dealings with; at least until Napier transferred to the 43rd in August, 1804. Certainly, if William Napier *did* possess a detailed knowledge of the events and personalities at Shorncliffe, it is odd that, given his nature, he of all people did not make more of it in his memoirs.

Indeed, this factor alone makes one seriously question whether William Napier ever was accurately informed about the origins of the various innovations that were introduced at Shorncliffe; and there were, in any case, other officers present at the time who, as well as being more impartial, were, because of their relationship with Moore or by virtue of their more senior rank in his brigade, somewhat better qualified to speak on these matters. These included Moore himself; Mackenzie – who had already excelled himself in training the 90th Regiment as a light corps and who Moore had, after all, brought in specifically to help form and instruct the 52nd; George Napier – who, unlike William, had been in the 52nd since it was first made a light regiment and who was later to serve as Moore's aide-de-camp; and Sir Thomas Graham who, with Macken-zie, had trained his own 90th Regiment, was an extremely close friend of both that officer and Moore, served as the latter's aide-de-camp in the campaign and was a distinguished lieutenant-general before William Napier was a major.

The views put forward by these officers in their writings on Shorncliffe are a good deal more specific than William Napier's generalized, 'rosy-tinted reminiscences' and present a markedly different picture of events. We have already noted the modifications made by Glover to Napier's assertion about Moore devising 'improvements in . . . discipline . . . [and] arms . . .'. And it would also seem that, similarly, Moore was not responsible for those innovations made in 'drill . . . formations and movements . . .'. This was the contribution of Colonel Kenneth Mackenzie. Indeed, as W.S. Moorsom – the 52nd Light Infantry's official historian – pointed out only three years after the aged William Napier produced his account of Shorncliffe in his brother's biography:

> The Royal Military Calendar of 1820 states: '. . . Letters from Sir John Moore are now extant which corroborate the assertion that the improved system of marching, platoon-exercise, and drill, were entirely Lieut.-Colonel (afterwards Major-General) Mackenzie's'.[110]

Unfortunately for present day historians, neither Moorsom nor the *Royal Military Calendar* revealed where the letters referred to were found or what became of them. However, they were probably once located amongst the papers of Sir Thomas Graham and those of Kenneth Mackenzie, which still contain other documents that do indeed support the view that Mackenzie and not Moore devised the drill introduced at Shorncliffe.

To begin with, however, let us examine the evidence on the camp left us by William Napier's brother, George. He had been an officer in the 52nd since it first became a light corps, and in his memoirs he stressed the fact that Moore went to extraordinary lengths to secure the services of Mackenzie as commander of his new light regiment. 'Colonel Kenneth Mackenzie', George Napier recalled,

> took the command of the regiment to which Sir John Moore had appointed him as the officer at that period best adapted to form a light infantry regiment, our's being the first of that description of force; and as Colonel Mackenzie was an old, experienced and skilful officer, and had served a great deal, and particularly distinguished himself in Egypt in command of the 90th Regiment, and, indeed, was generally considered the best commanding officer in the army, Sir John Moore was fully justified in his choice of such an officer to command his regiment . . .[111]

This, surely, reveals something not only about Mackenzie's capabilities as a light infantry commander, but also about the kind of role Moore expected him to fulfil at Shorncliffe. He is described as 'the officer at that period best adapted to form a light infantry regiment . . .'. Would Moore then – after having gone to the trouble of having him transferred to the 52nd because of his recognized ability in the training of light troops – be likely to take the rather contradictory step of reducing Mackenzie to a glorified head clerk who just unthinkingly relayed

Moore's instructions and generally conducted the administration of the 52nd on the general's behalf? No: Mackenzie was selected by Moore because of his peculiar talent for training soldiers, particularly light infantrymen. As Moore once explained to Thomas Graham:

> . . . He never met with anyone so perfectly qualify'd [as Mackenzie] to instruct officers and men in every part of their duty, whether as to accuracy of movement in close order and according to the Regulations, or as to steadiness and intelligence in the looser order requir'd of Tirailleurs, as well as in everything relative to the duty of outposts.[112]

We have already noted how, in 1860, W.S. Moorsom had pointed to the existence of some evidence for the belief that, far from being the work of Moore, the 'improved system of marching, platoon-exercise, and drill [devised at Shorncliffe] were entirely Lieut.-Colonel Mackenzie's'. And, indeed, it would seem reasonable to conclude that Moore summoned Mackenzie to the 52nd with the specific intention of allowing him to play a leading role in devising and teaching the regiment's system of drill and manoeuvres. Certainly, on closer examination, the available primary evidence does support this view. We will see in the next chapter that Mackenzie devised an improved manual exercise for the 52nd and, with regard to tactical drill, the colonel told Thomas Graham that he taught Moore's regiment

> what I thought a light Regt. should be taught. . . . Sir John . . . was convinced the sistem [sic] was a good one, but he gave strong opposition to the most material parts of it for some time during the instruction, and . . . thought little about it after I left the Regt.[113]

Similarly, Mackenzie's obituary in the *Gentleman's Magazine*, written in 1834, included the illuminating comment that the colonel

> commenced with the 52nd a system of movements and exercise in which Sir John Moore at first acquiesced with reluctance, the style of drill, march and platoon exercise being entirely new; but when he saw the effect of the whole in a more advanced stage, he was not only highly gratified but became its warmest supporter.[114]

Likewise, in his *Life of an Old Soldier*, Lieutenant-Colonel J. Leach – who had served as a lieutenant in the 70th Regiment when it formed part of Moore's brigade at Shorncliffe – recalled how:

> In the early part of the Spring in 1803, John Moore picked and culled the finest and most effective men of the two battalions of the 52nd regiment, the first of which Lieutenant-Colonel Kenneth McKenzie [sic] was appointed to command and organise as Light Infantry . . . The new system of drill which . . . McKenzie introduced at this period, and which has been adopted by other light infantry regiments, it will scarcely be denied by the most prejudiced persons, has been attended with the most complete success.[115]

Indeed, a striking feature of Moore's outgoing correspondence during this period is the absence of regular references to matters relating to tactical drill. Whilst one can find a good deal of material in his letters demonstrating that he was very active in procuring weapons and other equipment for his new corps and in the general administration of Shorncliffe and the rest of the Southern District, as Maurice – the editor of Moore's diary – noted in 1904, one will search in vain for any details of tactical training in Moore's papers.[116]

This can, surely, be taken as a further indication that Moore was not primarily concerned with this aspect of the camp's work and left it in the capable hands of Mackenzie.[117] Indeed, he once said of that officer that he was such an accomplished trainer of light troops that 'he did not know of his equal in the service',[118] and on receiving the congratulations of the Commander-in-Chief on the excellence of the 52nd in August 1804, issued an order to the regiment stating that:

> The officers owe it to their own good conduct, and to the attention they have paid to their duty, but above all to the zeal with which they have followed the instructions of Lieut.-Colonel Mackenzie, to whose talents and to whose example the Regiment is indebted for its discipline and the character it has so justly acquired.[119]

However, perhaps the most conclusive piece of evidence for the view that Mackenzie devised the Shorncliffe system of drill is furnished by a letter written by Sir Thomas Graham – an extremely close friend of both Mackenzie and Moore and the latter's aide-de-camp during the Corunna campaign – on 15 October 1811. This was actually a reference supporting Mackenzie's application for employment on the home staff as an inspector and trainer of light troops. It was, therefore, a confidential summary and assessment by General Graham of Mackenzie's service record, and included the statement:

> Now I have it from Sir J. Moore's own mouth, that he did no more than sanction and uphold with his authority, the system which Mackenzie, then commanding . . . [Moore's] own Regt. the 52nd proposed, and that he never met with anyone so perfectly qualify'd to instruct officers and men in every part of their duty . . .[120]

Indeed, that system became the envy of the entire service and, as Captain Cooke then of the 'York' Regiment recalled in his memoirs, earned the Shorncliffe light regiments 'the admiration of all, for their discipline, and the rapidity of their light movements . . .'.[121] But what was the drill system used by the 52nd, 43rd and 95th? In his book *Sir John Moore's System of Training*, J.F.C. Fuller quoted a letter – 'in the author's possession' – supposedly written by Moore to Mackenzie, in which the general remarks 'I mean, therefore, to make De Rottenburg the groundwork . . .'.[122] This, however, is a rather controversial piece of evidence. Firstly, Fuller gives no indication as to where he got this document from; there is no copy of it in the Moore correspondence in the British Library, and the original is not to be found amongst Fuller's own papers and book drafts in the Rutgers State University.[123]

Secondly, the content and date of this missive are also puzzling: Moore does not seem to have concerned himself very much with tactical drill, and for him to write in mid-August 1805 – some two-and-a-half years after the Shorncliffe camp was first placed under his supervision – that he intended making De Rottenburg's manual the *basis* of the system would seem both uncharacteristic and anachronistic. Moreover, neither Moore nor Mackenzie were particularly involved with the Shorncliffe camp by this time: Sir John had been sent on an intelligence mission to Ferrol in Spain at the end of 1804 and, thereafter, was repeatedly employed on foreign service;[124] while Mackenzie, seriously injured in a fall from his horse at the end of November 1803, had retired on sick-leave the following summer and, as his correspondence reveals,[125] was at his home in Dundee on 1 September 1805. Although he made several attempts to return to active service,[126] chronic ill-health prevented him from doing so until as late as 1811, when he took command of a light infantry camp at Brabourne Lees, between Shorncliffe and Canterbury.[127]

But it is entirely on this controversial letter that Fuller based his reasoning about the type of drill introduced at Shorncliffe. The system, he argues, was not that of David Dundas and was perhaps that of Mackenzie as referred to in the *Royal Military Calendar* of 1820. He then, however, goes on to assert that it was 'not a light drill at all'[128] and concludes that:

> This letter plainly shows that whatever the system originated, adopted, or developed by Lieut.-Colonel Mackenzie may have been, it was not simply, or chiefly a system of skirmishing, but in place a close-order drill, probably a simplified Dundas.[129]

This reasoning is, however, clearly open to serious criticism in a number of respects. Firstly, whilst Fuller claims that the system that was introduced was not 'a light drill at all', he fails to produce any primary evidence to support this assertion. Indeed, although he concludes that the system was 'probably a simplified Dundas', he later concedes that from his research he is unable to demonstrate with any certainty what form the drill took or even who its author was.[130]

Yet, simultaneously, he cites a letter – supposedly written by Moore – which, he argues, proves that Rottenburg's drill manual formed 'the groundwork' for the Shorncliffe system. But, as we have seen, Rottenburg's work was exclusively devoted to the duties of light troops and all of the drills that are described in it are solely for the use of skirmishers; facts that Fuller was apparently ignorant of.[131] And had Moore not written in spring 1803 of the need to devise for the newly formed 52nd Light Infantry 'a system of Light movements . . .'?[132] Certainly, the 52nd continued to be instructed in the close-order drills laid down in Dundas's *1792 Regulations* as well as in those more suited to skirmishing; for the regiment always was intended to be a fusion of the line and light services. But the system specially devised by Mackenzie for the 52nd and later adopted by other light infantry units was, as the memoirs of Captain Cooke and Lieutenant-Colonel Leach confirm,[133] a drill for skirmishers.

Besides these considerations, Mackenzie's papers also confirm that, contrary to Fuller's argument, the Shorncliffe light brigade did not use Rottenburg's system of drill. Mackenzie replaced it with something he devised himself which was appreciably different and, consequently, as he told General Gross in February, 1812,

'. . . There is not in the service one Regt. of Light or Rifle that have the same plan of movement, exercises or instruction as was established in the 43rd, 52nd and Ist Batt. 95th. . . . Although the Shorncliffe system introduced in those Regt's. . . . was much approved of, no step was taken to introduce it into other Regt's . . . I am preparing a paper to be sent to the Adjt. General on marching and the platoon exercise such as was established at Shorncliffe and approved by Sir John Moore, giving the strongest reasons I can for having it introduced in the Army. I shall send you a copy of both. The style of march has been adopted by many Regt's. but neither have ever been sanctioned by Head Quarters. I mean to detail a great part of the instructions for Light Troops, and will sent it to you for your opinion.[134]

Again, in May 1812, Mackenzie wrote to Thomas Graham on the subject:

I enclose you my plan of Marching and Platoon exercise with the correspondence I had on the subject with head quarters. Every Light officer in my division I have ordered to copy it in a Private Book which they are all ordered to have. The Light Movements I have explained generally to the Regt's. at Drill and I am preparing them in a regular shape to be entered in their Books with other general observations that every officer should know, . . . the result of my own observations on service that I have actually seen the bad effects of not attending to.[135]

Whilst, as he himself states in these letters, certain minor aspects of Mackenzie's drill were taken up by most of Britain's light infantry regiments, the colonel's efforts to get approval for the adoption of the work as a whole by the entire light infantry service apparently failed; probably because switching units to a new tactical system in the midst of a war would have proved an extraordinarily complex problem. Nevertheless, Mackenzie's drill did not remain the preserve of the 52nd Regiment for which it was originally devised. As he made clear in his letter to General Gross in February 1812, the 'Shorncliffe system' was introduced into all the light units that were trained at the camp: 'the 43rd, 52nd and 1st Batt. 95th. . . .' This is an important factor: for it largely explains how, whilst Mackenzie was only lieutenant-colonel of the 52nd and thus primarily concerned with the unit alone, the rest of the Shorncliffe light corps acquired the same excellence in tactical drills and manoeuvre that he taught his own regiment.

From the outset, Moore's own 52nd had been intended to serve as a prototype for any subsequent units of light infantry that the duke of

York chose to form from existing regiments of the line. Indeed, in his correspondence with York during January 1803 on the number of line units to be initially involved in the experiment, Moore had written that 'It is my intention that no alterations should be made in the movement or exercise of the Corps until it is fixed what those shall be.', and had recommended that:

'. . . Until a system of Light movements is determined, & ready to substitute for the present regular one, it will be advisable to confine the change to one, or to as few Corps as possible.'[136]

By summer 1804, however, Moore and Mackenzie had completed preparing the 52nd as the model on which further light units could be moulded: Mackenzie had devised the necessary system of light movements and drill; and the new patterns of clothing and weapons issued to the regiment had been adequately tested. York was suitably pleased and the planned expansion of the light infantry arm was now implemented: a second battalion – formed around an officer *cadre* drawn from the first – was added to the 52nd on 8 August and based at Newbury (later Hythe); while, shortly before, the 43rd Light Infantry was moved to Shorncliffe to be trained and equipped in the same manner as the 52nd. Indeed, several officers, including William Napier, were transferred to the 43rd from the 52nd to pass on the skills they had learnt there. Thus, the perfection achieved in the latter regiment was gradually extended to the 43rd, and subsequent light units such as the 68th and 85th were, likewise, 'assimilated with regard to their clothing, arming and Discipline to the 43rd and 52nd Regiments'.[138]

Similarly, the 95th, also based at Shorncliffe, was influenced by developments in the 52nd. We have noted how, long before Moore's regiment became light infantry, the rifle corps had attained a high level of proficiency under the guidance of Stewart and Manningham. Those officers continued to be active and most of the credit for the 95th's excellence rightly belongs to them. However, as Mackenzie's papers confirm, the regiment adopted his drill and this was probably due to the influence of Moore who, as the brigade commander, 'approved'[139] and upheld 'with his authority, the system which Mackenzie, then commanding . . . the 52nd, proposed . . .'.[140] What is certain, however, is that 'The new system of drill which . . . Mackenzie introduced at this period . . . [was] adopted by other light infantry regiments . . .',[141] though, as we have seen, the work was only taken up in its entirety by those units that had been instructed at Shorncliffe.

However, it was not simply through precise drilling and tactical instruction that such excellent troops were produced. 'It was', as another diarist observed,

the internal and moral system, the constant superintendance of the officers, the real government and responsibility of the captains, which carried the discipline to such perfection.[142]

This 'internal and moral system' had two basic components. Firstly, great emphasis was placed on the duties and attributes of the officers. They were required to be at all times respectful and considerate towards their troops, and were also expected to be very familiar with even the most mundane details of the work of light infantry. To this end, George Napier explained,

Colonel Mackenzie began by assembling the officers and telling them that the only way of having a regiment in good order was by every individual thoroughly knowing and performing his duty: and that if the officers did not fully understand their duty, it would be quite impossible to expect that the men could or would perform theirs as they ought; therefore the best and surest method was to commence by drilling the whole of the officers, and when they became perfectly acquainted with the system, they could teach the men, and by their zeal, knowledge and, above all, good temper and kind treatment of the soldier, make the regiment the best in the service; and, as he predicted, it did become the finest and best behaved corps . . .[143]

Similarly, Captain Cooke recalled the officer training procedure that was followed by the 43rd Light Infantry:

When an officer entered this corps it was an invariable custom to send him to drill with a squad, composed of peasants from the plough tail, or other raw recruits, first learning the facings, marching, and companies' evolutions. That being completed, the officer put on cross belts and pouch, and learned the firelock exercise; then again he marched with the same: and when it was considered that the whole was perfect, with, and without arms, they began to skirmish in extended files, and last of all learned the duties of the sentry, and to fire ball cartridge at a target. The officer after all this was not considered clear of the adjutant, until he could put a company through the evolutions by word of command, which he had already practised in the ranks. It generally took him six months . . . at four times a day (an hour at each period) to perfect him in all he had to learn. . . . Subalterns inspected squads on parade: the company was then formed and given over to the captain, who, with the rest of the officers, never quitted their company to lounge about, so long as the soldiers continued under arms. The corps paraded twice a week in heavy marching order, and the mess was equally well conducted, in a system of style and economy happily blended.[144]

Such policies were consistently pursued by the 43rd and the other light units that were trained at Shorncliffe. Indeed, little, including active service, was allowed to substantially interfere with the staging of the regular drills and inspections. As, for instance, Lieutenant George Hennell commented to his brothers in a letter from the Peninsula written during September 1812:

We have a great deal of duty to do here besides which I have to drill twice a day so that I have but little time to myself. There is no regiment [which] drills their officers so much as ours & for that reason it is the best disciplined in the service.[145]

Besides this constant, intensive training of the officers, the Shorncliffe system of education had one other basic component. This consisted of the cultivation of what, by the standards of the day, were quite revolutionary attitudes amongst the officers and NCOs towards the sensitive issues of crime and punishment. George Napier recalled that:

> The great thing that Sir John Moore and Colonel Mackenzie used to impress upon the minds of the officers was that our duty was to do everything in our power to prevent crime, as then there would be no occasion for punishment . . . [146]

This, of course, was very much a development of the philosophy followed by De Rottenburg who, as we have seen, maintained that he 'never flogged his men, . . . but governed them in a patriarchal manner, more as a father would his children, than as commanding officers used to do in those days'. By seeking to abandon the Frederickian school's 'rule of the lash' in favour of what William Stewart once described as 'authority . . . softened by the feelings of honour and affection'. Moore and Mackenzie refined this revolutionary concept still further and their policy paid enormous dividends. The Shorncliffe light regiments emerged as models of discipline and, encouraging as they did the development of personal initiative amongst their members, became schools in leadership, producing a remarkably high proportion of the soldiers and statesmen who were to dominate the British establishment during the first half of the nineteenth century.[147] Sadly, Moore perished in the Corunna campaign and thus did not live to see the full fruits of his work. However, it would not be an exaggeration to say that at Shorncliffe with Mackenzie he laid the foundations of the disciplinary practices of the modern British Army. Certainly, his ability to win the confidence and affection of his troops was enormous and, as George Napier concluded about him, it would have been

> impossible for any father to devote himself more to the welfare of his sons than did Sir John Moore to that of his officers, and no parent could be more revered and beloved than he was by us all – officers, non-commissioned officers, and privates.[148]

Indeed, it would seem to have been in the field of general discipline that Moore made his greatest contribution to the work of the Shorncliffe camp. Certainly, there is a good deal of truth in Glover's claim that:

> [the] far happier system of discipline . . . [Moore] maintained in his brigade was in large measure made possible by his good fortune in commanding picked officers and men – and for that . . . he had to thank the Duke of York, without whose authority he could not have done the picking.[149]

But whilst, as Glover emphasizes, it was from the Commander-in-Chief that Moore derived his authority to pick suitable men from whom to form the 52nd, it was Moore who actually exercized that power of selection.[150] And if the duke's choice of Moore as the officer who was to supervise the details of the project was a reflection of the 'soundness of

York's judgement of men',[151] then Moore's subsequent selection of talented officers like Mackenzie is clear evidence of his own ability to assess a man's worth.

But, more importantly, Glover's reasoning fails to account for the excellence of all the light units at Shorncliffe. Whilst Moore was allowed to pick officers and men for the new 52nd Light Infantry and, Manningham and Stewart were given the same privilege in forming the Experimental Rifle Corps that later became the 95th,[152] the 43rd was not composed of selected men. Indeed, on its arrival at Shorncliffe, this regiment was in a 'very bad state of discipline'.[153]

How then, did the 43rd come to be as disciplined a unit as the 52nd and the 95th? One can conclude that it was due to Moore's influence. He had first shown an interest in general disciplinary policy as early as 1796 when, as we have seen, he wrote to General Abercromby about the need for better officers and more 'discipline and interior economy' in the regiments he was then commanding in the West Indies.[154] 'The discipline of modern times', he had concluded,

> which consists of parades, firelock exercises etc. is easy to the officer as it takes up but an hour or 2 in the day. The machine is in other respects conducted by the commanding and staff officers.[155]

Moore found this rather leisurely approach to discipline highly unsatisfactory and, at Shorncliffe, sought to replace it with what he had once described to Abercromby as 'The discipline of the ancient'. The new light regiments were to be maintained in good order by constant exercise and 'by every individual thoroughly knowing and performing his duty . . .'.[156] Such dedication was particularly required of the officers attached to each company; for, as Mackenzie explained to George Napier and his colleagues in the 52nd: '. . . If the officers did not fully understand their duty, it would be quite impossible to expect that the men could or would perform theirs as they ought . . .'.[157] Indeed, it was, as another observer noted, this 'constant superintendance of the officers, the real government and responsibility of the captains, which carried the discipline to such perfection'.[158]

But in allocating Moore responsibility for any particular innovation that took place at Shorncliffe, we need to sound a note of caution; for there is little unambiguous evidence that one can examine to determine the general's exact role. The mere fact that he was the brigade commander and ultimately responsible for the Shorncliffe camp has too often been assumed to be conclusive proof for the notion that he was the originator of all the various improvements in discipline, arms and movements that were introduced there. But it is clear that other people were also deeply involved in this work and, in some respects, were of as much significance, if not more, than Moore himself. We have seen, for example, how the notion of forming light regiments from units of the line was not originally devised by Moore at all. The policy had been advocated by several military thinkers – including General Money in England – for some considerable time and, indeed, had already been adopted by a number of European Armies. The idea of conducting a similar experiment in Britain was, as the memoirs of Moore's brother confirm,[159] put forward by the duke of York who originally suggested that these corps should – like the Experimental Rifle Corps he had formed three years before – be marksmen, armed with rifles. Moore's counter-suggestion that they should be armed with 'the usual muskets' instead was only a minor modification to York's original idea[160] and, strictly speaking, was not taken up; for the new light infantry regiments were not subsequently equipped with 'the usual muskets', but with a specially produced, lightweight fusil.[161]

Likewise, whilst the duke of York clearly valued Moore's expert opinion, entrusted the general implementation of the scheme to him and asked him to provide 'some detailed plan as to the manner of carrying the measure into execution',[162] the general was, for all his talents, not left completely to his own devices. York was not, as Glover points out, 'a meekly suggestible Commander-in-Chief [who merely] followed Moore's advice',[163] but was himself an experienced, imaginative soldier who continued to take an active part in formulating the details of the scheme which he had, after all, first suggested to Moore and the other members of the Board of General Officers. It seems to have been York who was responsible for the new light regiment being equipped with the special fusil[164] and some of the other innovations were probably his ideas, too. He was, as we have seen, implementing reforms in every branch of the Army at this time and, as Moore himself was to acknowledge to the duke's secretary in furnishing the requested 'detailed plan' for the formation of the new 52nd:

> I have confined myself . . . merely to the selection of men & officers; leaving what relates to their armament, appointments & movements . . . until after I have had the honour of conversing with His Royal Highness, & receiving his commands.[165]

Thus, the duke of York evidently played an important role in determining the shape of the new light regiments and, in other respects, what has often been attributed solely to Moore was, perhaps, partly or wholly the work of other officers. Moore's views on general discipline, for example, were reflected in the disciplinary policies followed by the light regiments trained at Shorncliffe, and there is some evidence to support the belief that he did take an active interest in this aspect of the camp's work. But such a system of discipline had been experimented with by De Rottenburg's Fifth Battalion of the 60th for some years and, more significantly, Stewart and Manningham had adopted it in the Experimental Rifle Corps which later became the 95th and was stationed at Shorncliffe. It is far from inconceivable, indeed it is likely, that Moore was influenced by the thinking of these other eminent trainers of light troops and may well have adopted for use in the 52nd many of the ideas that Stewart, for instance, had alredy tried and tested in the 95th.

Similarly, it would appear that Moore played an important part in extending the 52nd's system of drill to the other light regiments in the Shorncliffe camp. But, as we have seen, it was Mackenzie rather than Moore who devised that system and took the leading role in its instruction. Indeed, at first, Moore seems to have had grave doubts about the drill and accepted it only with reluctance.[166] However, he later became its 'warmest supporter' and, as Sir Thomas Graham told Calvert, was to 'sanction and uphold [it] with his authority . . .'

Nor should Mackenzie's contribution to general discipline be over-looked. He had turned the 90th into a model corps many years before the 52nd Light Infantry was formed and, at Shorncliffe, apparently concerned himself nearly as much with this aspect of the work as he did with tactical training. George Napier's memoirs confirm that Mackenzie *began* his instruction of the 52nd by gathering the officers together and lecturing them on the disciplinary policy that was to be followed: '. . . By their zeal, knowledge, and, above all, good temper and kind treatment of the soldier', he told them, they would 'make the regiment the best in the service; and', George Napier concluded, 'as he predicted it did become the finest and best behaved corps . . . '.[167]

The available evidence for either interpretation being inconclusive, it is possible that here Mackenzie was either doing nothing more than passing on Moore's opinions or, on the other hand, was, as with the tactical training, playing the leading role in determining the system of discipline. What is more likely, however, is that Moore and the colonel held views on these matters that were generally similar and both took a share in teaching them to the 52nd's officers. Moore then used his authority to extend the basic principles to the 43rd.

Certainly, when taken in conjunction with the influx of officers trained in the 52nd, this would explain how the 43rd progressed from being in 'a very bad state' to being what Lieutenant George Hennell was later to describe as the 'best disciplined [regiment] in the service'.[168] But care must be taken in regarding the high quality of all the light units trained at Shorncliffe as a reflection of the effectiveness of Moore's personal role; the 95th, for example, had acquired much of its proficiency long before Moore had any connections with the regiment and much of what was done in the 52nd was the work of Mackenzie. And if Moore is to be given the credit for personally inspiring similar excellence in the 43rd, then he is perhaps to be criticized for his failure to extend that perfection to all the units under his command; for it is a frequently overlooked fact that, besides the three light corps, there were three other units at Shorncliffe – the 70th, 59th and 4th Regiments – which formed part of Moore's brigade and for which he was ultimately responsible.[169] Yet, unlike the skirmisher units, these three regiments of the line apparently remained much as they had been before Moore took command of them. Many of the reforms introduced in the light regiments were, of course, not applicable to regiments of the line. But in the case of general discipline, for example, Moore's apparent failure to raise these units from relative obscurity to the same celebrated position that his other corps ultimately enjoyed is an interesting point. As he confessed to the adjutant-general late in 1803:

> I had hopes, from the pains I have taken, and the mode I directed to be followed in the instruction of the regiments of my brigade, to have made much progress, and if honoured with another visit from H.R.H. to have shown him something tolerably perfect, but except in the 52nd the progress has been trifling. The other commanding officers, though many of them good enough men, have not military heads, and seem incapable of acting from general instruction.[170]

Indeed, this concluding remark by Moore about the other commanding officers' inability to act 'from general instruction' provides what is perhaps a valuable, if small, insight into the way training was organized at Shorncliffe; for it seems to confirm that Moore's role was primarily to give guidance of a general nature, leaving the detailed instruction to the officers of the respective regiments. The ultimate success of that instruction, therefore, rested as much on regimental officers like Mackenzie as it did on Moore himself.

Thus, one can conclude that in the past Moore's role at Shorncliffe, though of great importance, has, in many respects, been misrepresented or over-emphasized. Certainly, the situation was rather more complex than has often been allowed, and the notion that Moore alone was responsible for the creation and shaping of Britain's first permanent light infantry regiments stands in need of considerable modification. The earlier work done by other officers such as Manningham and Stewart was not without significance, nor was the role of the duke of York.

But, above all, the contribution of Kenneth Mackenzie to the training of the British light infantry arm has been grossly undervalued. He played an important role in formulating the Shorncliffe systems of both discipline and drill and, indeed, it would seem that he was the principal architect of the latter. Nor were his successes confined to that camp alone. He had first distinguished himself with Graham's 90th Regiment and, although crippled by the injuries he sustained when he fell from his horse in November 1803, was promoted to major-general and continued to be intermittently employed as a trainer of skimishers until the very end of our period. Indeed, in 1815, only days before the Waterloo campaign, he was recalled from active service with the duke of Wellington's army by the Commander-in-Chief and appointed to 'the command of the Light Troops in England, for the purpose of organizing and disciplining those corps'.[171]

That York should select him as the officer best qualified to supervise this latter-day Shorncliffe is ample testimony to Mackenzie's ability as a trainer of light troops. Indeed, had the struggle against Napoleon dragged on, his reputation in this field may well have come to overshadow Moore's. But it was not to be and Mackenzie's greatest work remained that which he had undertaken at Shorncliffe where he played a major role in shaping the 52nd and its sister regiment the 43rd. They, along with Stewart's rifle corps, became the *élite* brigade of the whole British Army and eventually took pride of place as the nucleus of the celebrated Light Division of the Peninsular War. Promoted to lieutenant-general and knighted for his services, Kenneth Mackenzie took the Scottish title 'Douglas of Glenbervie' and retired from the forces shortly after the end of the Napoleonic Wars. He died in 1834.

As, in 1803, the work of transforming the 52nd into the prototype light infantry corps began at Shorncliffe, a distinguished French *émigré* officer arrived in England and took up a post as an adviser to the War Office. Born in Cambrai in 1739, his name was Charles François Dumouriez – the former commander of the French '*Armée du Nord*' who, in 1792, had won the Battle of Jemappes and had thus made a significant contribution to the survival of the new-born French Republic.

Within months of this victory, however, Dumouriez, accused of treason by his Revolutionary masters and bitterly disillusioned with the trend of French politics, had deserted to the Allies and had gone into exile, eventually settling near Hamburg in 1795. Here, he spent much of the next seven years in writing his memoirs and other works in which his views on military affairs figured prominently. As the commander of the '*Armée du Nord*', he had been intimately involved with the development of the new French mode of warfare and had witnessed its impact on the battlefields of Flanders. Consequently, he possessed a knowledge of French tactical methods that few could rival and, like his countryman General Money, was well aware of the central role that light troops played in those tactics.

Dumouriez steadily grew into a fanatical hater of the Republic and its leaders and, as Napoleon's star began to rise, he devoted himself increasingly to the exiled Bourbons' cause. In October 1800, he met Nelson at Hamburg and had a lengthy discussion with the admiral, impressing on him the need for Britain to prepare to resist a French invasion. This conversation led to further correspondence between the two men and, during August 1801, Nelson wrote to Addington, the Prime Minister, enclosing letters written by Dumouriez regarding the danger of a French attack on England. The opening of negotiations – which eventually culminated in the signing of the Peace of Amiens with France – gave the British cabinet some hope that the threat of invasion could be removed through diplomatic channels alone. But within months it was clear that the Amiens pact was destined to collapse and, as the danger of a French landing rose again, the War Office became increasingly interested in Dumouriez as a potential adviser on defence affairs.

Accordingly, once hostilities had resumed in May 1803, a suggestion by Nelson that Dumouriez be brought to England was taken up. It is not clear exactly when the general arrived, but it is known that he appeared alongside other prominent *émigrés* at a military review held in October

and commenced a large, written study of Britain's defences during that
same month.[172] However, his reference in this manuscript to an earlier
memorandum, written 'by order of the Commander-in-Chief, on the
need of forming corps of light troops,'[173] suggests that he had been
undertaking written work for the Horse Guards for some time. Indeed,
in the Public Record Office, appended to Dumouriez's work on the
defence of England, are two collections of *Notes* relating to *Corps des
Chasseurs*. Covering letters enclosed with these interesting documents
suggest that they were composed at some time prior to September 1803;
and they form, almost certainly, either a part or the whole of the
memorandum to which Dumouriez refers in his *Mémoir militaire sur
l'Angleterre*.

This memorandum on the need to form corps of *chasseurs* must have
been submitted during the period when York was finalizing his plans for
the conversion of the 52nd to light infantry and, doubtlessly,
Dumouriez's opinions were sought in order that they could be taken into
consideration as the scheme was implemented. His most important
work, however, was the large study of British defence policy – the
Mémoir militaire sur l'Angleterre – that he undertook between October
1803 and May 1804, and it is in this manuscript that most of
Dumouriez's more interesting comments on light forces are to be found.

To begin with, Dumouriez warned of the effectiveness of the French
light troops in enclosed terrain and stressed the significance this would
have should southern England be invaded. Referring to his earlier
memorandum, he wrote:

> I again express the hope that there may be raised a large amount of light
> infantry and horse artillery, for these are beyond a doubt the kind of
> defenders most usefully opposed to the French sharpshooters in so cut-up and
> enclosed a country as England. . . .
>   The French have conquered all Europe with their sharpshooter methods;
> and here the advantage would lie with them, seeing that the English would
> come up against them in [serried] masses, and the greater their dash the
> greater their losses – that is what happened to the Russians in Switzerland.
> The French would make their way more easily in a country cut up by hedges,
> trees, parks, fences, where each estate acts as a kind of entrenched position,
> . . . than across more open ground; they would show to advantage there
> against massed troops unaccustomed to the same style of fighting.[174]

These observations were essentially similar to those that had been
made by Money, Jarry and other theorists over the previous five years;
and, like those thinkers, Dumouriez called for the creation of large
numbers of light infantry to counter those of the French – seeing 12,000
chasseurs and numerous companies of marksmen and rangers as the
minimum requirement.[175] But in his detailed analysis of what light
troops were for and how they should be deployed Dumouriez went on
to imaginatively combine established notions with some of his own;
producing concepts which, if not wholly revolutionary, were certainly

remarkable milestones in the history of the development of light forces. Indeed, it can be argued that Dumouriez was the original innovator of such concepts as the 'Island of Resistance' – developed and used to such effect by the Germans in the *Blitzkrieg* battles of World War II[176] – and rapid deployment forces – such as those currently being assembled by the United States of America for swift military intervention in troubled areas of the globe.

From the outset, Dumouriez stressed the importance of combining the various arms – infantry, cavalry and artillery– into self-reliant units. This had first been advocated by Bourcet in 1775,[177] and the legions of the American War of Independence were early examples of such combined-arm forces – the forerunners of the present-day army division. But Dumouriez urged that the principle of integrating different types of units should be carried to the lowest level and, by so doing, firmly established the precedent for the modern, tactical combat team. 'I have insisted', he wrote,

> upon the amalgamation of the light artillery and light cavalry with the infantry of the same species, thus constituting new bodies . . . which may be approved.
>
> . . . It would be . . . advisable to divide the whole army in divisions of 12,000 men, whereof at most an eighth should be cavalry, one half heavy infantry fighting stoutly in battalions and the remainder rangers, sharpshooters and light infantry fighting irregularly in the French way, as sharpshooters. Each division must have eight field guns, four howitzers, four mortars, and two pieces of cannon *per* infantry battalion and two companies of mounted artillery to form the vanguards with the light infantry and the light cavalry.
>
> . . . In a country so destitute of open plains and cut up by countless hedges that are all so many impediments, one must parcel out each of the five arms – heavy infantry, light infantry, heavy cavalry, light cavalry and artillery – in small portions and amalgamate these. Thus, in every case there must be some light cavalry with light infantry and mounted artillery.[178]

The system of defence advocated by Dumouriez for use in southern England was founded on quite a revolutionary idea. The defence was to be based on lines of positions – fortified camps or villages – garrisoned by heavy forces with mobile light divisions acting in support:

> The whole defence should be divided in first and second lines, or in *stationary* divisions intended to dispute foot by foot the different [strong] points, . . . and *mobile* divisions meant to afford them immediate support.[179]

'These fixed camps', Dumouriez explained,

> are pivots on which must turn the whole defence. . . . [They] must be set out in a chess-board manner, so that, whatever the direction in which [the enemy] . . . attempts to go through, he shall always find himself in a re-entering angle of which the apex is a camp intended to resist him and the . . . sides bodies of troops supported by other camps . . . These mobile side-lines are meant to press, harass and attack him on the flank or in the rear,

. . . prevent him extending his battle-line, starve him, and drive him against the army posted at the apex of the angle that shall stop him and fight him in superior numbers. By this arrangement, if he pierces the first line, he will still wedge himself in the re-entering angle of the second line and so on . . . His progress will be very slow, his losses many and irreplaceable, and he will end by being quite unable to withstand a general attack . . .[180]

This particular concept of offensive-defensive fighting was essentially the forerunner of the German 'Island of Resistance' – used to great effect in World War II engagements like Operation 'Goodwood' and now attracting interest in the current debate about the potential uses of light troops in the defence of the Federal Republic of Germany.[181] Like southern England in Dumouriez's time, the West Germany of today is ideally suited to the operations of light forces. Having been increasingly urbanized and enclosed, some 60 per cent of the terrain is now covered in forests and settlements. Indeed, a typical brigade sector on NATO's German front contains no less than 85 villages, each separated from its neighbours by an average distance of only three-and-a-half kilometres.[182]

In such countryside, Dumouriez's notion of a 'sword and shield' defence was – and still is – perfectly feasible. Light, mobile divisions could strike at the enemy's flanks and rear as he struggled to make headway through a web of settlements and redoubts. Using these 'fixed points' as bases for their operations, tactical combat teams of light troops could penetrate into the intervening territory to harass the enemy from all directions. If severely pressed the teams could take refuge in the villages, poised to re-emerge and take advantage of any opportunity that presented itself. Heavy infantry and guns would help to retain control of the fixed points themselves while, deployed in the second line, ready 'either to restrain and stop the enemy's rush or to charge him by lashing through the intervals between [the villages]', would be units of heavy cavalry – the Napoleonic period's equivalent of the modern armoured division. Manned by a relatively small number of troops, such a defensive web could, at the very least, contain an attacking army for several days and Dumouriez – faced by similar problems to those confronting the NATO planners of today – saw it as a simple means of buying time in which the country's armed forces could be fully mobilized to meet any invasion. 'If the French carry out the expedition', he warned,

all their movements are sure to be abrupt. Eight days will decide the fate of the war: it is only by meeting them with similar promptitude that their first onrush can be checked . . . The enemy would take advantage of [any] . . . disorder and irresolution, augmenting them by the celerity of his march, and would soon overthrow, one upon the other, several armies, mixed up with baggages, field carts, cattle, inhabitants in flight, etc. Numbers and bravery would be beaten by their own disorder far more than by the strength and talents of the foe.[183]

Part of Dumouriez's plan for coping with invasions and other such sudden military threats was to create substantial units that could be quickly mobilised and moved to any trouble spot. Twenty-five per cent of every army should, he argued, be formed into these latter-day rapid deployment forces and kept in reserve. 'Composed chiefly of horse artillery and light infantry and cavalry,' they should, he urged, be 'ever ready to march, capable of mustering speedily and proceeding to the help of a threatened, attacked or invaded country'.[184] In current-day warfare planning, light forces that can be 'plugged' into areas of conflict at high speed are becoming increasingly commonplace; the new US light divisions and the French Rapid Action Force being good examples.[185] Modern technology – notably aircraft and helicopters – have enabled this concept to be refined and extended to a degree hitherto impossible, but the concept itself was first thought of at least 180 years ago.

Indeed, in his writings on the defence of Britain, Dumouriez was to exhibit a remarkable amount of foresight in outlining the potential roles of light troops. But many of his ideas were not to be put to the test in his own lifetime; the French never landed in England and his defence '*en échiquier*' remained untried. Indeed, as the threat of invasion receded, Dumouriez found himself increasingly redundant and, in the later years of the Napoleonic Wars, took to bombarding military celebrities – notably Wellington – with his views on every strategic and tactical issue that came to prominence. This constant stream of advice – mostly unsought – eventually irritated a number of recipients and Dumouriez became somewhat unpopular with many members of the Allied military hierarchy. With the final defeat of Napoleon in 1815, he found himself relegated to almost complete obscurity and died, at Henley-on-Thames, in 1823. It was a rather unglamorous end for a man who, besides producing some ingenious written work on light forces and other aspects of military theory, had also led an active military career lasting 45 years, served as the commander-in-chief of two major armies, won one of the most famous victories in the history of war, and had also, at one time, been France's Minister of Foreign Affairs and Minister of War.[186]

Another officer who came to prominence through his links with Britain's light infantry arm during this period – and whose fame proved more durable – was Robert Craufurd. He was born in 1764 at Newark Castle in Ayr and first joined the armed forces at the age of fifteen; becoming subaltern in the 25th Foot. A keen student of his profession, he devoted a great deal of time over the next few years to the study of military theory and even travelled to Potsdam to observe the Prussian Army's annual training camps. By 1783 he had attained the rank of captain and, after seeing service in India and Ireland, was dispatched to Switzerland as an official observer to report on the Austrians' campaign against the French in 1799. On his return from that mission, he was immediately posted overseas again, this time taking part in the duke of York's ill-fated expedition to Holland.

There followed a period of uncertainty in Craufurd's life. Deeply devoted to his wife, he found himself torn between his allegiance to her and the demands his chosen profession made upon him. For some time, his family commitments proved the stronger attraction and Craufurd, setting aside his military career, entered politics and was elected to the House of Commons. However, he soon became bored with domestic life and, resolving to devote himself to the Army once more, resigned his seat to go on foreign service.[187] Appointed to the rank of colonel, he subsequently sailed to Montevideo to take part in General Whitelocke's 1806 campaign against the Spanish. Demonstrating great ability as a light infantry officer, he was entrusted with the corps' flank companies and saw appreciable action in the later fighting about Buenos Aires before being taken prisoner in the concluding battle of the campaign.

On his return to Europe his talents as a commander of skirmishers were acknowledged and he was appointed to lead the light brigade of General Baird's corps in Sir John Moore's Corunna campaign. This marked the beginning of his long and famous association with the forces serving in the Peninsula. Later in 1809 at the head of the units Moore and Mackenzie had trained at Shorncliffe, 'Black Bob' – as his troops dubbed him – executed the most celebrated forced march in modern military history, covering the 53 miles between Plasencia and the battlefield of Talavera in only 24 hours.[188] The following February, Wellington created the famous Light Division by supplementing Craufurd's existing command of the 95th, 52nd and 43rd Regiments with two battalions of Portuguese *cacadores*.[189]

Under 'Black Bob's' inspired leadership this formation became the *élite* division of the British forces in the Peninsula, playing a key role in most of Wellington's engagements and providing a model of discipline for the rest of the service. Of course, much of Craufurd's success with the Light Division cannot be attributed directly to him: the nucleus of the formation had been trained at Shorncliffe by Mackenzie and Moore, and the foundations of its excellence were laid by them. Furthermore, Craufurd had very different attitudes from those other two officers – or, indeed, from Jarry and Rottenburg – in several important respects, notably on the question of general discipline. We have already seen how the Shorncliffe system was essentially based on the creation of a mutual respect between officers and men. Moore and his colleague took the view that bad behaviour could be obviated simply by treating the troops in a humane way and by developing their sense of personal and regimental pride. Craufurd, on the other hand, had little time or interest for such niceties. More like Wellington who, to a Royal Commission, once expressed the opinion that 'I have no idea of any great effect being produced on British soldiers by anything but the fear of immediate corporal punishment',[190] Craufurd preferred to flog and hang his regiments into order, often inflicting the most hideous punishments for the slightest deviation from the very strict standards that he demanded.

Little wonder, therefore, that many in the army came to detest him and even George Napier – one of his closer friends – was forced to concede that:

> Brilliant as some of the traits of his character were, and not withstanding the good and generous feelings which often burst forth like a bright gleam of sunshine from behind a dark and heavy cloud, still there was a sullenness which seemed to brood in his innermost soul and generate passions which knew no bounds.[191]

But the crude and unenlightened system of discipline followed by Craufurd had been the standard one of the Frederickian school, and it was to be pursued by many officers for decades after the end of the Napoleonic Wars as the most effective way of obtaining obedience from their troops. Moore and Rottenburg had suggested a different approach, but Craufurd – often suddenly confronted by the serious indiscipline that years of gruelling active service could give rise to – clung to the old methods that had stood the test of time. In his defence, Captain Kincaid of the 95th observed that

> While he exacted from . . . [the soldiers] the most rigid obedience, he was, on his own part, keenly alive to everything they had a right to expect from him in return, and woe befell the commissary who failed to give a satisfactory reason for any deficiences in his issues. It is stated that one of them went to the commander-in-chief to complain that he had been unable to procure bread for the light division, and that General Craufurd had threatened that if they were not supplied within a given time, he would put him in the guard house.* 'Did he?' said his lordship; 'then I would recommend you to find the bread, for if he said so, he'll do it!'[192]

'. . . If this does not redeem Craufurd and his cat [-o'-nine-tails],' Kincaid concluded, 'I give it up'.

Nor did the general's methods prove ineffective. The Light Division came to be regarded as the finest in Wellington's army and Craufurd's reputation as a commander of light troops continued to grow. He was particularly envied for his skill in aspects of *la petite guerre*. George Napier recalled that:

> As a general commanding a division of light troops of all arms, Craufurd certainly excelled. His knowledge of outpost duty was never exceeded by any British general, and I much doubt if there are many in any other service who know more of that particular branch of the profession than he did. . . . His mental activity was only surpassed by his physical powers. The moment that his division was at its ground for the night he never moved from his horse until he had made himself master of every part of his post, formed his plans for defence if necessary, and explained all his arrangements to the staff . . . and the field officers of each regiment, so that if his orders were strictly obeyed a surprise was impossible.[193]

---

*In some accounts, Craufurd threatened to hang the commissary.

In view of all this, it is a little surprising that Craufurd never devised any improvements in the tactics and drill of the light infantry that he commanded. He did, however, contribute an invaluable work to the general military library: a collection of standing orders that he enforced in the Light Division until he was mortally wounded at the storming of Ciudad Rodrigo in 1812. Containing highly detailed sections on such topics as the preparation and execution of marches, duties in camps or quarters, fatigue and foraging parties, pickets, inspections and general administration, these regulations enabled the Light Division's day to day business to be conducted with the utmost efficiency. '. . . By long experience, unwearied zeal and constant activity, united to practice', recalled George Napier, Craufurd had

> founded a system of discipline and marching which arrived at such perfection that he could calculate to the minute the time his whole division, baggage, commissariat etc would take to arrive at any given point, no matter how many days' march. Every officer and soldier knew his duty in every particular, and also knew how he must perform it.[194]

Rapidly emulated by other corps in the Peninsular Army, Craufurd's *Standing Orders* served as the informal basis for the conduct of troops on the march throughout the Napoleonic Wars. Indeed, so good were they found to be that in 1844 and again in 1880 they were republished and enforced as official regulations for the British forces in Ireland.[195] Fittingly, one of 'Black Bob's' old units, the 43rd Light Infantry, even continued to follow them until well into the 1890s, when only growing obsolescence in the face of improved military technology finally led to their replacement.

Having examined the major written works on the duties of the light infantry, before concluding this section we should acknowledge the smaller role of the minor English studies that also appeared during this period.

The first of these was composed by Baron Gross, a field officer in the Dutch Brigade of the British Army. His book, *Duties of an Officer in the Field and Principally of Light Troops*, was published in 1801 and was similar in style and content to the earlier study *The Partisan in War* by Andrew Emmerich. Containing sections on the conduct of retreats, vanguards, sentries and patrols, there was, at least from the point of view of instruction, little in it that had not already been covered far better in Jarry's manual. Nevertheless, it contained a few astute observations on the importance of having skilled light infantry and made a useful if limited contribution to the literature available to British officers on the work of such troops.

A similar work was that published in 1804 by Captain T.H. Barber, the commander of the 'Duke of Cumberland's Sharpshooters'. Barber's *Instructions for the Formation and Exercise of Volunteer Sharpshooters* was largely a summary of official doctrine on the duties and training of light troops. In addition to quoting Jarry's manual at length it contained a detailed examination of Rottenburg's drill system, supplemented with general comments on tactics. The section covering aimed fire and target practice, however, was more detailed than anything found in previous works and contained lots of useful hints and observations on this important aspect of the skirmisher's art. At a time when, as we shall see in the next chapter, the significance attached to the concept of aimed fire was growing in Britain, such a study formed a useful addition to the written material available on the subject.

Lastly, Captain T.H. Cooper's *Practical Guide for the Light Infantry Officer* merits some comment. Published in 1806, this work appeared at a time when the development of the British light infantry arm was well under way and the demand for officers' handbooks and the like was steadily mounting. Noting that:

> The great importance of a well disciplined Light Infantry is no longer disputed, though it had, till lately been either too little attended to, or too little valued,[196]

Cooper produced a study that was a blend of useful factual information and perceptive observations on the important role of light troops. Containing a full explanation of Rottenburg's tactical drill – including the various bugle-calls – as well as sections on such subjects as aimed fire, it proved very popular as a book of basic instructions for light infantry officers and remained so throughout the Napoleonic Wars.

CHAPTER V
Aimed fire

As we have seen, the Frederickian school of tactics that dominated European military thought from 1740 until the beginning of the nineteenth century placed little emphasis on the concept of aimed fire; infantry were trained to fire massive, controlled volleys and to deliver as many of these salvoes in a given period of time as possible. Little importance was attached to the accuracy of this musketry. Indeed, aiming was usually deliberately discouraged because it tended to slow down the rate of fire.[1] As Scharnhorst was to comment after Prussia's disastrous war with France in 1806: 'Before the war we taught the men to load quickly, but not well, to fire quickly, but without aiming. This was very ill-considered.'[2]

This policy can be at least partly explained by the technological crudity of the firearms that were in use at this time. As we saw in Chapter III, the principal weapon of the infantry throughout the French Revolutionary and Napoleonic period was the smoothbore, flintlock musket; a firearm which was, for a number of reasons, highly inaccurate. In the first place the standard-issue musket lacked any real sights. The clip near the muzzle to which the bayonet was fixed served as a rough guide to the soldier, but this was completely obscured when the bayonet was in place and, other than the breech pin, there was nothing to use as a rear sight whatsoever.[3]

Secondly, the construction of the barrel and the design of bullet used did little to improve the accuracy of the flintlock. The lack of rifling and the large windage in the barrel, coupled with the employment of a spherical, heavy shot, led to a low muzzle velocity and a poor ballistic performance. The bullet followed an increasingly curved and erratic trajectory and, over a distance of around 120 yards, could be expected to fall some five feet on the vertical axis.[4] Thus, we find the great French tactician Guibert advising:

> Suppose a battalion of the enemy to be before you. If the distance is three hundred toises*, the soldier should be told to aim three feet above the battalion; if at two hundred, about a foot and a half; one hundred and fifty, at

---

*A *toise* was approximately two yards.

the hats; one hundred, at the middle of the body; fifty or sixty, at the knees
. . . but never lower.[5]

'This principle of not levelling precisely on the mark,' he continued,

is confirmed by all chasseurs. Those who kill game at almost every shot,
never fire in having their game full on the line of level of their pieces; they not
only fire on the spot where their game is at the time their shot arrives; but
they aim more or less above it, according to the distance it is from them.[6]

Thus, the standard weapon of the infantry during this period was
remarkably inaccurate and any attempt to aim such a firearm was an
extremely haphazard affair. As Colonel Hanger commented in 1808:

A soldier's musket, if not exceeding badly bored, and *very crooked, as many
are*, will strike the figure of a man at 80 yards, it may even at 100 yards; but a
soldier *must be very unfortunate indeed* who shall be wounded by a *common
musket* at 150 yards, PROVIDED HIS ANTAGONIST AIMS AT HIM; and
as to firing at a man at 200 yards with a common musket, you may just as
well fire at the moon, and have the same hopes of hitting your object. I do
maintain . . . that NO MAN WAS EVER KILLED AT TWO HUNDRED
YARDS by a common soldier's musket, by the person who aimed at him.[7]

In addition to being often 'badly bored' and 'very crooked', flintlock
muskets and rifles suffered from other technological drawbacks which
did little to promote accurate and consistently effective firing. As the
slightest dampness could render the flint mechanism useless, a sudden
fall of rain, for example, could leave dozens of troops virtually
weaponless. In his description of the action at Sabugal in Spain in 1811,
for instance, one eye-witness reported that there was 'A heavy fall of rain
in the middle of the fight, and for a short time not a musket would go
off.'[8] Flints worn with use could produce similar difficulties, as could the
rather coarse gunpowder that gradually clogged up the firing mechanism
with each discharge. Lieutenant George Bell of the 34th Foot, for
instance, complained how

Our wretched old flint firelocks would not burn powder at times until the
soldier took from the pocket in his pouch a triangular screw, to knock life
into his old flint, and then clear the touch-hole with a long brass picker that
hung from his belt.[9]

Another diarist also noted how 'Sometimes after a volley nearly a fourth
of the muskets were still loaded, owing to the inferiority of the flints
then supplied.'[10]

Also of great significance, particularly when it came to the accurate
aiming of these weapons, was the fitting of badly designed stocks.
Following an inspection of the First Battalion of the 95th Regiment in
May 1809, Major-General Thomas Graham wrote of their Baker Rifles,
for example, that:

These arms, tho' seemingly of an excellent quality in other respects are *most inconveniently* stocked – being *so straight* that the men can scarcely bring down their eyes so as to use the sights.[11]

However, even when they were fitted with a better designed stock, the 'kick' of the heavily charged[12] flintlock remained exceptionally powerful and prolonged periods of firing could cause severe bruising to the marksman's shoulder – rendering any attempt at taking aim downright painful. After the Battle of Fuentes d'Oñoro, for example, one light infantryman complained in his diary that:

> My shoulder was as black as coal, from the recoil of my musket; for this day I had fired 107 round of ball-cartridge.[13]

Likewise, the uncased, flintlock mechanisms that detonated the powder used in all the firearms of this period could only have served to deter the troops from taking proper aim at their targets. When firing the gun, particularly when facing into the prevailing wind, the soldier had to be careful 'to take precautions against getting his face scorched and his eyes injured by the back blown flare from the touch hole'.[14] Indeed, after the Battle of Vitoria in 1813, Lieutenant George Bell, for instance, noticed that many of the troops had had their faces blackened with powder in this way.[15] Such unpleasant side effects could have done little to encourage men to aim their weapons properly when firing.

In view of all this, it is not surprising that troops tended to expend a colossal amount of ammunition in relation to the total number of casualties they inflicted on the enemy. Henegan, who served as a senior officer in Wellington's commissariat, noted how at Vitoria in 1813, for example,

> . . . Each infantry soldier had sixty rounds of ball cartridges . . . making a total of three million rounds; . . . from the commencement to the close of the engagement, one million, three hundred and fifty thousand rounds of ball cartridges were issued . . . to the troops. Now allowing one half of these [one million three hundred and fifty thousand rounds] to have been expended at the termination of the battle, there was still a total of three million, six hundred and seventy-five thousand rounds fired against the enemy. The French lost in killed and wounded, eight thousand out of ninety thousand combatants; therefore it follows that only one musket-shot out of four hundred and fifty-nine took effect! and this calculation excludes altogether the injury inflicted on the enemy by ninety pieces of Artillery, which had fired nearly seven thousand rounds between them![16]

However, far from all of this tremendous imbalance between the number of shots fired by a unit and the number of casualties it inflicted was due to the poor quality of the weapons alone; much of it was attributable to the constraints imposed on the soldier by the rigid linear tactics in common use at this time. Frederickian tactical doctrines discouraged aiming and preached that the maintenance of 'a continual discharge at a high rate' was of paramount importance.[17] Infantry, therefore, were deployed shoulder to shoulder and delivered controlled volleys by platoons, companies or battalions with the minimum amount of time and effort being devoted to the aiming of their muskets. Indeed, the dense, lingering clouds of smoke generated by such salvoes usually masked the target very quickly and thus any attempts to take aim would rapidly have become quite futile. As the widely experienced soldier J.F.C. Fuller commented in 1925: '. . . It was, and still is, utterly impossible to deliver aimed fire from platoons of men packed together like herrings in a barrel'.[18]

The Frederickian system for delivering musketry was adhered to by the heavy infantry of all European armies throughout the eighteenth century. In the British service, for example, where, even before Dundas's Prussian-inspired drill was adopted, Frederickian fire tactics were in common use,[19] the infantry training manuals contained little guidance – if any at all – as to how the soldier could derive as much accuracy from his firelock as was possible. It is interesting to note, for instance, that none of the plates illustrating these books show the musketeer, while firing, actually taking aim along the barrel of his musket. Rather, he invariably appears with his gun pressed against his right shoulder and his head held erect. It was not until 1800 that this policy was changed and such plates began to depict the soldier taking proper aim at the target.[20]

Similarly, it was not until after 1786 that the British high command began issuing even modest quantities of live ammunition to the troops for target practice; for, as the rate – rather than the accuracy – of fire was seen as the vital issue, blank cartridges were regarded as being perfectly adequate for such training.[21] As Guibert concluded about the practice of the Frederickian system in European armies in general:

> The fire of the musketry may be deduced to a theory, but far from that being the case, it is always practised at hazard, and its execution rendered nothing more than merely mechanical. The reason is . . . that . . . there are so few officers who understand the construction of the pieces, and who have studied the jet of the motional bodies which are impelled from them. The soldier has likewise no principle given him whereby he can adjust himself, for let the distances or the situation of objects be what they will, he fires at random. It is particularly owing to the exercise of the target being so little practised, that this ignorance and deficiency of principles is so severely felt.[22]

As much as a quarter of a century after Guibert first wrote these words, Captain T.H. Cooper was to restate them in his *Practical Guide for the Light Infantry Officer* when attacking the lack of aimed fire training given to British troops.[23] Indeed, disillusionment with the Frederickian system of musketry practice had been gradually growing ever since 1780, when Guibert – who had a tremendous influence on later military thought and who, as we have seen, provided the basis for the French Army's drill in the 1790s – had commented that:

> Those Prussian battalions, so famously esteemed for their order and

execution, are those whose fire is less galling; their first discharge has precision and effect because this first shot is loaded out of action, and done with more attention and regularity; but afterwards in the heat and confusion of an engagement, they load in haste, and are inattentive to the well ramming of their charges. They are told that the great perfection of their exercise consists in making the most fires in a minute; no wonder then if they pay such little attention to the leveling (sic) of their pieces. Busied with this imaginary effect of celerity, at the expense of teaching the true position of adjusting the aim, they have acquired no proper idea of the true theory of their shot or fire.[24]

However, with the steady increase in the importance attached to light infantry which occurred in the closing years of the eighteenth century, criticism of the Prussian system of firing and calls for new, more accurate methods became more intense. In his (1780) *Abhandlung von dem Dienst der leichten Truppen*, Oberst-Leutnant von Ewald, for example, urged that all troops should be instructed to aim their weapons properly.[25] Similarly, in Britain the growing use of aimed fire by the French was particularly noticed and, especially after the bitter experiences of the duke of York's campaigns during the 1790s, several soldiers and theorists began to call for drastic reform. Noting the rise of the French *tirailleurs* and *chasseurs*, General John Money, for instance, complained in 1794 of the inability of British light infantry to match them for want of training in marksmanship:

> Light infantry men, who have been trained on the parade ground to load and fire in platoon etc., are sent forward to line hedges, to oppose the enemies (sic) chasseurs, who are all marksmen; the first shot one of them hears pass him (if he has the good fortune not to be hit) he runs his firelock through the hedge, and fires where he sees smoke, and continues to do so, as long as his ammunition lasts, or he sees the smoke continue. What does a chasseur do? When he hears a ball whistle by him, he conceals himself immediately, peeps through the hedge and never fires till he sees an object to fire at, then he takes a deliberate aim, and is almost sure . . . to kill or wound the man he fires at. He fires perhaps five or six shots in an hour with effect, when a light infantry soldier fires thirty without doing any execution.[26]

Again, in his (1804) *Instructions for Sharpshooters*, Captain T.H. Barber warned that 'Noise and smoke are not sufficient to stop the advance of soldiers accustomed to war: they are to be checked only by seeing their comrades fall',[27] whilst, the previous year, a Lieutenant-Colonel Robertson had advised the Secretary at War that:

> Although bred in the Prussian military System I think it certain that troops will learn the essential part of the use of Arms more effectually by . . . shooting at a Mark than by all that I have ever seen them taught.[28]

The high command attempted to respond to this pressure by improving the appropriate instructions in the *Manual and Platoon Exercise*. The 1800 edition of this handbook, for example, directed that when firing the soldier was to '. . . Look along the barrel with the right eye from the breach pin to the muzzle and remain steady. Pull the trigger strong with the forefinger'.[29] Although the 1803 and 1805 versions of this work simply reproduced this instruction almost word for word, the copy that appeared in 1807 was a little more detailed: 'In taking aim', it instructed,

> . . . Look along the barrel with the right eye from the breech pin to the muzzle, and remain steady. Pull the trigger strong with the fore-finger and, when fired, remain looking on the aim while you can count one-two.[30]

Also of interest in the 1807 edition was the inclusion of a paragraph of aiming and firing directions specifically for the use of light infantry men:

> On the word *present* both ranks bring their firelocks to the present, each man slowly and independently levelling at the particular object which his eye has fixed upon; and as soon as he has covered his object, each man fires of his own accord, without waiting for any word of command.[31]

These new instructions were highly significant, for they accelerated moves towards a practice that had first been suggested by the Horse Guards in 1801. Then, a circular order had recommended that:

> Individuals . . . [should be] occasionally detached and instructed how to act as Flankers, and as skirmishers in attacking, or repelling those of the Enemy; . . . accustomed not to fire, but when they have a good Mark and Aim.[32]

The individual soldier was thus being released from the usual rigid constraints of the linear drill and, acting independently from the other troops about him, permitted to take time in aiming and firing his firelock at 'his own accord'. Such changes in the tactical principles governing the firing of musketry were, when linked with more opportunities for practice with live ammunition and the drill manual's improved guidance on how to aim, instrumental in enabling the light infantryman to achieve as much accuracy with his firelock as its primitive design would allow. Skirmishers armed with ordinary muskets rather than rifles were thus able to obtain sufficient accuracy from their crude weapons to carry out their role as marksmen with a satisfactory degree of success.

These important amendments to the earlier instructions followed yet another attack on the system embodied in the *1792 Regulations* of David Dundas. This latest onslaught came from Lieutenant-Colonel John Macdonald who, in 1807, published a set of instructions for use by infantry on actual service. 'It has been found by experiment,' he wrote, that:

> not above one shot out of five, at the distance of 120 paces, hits an extended object as tall as a horse. At a period when the Enemy, from training and practice, have attained . . . an extraordinary degree of expertness, as general, and individual marksmen, this branch of exercise demands an unremitting perseverance.[33]

Going on to deplore the *1792 Regulation*'s lack of a section on target practice as was to be found in the French *ordonnances*,[34] Macdonald concluded with a criticism of the inadequacies of the official manual's scanty clauses relating to light infantry training,[35] before calling for a dramatic increase in the number of British troops armed with rifles.[36]

As we have seen, riflemen were regarded as the élite marksmen of the light infantry arm. In terms of accuracy, their weapons were markedly superior to the ordinary smoothbore muskets, and an expert rifleman could, under ideal conditions, hit a target at ranges of up to as much as 300 yards. To encourage the troops to perfect their skills, rifle units – following the system established in the 95th Regiment by Colonel William Stewart – organized regular shooting competitions in which the riflemen vied with one another for medals and positions in three 'classes'. Under this system, to qualify for entry to the third (lowest) class, the soldier had to put '*five* shots out of *six* in the target two days out of three, firing from the shoulder at the distance of 100 yards . . . .'. Once in the third class, the riflemen had to repeat this feat, but at a range of 150 yards, to qualify for the second class. Soldiers in this group fired at targets 200 yards away to graduate into the first class, where they were required to shoot at ranges of 300 yards and often at moving targets '. . . As a further inducement to the acquirement of skill', a gold medal was competed for on a monthly basis between the first and second classes of riflemen. After six such monthly trials, the medal would be awarded to the most deserving marksman and a new one produced for the next competition. Riflemen of the first class were also permitted to wear a distinctive green silk cockade on their hats.[37]

To enable them to carry out this constant target practice, rifle units received a larger than usual allowance of live ammunition.[38] However, the additional need for suitable firing ranges occasionally presented difficulties. In a report on the Second Battalion of the 95th Regiment, for example, Rottenburg noted that the battalion's barracks lacked an area that was extensive enough to permit the practice of skirmishing drill 'even for [a] company, in extended order'. 'This corps', he continued, 'is also precluded from the essential practice of firing at the Target'.[39] And whilst the degree of accuracy maintained by the average rifleman was doubtlessly superior to that of the average musket-armed sniper, the quality of shooting achieved on these practice ranges should be seen in perspective. Hitting selected targets at 300 yards, at least by the standards of the day, sounds impressive, but it is improbable that, under battlefield conditions, such standards of marksmanship were often attained.

A number of reasons can be put forward for this. Firstly, the majority of soldiers in a rifle unit would not qualify for the green silk cockade of the *élite* class; they would belong to the third and second classes of marksmen as defined above: that is to say, that the *maximum* range at which the best of them could regularly hit an individual target would be 200 yards. It should also be remembered that, in keeping with

Rottenburg's suggestion,[40] practice targets would be at least five feet in diameter and, whilst this meant that they presented a smaller target than, say, a close-order column of troops, they were appreciably easier to hit than an average sized man standing alone. George Hanger firmly believed that, from 200 yards, no musketeer could kill a man he specifically aimed at;[41] and it would seem improbable that most riflemen could either. Against a large target like a column, a sniper armed with either a smoothbore or a rifle would probably succeed in hitting something. But, from 200 yards; he would be unlikely to prove capable of picking out an individual from amongst a mass of marching men – and, even if he did, his fire would probably miss the mark by a sizeable margin, striking, by luck rather than design, another individual elsewhere in the formation.

This meant that against single, man-sized targets like enemy skirmishers even rifle fire was unlikely to actually strike the target at distances much over 150 yards, though it might come sufficiently close to make the soldier fired on feel menaced. And, away from the ideal conditions of the practice ground where men could load, aim and shoot at their ease, effective ranges were probably still shorter. A principal role of the light infantry was to harass the enemy's skirmishers with aimed fire; but there was a great deal of difference between shooting at leisure into a large, inanimate target and attempting to hit such troops: practice targets – though some, used by the better marksmen, were mounted on wheels and drawn backwards and forwards – did not weave erratically and unpredictably across the firing range, taking shelter behind any available cover; they were not shrouded in the dense smoke that hung everywhere in Napoleonic battles; and, above all, they did not have the very disturbing habit of shooting back.

Under such circumstances, a sniper's accuracy and speed in firing could drop significantly. Fear and smoke could blur his senses and, once he had drawn the enemy's attention, their return fire was a constant threat. Evasive action often consumed valuable shooting time and led to missed opportunities, while the skirmisher's usual forward position in 'no-man's-land' could give rise to a demoralizing sense of isolation. Operating under these conditions, even soldiers armed with rifles might prove unable to do more than molest other skirmishers at all but the shortest ranges.

Riflemen, however, as we have seen, were very much a minority in the British Army at this time and, armed with rifles or not, the whole of the light infantry arm was expected to fulfil the same sort of tasks as the 95th Regiment. Sound marksmanship was increasingly seen as an essential quality of all good skirmishers and, obliged to make the most of their rather crude weaponry, the 52nd Light Infantry, under the guidance of the able Kenneth Mackenzie, devised a new system of training their men to take aim that sought to improve on the one laid down in the existing *Manual and Platoon Exercise*. Colonel Mackenzie was himself an expert marksman. Throughout his life his favourite recreation was hunting and, indeed, training gun dogs and shooting were his principal pastimes following his retirement from the Army.[42] Like the *Jäger* and *chasseurs* of Prussia and France who were called into the military forces of their respective states because of their professional skills, Mackenzie's expertise in hunting and field-crafts made him ideally equipped for the instruction of light troops.

On the crucial issue of aimed fire, he regarded a light infantryman who was 'ignorant of this branch of his Duty [as being] of very little use in the field'.[43] Predictably, therefore, he was highly critical of the type of manual exercise in common use within the British Army at this time and, in January, 1808, wrote at length to Sir John Moore on the issue:

> I have been a shooter from the time I could carry a pistol, and have long thought the present system of platoon exercise the very worst possible to teach soldiers to do that for which they are intended, (to shoot their Enemy). Were I ordered to drill men to shoot in such a manner as to fire in their ranks . . . with the least possible chance of killing, I would adopt what is looked upon, at this period, as the most essential parts of the present system. I need say no more to you on this subject, as we had many a conversation on it before the new plan was introduced in the 52nd. I have conversed with many, but I have never yet found one person . . . that could object to the material parts of the system . . . practised by the 52nd.[44]

Mackenzie also objected to the paltry allowance of live ammunition that was issued by the Army authorities to units to practise with every year and felt that, given the poor training of the men in the basics of aimed fire, even much of this valuable shot was simply wasted. As he once explained in an order to his subordinates:

> '. . . Unless they practise so frequently as to acquire the habit of covering any object the eye may fix on, . . . merely firing the regular allowance of Ball Cartridge will never perfect any man. For at most a Light Infantry Soldier can only fire 30 rounds from 25th March till 29 Sepr. and 20 rounds from the latter period till the 25th March again, . . . and for the other Battalions of Infantry the allowance is 20 rounds a man less. . . . It must appear evident that something more is necessary to make a man aim with correctness (which is hitting the object aimed at) than merely firing these 50 or 30 rounds in 365 days – and the only method which seems adequate to attain this correctness is by making him constantly practise bringing his firelock in a line with an object, and instead of his only firing . . . 30 or 50 rounds in 365 days, he may cover an object . . . 365 times in half an hour. When a Regiment or company goes out to fire Ball each Man has perhaps but six Cartridges to fire that Day, & consequently only takes aim six times; this will do very well after the Man has acquired the habit, but till this is known the few rounds of Ball Cartridge annually issued by Government will be carefully preserved for the purpose of ascertaining if the Soldier has acquired the habit of bringing his firelock in a correct Line with the object he fixes his eye on – or in other words, to prove if he is a good Shot, as otherwise 'tis only throwing away the means of ascertaining his proficiency in this most essential part of his Duty. If it is

found that he is not a good Shot, let him be sent to practise bringing his Firelock in a line with an object for an hour or two every Day, & let him be kept at that alone till he becomes a good one, which he assuredly will be if he has no defect in his eye (however awkward he may appear for a time) if kept constantly to it, & not allowing his attention to be otherwise occupied while at practice. I would keep him at practice even for six months & indeed till he became proficient, as I should consider a Soldier ignorant of this branch of his Duty of very little use in the field.[45]

Thus, Mackenzie's system for promoting aimed fire consisted of removing the soldier from the ranks – and, by so doing, the constraints of linear tactics – and giving him constant practice in focusing his musket on targets selected by the eye. Eventually, as he explained to Moore, this would become an automatic response in the soldier and would enable him to take a surer aim even in the heat of battle. Then, once this habit was developed, he was ready to practise with live ammunition:

A soldier who from habit, can bring his firelock in a line with the object he is looking at, has a good chance of hitting the Enemy . . . even in the hurry and confusion of action because he is so instructed, that his firelock mechanically comes . . . in a direct line with the object he is looking at. What a difference there is between this and that part of the present mode, wherein he is instructed, and acquires the habit of bringing his firelock to a particular level. What is the chance that this level answers the distance or position of the Enemy? Very little – I believe that the reason any part of the fire of men so instructed has effect is that they are so ill drilled that they are not . . . perfect in their bad habit, and that some few go in the direction of the Enemy: for the eye naturally directs the hand to the object it is looking at.[46]

However, as we saw was the case with his system of tactical drill, Mackenzie's efforts to improve on official doctrine in the practice of musketry had little effect beyond those few regiments that came under his immediate superintendance. The directives laid down in the *Manual and Platoon Exercise* remained essentially unchanged throughout the years following 1807 until the end of our period, as did the general policy of training and instruction on musketry. Similarly, although in 1809 a rear sight was added to the pattern of musket used by the British light infantry regiments,[47] the inherent limitations of the smoothbore flintlock continued to act as a most effective brake on any attempts to carry the practice of aimed fire particularly far.

Indeed, what degree of accurate shooting was achieved was primarily secured through changes in the tactical principles on which skirmishers operated, rather than through improvements to their weaponry. Light infantry who, like the ordinary heavy infantry, had been 'trained on the parade [ground] to load and fire in platoon', gave way to a new generation of genuine marksmen who functioned individually on the battlefield. This, coupled with improved drill manual guidance and more opportunities for target practice, led to appreciable progress in the field of aimed fire and, by the outbreak of the Peninsular War, even those light infantrymen that were armed with ordinary muskets were no longer to be dismissed as 'perfectly unacquainted with the system of sharp-shooting . . .'.[48] Indeed, some of these musketeers became such accomplished snipers that, up to a certain distance, they could be sure of killing a man with one shot. Such 'Dead Shots' as they were known in the light infantry[49] were relatively few and far between. But most British skirmishers did acquire sufficient skill in aimed fire to hit, or at least be able to molest and thus pin down, individual members of opposing forces operating at fairly close range.

When it came to countering the French skirmishers, this limited capability in sharp-shooting was of crucial significance. As Colonel Hanger observed, when troops fired with any degree of precision even if the man shot at

> be not wounded, yet the ball passes so close to him as to intimidate, and prove . . . how skilful an opponent he is engaged with . . .[50]

The French *voltigeurs*, finding themselves opposed by equal – if not greater – numbers of British light troops, were thus prevented from carrying out their all-important role. Instead of being able to concentrate on molesting and reconnoitring the enemy's main force, they often became embroiled in defending themselves in a fire-fight with his protective sheath of light infantry. This effectively left the French heavy formations without skirmisher support – the vital element in their tactical system that had secured so many victories – and, as we shall see in the next chapter, was a key factor in their regular defeats by British defensive lines.

CHAPTER VI
The British light infantry at war, c. 1809–1815

The Light Infantry in the Guerre des Postes

The instruction the British light infantry received on the important subject of outpost duties was, as we have seen, primarily derived from the written works of Rottenburg and Jarry. And, having examined some of the basic, theoretical principles that those officers provided on such matters, we should say something about the manner in which the light infantry performed these duties in the field.

As we saw in Chapter I, the *petite guerre* was an extremely important feature of such eighteenth-century conflicts as the American War of Independence, and substantial numbers of troops were devoted to its prosecution on an almost day-to-day basis. Legions of light troops, like those of Tarleton and Simcoe, were raised with this kind of warfare specifically in mind and, whilst they occasionally took part in major engagements, their activities primarily consisted of raids on the enemy's communications, attacks on supply convoys, ambushes and similar small scale operations often carried out at considerable distances from the main armies. Indeed, in his work *The Partisan* written in 1760, De Jeney stressed the rather independent role that light troops fulfilled for most of the eighteenth century when he summarized their principal duties as being to separate

> from the Grand Army to secure its March; to protect the Camp; to reconnoitre the Country or the Enemy; to surprize their Posts, or their Convoys; to form Ambuscades; and, in short, to put in Practice every Stratagem that may harass or disturb them.[1]

But whilst, even today, the activities of light units operating at considerable distances from their parent armies remain an important feature of many conflicts, the scope for such independent action varies from theatre to theatre. The general political, military and geographical conditions under which the American War of Independence, for example, was fought, permitted the British light legions to operate in such a manner and, likewise, during the German War of Liberation of 1813, the Prussian *Freikorps* and Russian cossacks were to function in this way. Elsewhere, however, *kleiner Krieg* operations mounted behind enemy lines were more unusual. In the Peninsular War – the conflict that we are primarily concerned with here – the French found few favourable opportunities for such activities and, consequently, their light troops were primarily used in close co-operation with their main forces as reconnaissance units, pickets, and rear, flank and van guards. Similarly, Wellington declined to risk his own regular light troops in traditional, *petite guerre* operations against the enemy's communications. His irreplaceable army was relatively small and light infantry, having ceased to be mere auxiliaries who primarily functioned on the edges of battlefields, now played a crucial role in major engagements. As we shall see, numerous skirmishers were a key element in Wellington's tactical thinking and they thus formed an essential and integral part of all his divisions. He was, therefore, unwilling to see them separated from his main forces which, in any case, usually confronted the French in a general strategic framework that offered both sides few opportunities for blows against the enemy's communications. Wellington invariably entrusted long-range scouting and reconnaissance work to his cavalry, while the harassment of the French armies' rear areas was left to Portuguese militia units and, above all, the Spanish guerilla bands who carried out this work with legendary success.

Thus, the *guerre des postes* duties performed by Wellington's light infantry in the Peninsular War essentially consisted of local reconnaissance in terrain where cavalry could not act; the formation of van, rear and flank guards; and the provision of outposts, pickets and sentries, often in support of vedettes. Such work was, as Baron Gross concluded in his work on the duties of light troops, 'most essential'. Being nearest to them, it fell to the light infantry to

> follow and observe every motion of the enemy, and transmit notice thereof to the General, . . . [who] according to such reports . . . [would] frequently determine his plan of operations.

The light infantry were, furthermore, to 'secure the army from any surprise or sudden attack'.[2]

This *guerre des postes* was, however, usually carried on with a remarkable degree of civility. Whilst never losing sight of the fact that they were at war, opposing sentries and picket lines rarely made any real effort to molest one another except, perhaps, as a prelude to a general action. The suffering that would have been caused to both sides was simply regarded as unjustifiable by many officers and, consequently, the notion that advanced posts were not to harass one another became something of a convention. As Wellington himself explained,

> I always encouraged this; the killing of a poor fellow of a vidette or carrying off a post could not influence the battle, and I always when I was going to attack sent to tell them to get out of the way.[3]

Thus, in the various memoirs of the Peninsular War, one rarely comes across accounts of genuine *petite guerre* clashes between outposts, whilst there are numerous references to the civility exhibited by both sides. Captain Kincaid of the 95th, for instance, recalled how, at the end of the 1810 campaign in Portugal,

> Our battalion was stationed in some empty farm-houses, near the end of the bridge of Santarem, which was nearly half a mile long; and our sentries and those of the enemy were within pistol-shot of each other on the bridge.

'I do not', he explained,

> mean to insinuate that a country is never so much at peace as when at open war; but I do say thatr a soldier can nowhere sleep so soundly, nor is he anywhere so secure from surprise, as when within musket-shot of his enemy.
>   We lay four months in this situation, divided only by a rivulet, without once exchanging shots.[4]

Kincaid further recalled that:

> Repeated acts of civility passed between the French and us during this . . . [period]. The greyhounds of an officer followed a hare, on one occasion, into their lines, and they very politely returned them.[5]

Indeed, he observed,

> Our piquet-post, at the bridge, became a regular lounge, for the winter, to all manner of folks.
>   I used to be much amused at seeing our naval officers come up from Lisbon riding on mules, with huge ships' spy-glasses like six-pounders, strapped across . . . their saddles. Their first question invariably was, 'Who is that fellow there?' (pointing to the enemy's sentry, close to us), and, on being told that he was a Frenchman, 'Then why the devil don't you shoot him!' I was one night on piquet, at the end of the bridge, when a ball came from the French sentry and struck the billet of wood round which we were sitting, and they sent in a flag of truce, next morning, to apologise for the accident, and to say that it had been done by a stupid fellow of a sentry, who imagined that people were advancing upon him. We admitted the apology, though we all knew well enough that it had been done by a malicious rather than a stupid fellow, from the situation we occupied.[6]

Similarly, Captain John Cooke of the 43rd Light Infantry recalled that, at the commencement of the Battle of the Nive at the end of 1813, the French outposts began to call on his picket to retire and:

> At half past nine a.m., the enemy's skirmishers came forward in a careless fashion, talking to each other, and good naturedly allowed our sentinels to retire without firing at them.[7]

Likewise, of the same battle, a soldier of the 71st Light Infantry recalled how, in the fighting around Cambo, the French

> blew up the bridge over the Nive and retired out of the town. We then marched into it and were cantoned, and lay there for a considerable time, the French on one side and we on the other, our sentinel and their's, on the

bridge, not five yards asunder. The night before we crossed the French came down on the banks of the river with their music and gave us a tune or two. . . . About nine o'clock the whole of our . . . picquets were called to cover a party of sappers and miners in raising a battery to cover our fording ground; and the sentinel on the broken bridge received orders to shoot the French sentinel on the first gun . . . being fired. Both were walking from one parapet to another, the Frenchman unconscious of any unusual danger, the English sentinel listening and often looking to the victim, his heart revolting from the deed he dared not disobey. The match touched the signal gun; next moment the French sentinel fell into the river, pierced by a ball.[8]

But this particular incident marked the beginning of a full scale attack by Wellington's army. Indeed, skirmishes between light infantry picket lines were relatively unusual during the Peninsular War and, when they did taken place, they were almost invariably overtures to major engagements rather than the self-contained episodes of a traditional *guerre des postes*. As, for example, Captain Kincaid was to record about his regiment's day to day activities when it formed part of Wellington's vanguard in Portugal during 1811:

March 11th: [the French] retired yesterday to the heights behind Pombal, with their advanced posts occupying the town and moorish castle, which our battalion, assisted by some Cacadores, attacked this morning and drove them from with considerable loss. Dispositions were then made for a general attack on their position, but the other divisions of our army did not arrive until too late in the evening. We bivouacked for the night in a ploughed field, under the castle, with our sentries within pistol shot, while it rained in torrents. . . . March 12th: We stood to our arms before daylight. Finding that the enemy had quitted the position in our front, we proceeded to follow them; and we had not gone far before we heard the usual morning's salutation, of a couple of shots, between their rear and our advanced guard. On driving in their outposts, we found their whole army drawn out on the plain, near Redinha, and instantly quarrelled with them on a large scale.[9]

There is no better illustration of the whole range of duties performed by light troops in the field during the Peninsular War than that furnished by General Robert Craufurd's operations along the Beira frontier of Portugal during the spring and early summer of 1810. At this time, the French marshal André Massena had assembled three *corps d'armée* for an invasion of central Portugal and was planning to advance via the fortresses of Ciudad Rodrigo and Almeida on Lisbon.

To resist this offensive, Wellington, having sealed off Lisbon itself with the Lines of Torres Vedras, deployed the bulk of his army along the upper reaches of the River Mondego west of Almeida, with Craufurd's forces holding an outpost line along the Beira frontier with Spain. Initially, Craufurd's command consisted of the First Hussars of the King's German Legion, Ross's troop of Royal Horse Artillery and the Third Division. At the very beginning of 1810, the last of these units had two infantry brigades: one commanded by Craufurd himself and consisting of the three light battalions trained at Shorncliffe (1/95th,

1/52nd and 1/43rd); and that of Major-General Mackinnon, which comprised the 5/60th and two line battalions – the 1/54th and the 1/88th. Towards the end of February, however, Wellington reorganized some parts of his army. Craufurd's light brigade was removed from the Third Division and replaced by other troops, and on 22 February a General Order announced that 'The 1st and 2nd battalions of Portuguese Chasseurs (Cacadores) are attached to the Brigade of Brigadier-General Craufurd, which is to be called the *Light Division*'.[10] General Picton then superseded Craufurd as commander of the reformed Third Division.

The region over which Craufurd's line of outposts extended was the undulating plateau east of Almeida between the rivers Coa and Agueda, both of which flow northwards to join the Douro. The plateau between them is, on average, about 20 miles wide and is dissected by three smaller, parallel streams which, from west to east, are the Turon, the Duas Casas and Azava. At the start of the 1810 campaign Ciudad Rodrigo was still under Spanish control and was one of only four places at which the Agueda was spanned by a bridge; the other three being Barba del Puerco, Villar and Navasfrias. Elsewhere along its 25 mile length the Agueda was fordable in a number of places, particularly during periods of dry weather. But, as is the case with most mountain streams, a brief rain or snow fall could cause the water level to rise by several feet and thus such fords were frequently rendered impassable.

Wellington explained the role he expected Craufurd to fulfil in a number of letters written between the end of January and the beginning of March. 'As my views in the positions which the army now occupy, are', he wrote on 4 February,

> to take the offensive in case of the occurrence of certain events, I wish not to lose possession of the Coa; and I am anxious, therefore, that you . . . should maintain your positions upon that river, unless you find that the enemy collect a force . . . which is so formidable as to manifest a serious intention of invading Portugal.[11]

'If that should be the case,' he explained to Craufurd in a second missive,

> I don't propose to maintain the Coa, or that you should risk anything for that purpose; and I beg you to retire gradually to Celorico, where you will be joined by General Cole's Division. From Celorico I propose that you should retire gradually along the valley of the Mondego upon General Sherbrooke's Division and other troops which will be there. If you should quite the Coa, bring the [K.G.L.] Hussars with you.[12]

Finally, on 8 March, Wellington sent Craufurd a third dispatch in which he provided him with further information on the role his operations were to play in broader, strategic plans and gave him full responsibility for deciding the details of the dispositions to be made along and to the east of the Coa:

> The line of cantonments which we took up, principally with a view to the accommodation of the troops during the winter, and their subsistence on a

point on which it was likely that it might be desirable to assemble the army, will not answer our purpose of assembling on the Coa, if eventually that should be deemed an object. . . . I have long intended to alter our dispositions, as soon as the season would permit the troops occupying the smaller villages on the Coa, and as [soon as] I should be able to bring up the Portuguese light troops of your Division to the front. Since we took the position which we now occupy, our outposts have come in contact with those of the French; and although there is some distance between the two, still the arrangement of our outposts must be made on a better principle, and the whole of them must be in the hands of one person, who must be yourself. I propose, therefore, as soon as the weather will allow of an alteration of the disposition of the advanced corps, that your Division, with the Hussars . . . under your orders, should occupy the whole line of the outposts, and, with this, the Portuguese corps shall be brought up to the front as soon as the state of the weather will allow them to march. I am desirous of being able to assemble the army upon the Coa, if it should be necessary; . . . and till we shall see more clearly than I can at present what reinforcements . . . [the French] have received, and what military object they have in view, . . . I am adverse to withdrawing from a position so favourable as the Coa affords, to enable us to collect our army and prevent the execution of any design upon Ciudad Rodrigo. I wish you, then, to consider of the parts to be occupied in front of and upon the Coa, to enable me to effect that object. . . . You must be a better judge of the details of this question than I can be; and I wish you to consider it, in order to be able to carry the plan into execution when I shall send it to you.[13]

Thus, Craufurd was entrusted with a key role in Wellington's plans. As the commander of the Light Division he was expected to deploy and supervise the whole outpost line, observe the French beyond the Agueda and send Wellington accurate reports of their numbers and movements, and organise the other reconnaissance and survey work that was usually performed by an army's light troops. As, for instance, Wellington told him on 3 January:

I wish that you would desire Captain Campbell, and any other officers in your Division that are capable of it, to examine the course of the Coa which runs by Almeida, and to report upon it, and if possible let me have a plan of it; likewise, if the position of the enemy will allow of it, the course of the Agueda . . .[14]

Furthermore, Craufurd was also to analyse the intelligence his patrols were gathering and to deduce whether the French were preparing to advance into Portugal in force. If they were, his orders required him to evacuate the east bank of the Coa. Craufurd was, therefore, given the responsibility of taking a most crucial strategic decision.

Throughout February, Craufurd slowly moved his forces across the Coa towards the Agueda. In his diary, the general's aide-de-camp, James Shaw-Kennedy, reveals that Craufurd, in order to encourage the Spanish garrison of Ciudad Rodrigo and to keep it in communication with Almeida for as long as possible, had decided to occupy the whole of the plateau between the Coa and the Agueda.[15] This was a very extensive area and, even after his force had been augmented by some squadrons of the 16th and 14th Light Dragoons, Craufurd's forces totalled less than 5000 men. As Captain Kincaid commented:

> . . . They had more than enough of play in occupying a front of twenty-five miles with . . . [a] small division and some cavalry. The chief of the 1st German Hussars meeting our commandant one morning, 'Well, Colonel', says the gallant German in broken English, 'how do you do?' 'O, tolerably well, thank you, considering that I am obliged to sleep with one eye open'. 'By . . .,' says the other, 'I never sleeps at all'.[16]

At the end of February, Craufurd was ready to begin his allotted task in earnest. On the 27th of the month, Captain Creagh's company of the 95th was sent to reconnoitre the village of Barba del Puerco which commanded one of the four bridges which crossed the Agueda. Creagh's troops clashed with a large force of French cavalry and infantry in the settlement and, reporting their findings to Craufurd, retired on the village of Escarigo where they were reinforced by two more companies of riflemen. The next day, this force, commanded by Captain Leach, was sent forward to reconnoitre Barba del Puerco once again and, finding the French to have withdrawn beyond the Agueda to St Felices, established a picket in the village with an outpost at the bridge. Leach then interrogated a number of local residents and, from the information they gave him, was subsequently able to advise Craufurd that the French force in St Felices was part of General Loison's division and consisted of 3000 infantry, cavalry and artillery commanded by General Ferrey.[17]

In order to secure the various crossings over the Agueda between Ciudad Rodrigo and the Douro, Craufurd now dispersed the whole of the 95th in a chain running parallel to its western bank: one company held Escalon near the Agueda's confluence with the Douro; the bridge at Barba del Puerco – the only post actually on the river's edge – was occupied by four companies under Colonel Beckwith; four more companies were positioned about Marialva, with the remainder of the battalion deployed between the Azava and the Duas Casas to link Beckwith with Marialva and watch the fords near Gallegos. To keep the riflemen alert and to enable their officers to familiarize themselves with the local countryside, the various companies frequently exchanged positions.[18]

Communications between the 95th's outposts were largely maintained by patrols of the First Hussars of the King's German Legion who were also required to observe the Agueda between Navas Frias and Ciudad Rodrigo. Just as German *Jäger* generally enjoyed an enviable reputation as masters of *la petite guerre*, this German hussar regiment was also regarded as being particularly adept at picket and reconnaissance duties. Craufurd, however, provided them with detailed supervision for their more demanding tasks and, indeed, speaking German, tended to deal directly with the patrol commanders.[19]

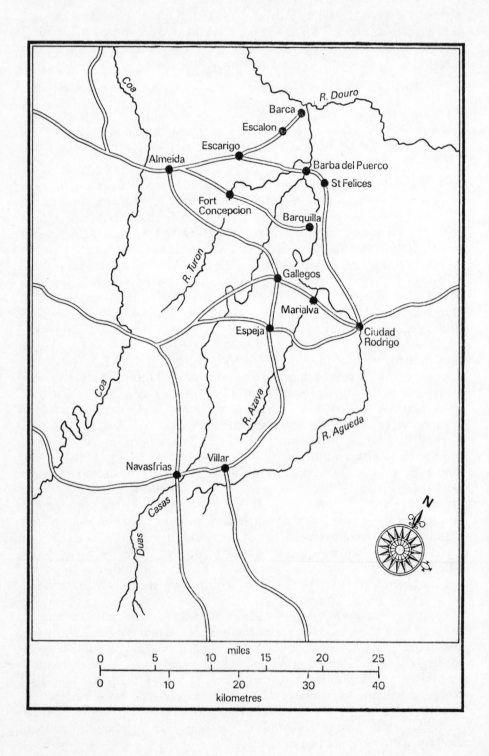

The rest of Craufurd's forces were deployed in support of the screen formed by the hussars and riflemen: the companies of the 43rd Light Infantry and 52nd Light Infantry were scattered in villages just west of the Agueda, while Ross's artillery battery took up a central position at Fort Concepcion. When they were in the area, the two regiments of Portuguese *cacadores* were also kept in this latter place as a general reserve. These dispositions enabled the Light Division to maintain the line of the Agueda and, thus, screen any deployment by Wellington on the Coa, encourage the garrison of Ciudad Rodrigo, observe Massena's army and control the movements of his foraging and reconnaissance parties. They were, furthermore, based on Craufurd's calculation of the amount of time needed to withdraw his division beyond the Coa after hearing of a major French advance. As Shaw-Kennedy explained:

> If we are to properly understand the operations of General Craufurd, the *calculation* as above stated, must never be lost sight of; for it was upon the *calculation* that he acted all along. The cause of hazarding the four companies at Barba del Puerco forms a separate consideration. It was formed upon the belief that the pass there was so difficult that four companies could defend it against any numbers, and that, if turned higher up the river, the Hussars would give Colonel Beckwith warning in ample time to make a safe retreat.[20]

Whenever the level of the Agueda fell sufficiently to render the various fords passable, Craufurd took the precaution of concentrating his units for action. This, as Captain William Napier of the 43rd Light Infantry recalled, was carried out by the troops with

> a promptitude and intelligence the like of which had seldom been known. Seven minutes sufficed to get under arms in the night, a quarter of an hour, night or day, to gather them in order of battle at the alarm posts, with baggage loaded and assembled at a convenient distance in the rear; and this not upon a concerted signal and as a trial, but at all times certain and for many months consecutively.[21]

The Light Division's ability to prepare for action with such consistent promptness and efficiency was largely due to their following the collection of standing orders which Craufurd had devised.[22] It was also to the rigid enforcement of this system that Craufurd owed his ability to 'calculate to the minute the time his whole division . . . would take to arrive at any given point, no matter how many days' march'.[23] As Captain Kincaid explained,

> [Craufurd] suffered neither mire nor water to disturb the order of his march with impunity. . . . Filing past dirty or marshy parts of the road in place of marching boldly through them or filing over a plank or narrow bridge in place of taking the river with the full front of their column in march, he proved to [his troops] . . . on true mathematical principles, that with the numbers of those obstacles usually encountered on a day's march, it made a difference of several hours in their arrival at their bivouac for the night. That

in indulging by the way, they were that much longer labouring under their load of arms, ammunition, and necessaries, besides bringing them to their bivouac in darkness and discomfort; it very likely, too, got them thoroughly drenched with rain, when the sole cause of their delay had been to avoid a partial wetting, which would have long since dried while seated at ease around their camp-fires . . .[24]

The practice of this system, however, took some time to perfect and Craufurd, as we have seen, tended to obtain obedience from his men by the threat of the lash and the noose. 'The general and his divisional code', commented Kincaid, were

at first much disliked . . . He enforced it, in the first instance, with unnecessary severity, and it was long before those under him could rid themselves of that feeling of oppression which it had inculcated upon their minds. . . . However, . . . punishment for . . . disorders was rarely necessary after the first campaign; for the system, once established, went on like clockwork . . .[25]

This precisely regulated, clockwork-like march system was not, of course, impervious to the glue of 'friction' – the unpredictable, disruptive problems encountered in attempting to implement any military operation, no matter how simple it might look on paper. Certainly, it broke down on a number of occasions, throwing Craufurd's detailed calculations on 'the time his whole division . . . would take to arrive at a given point' into utter confusion. But, under most conditions, the system worked sufficiently smoothly for the general to have confidence in his soldiers' capability to meet demanding schedules and, in his defence of the Agueda, the Light Division's ability to concentrate for action in a remarkably short period of time enabled Craufurd to take the risk of spreading his relatively few troops along a 25-mile front in the face of powerful enemy forces. However, major clashes between his outpost line and the French beyond the river were, until June at least, relatively rare. During the early months of 1810 the Imperial forces were too concerned with other matters to make any serious advance against Craufurd. Furthermore, the river remained at a high level for most of the time and could only be traversed by the few bridges along its length; all of which were heavily guarded. But in the middle of March one significant action took place which, as a typical *petite guerre* clash between light infantry forces, merits some examination. Indeed, it is one of the Peninsular conflict's very few examples of such warfare and provides us with an interesting glimpse of how the light infantry outpost system devised by Rottenburg and Jarry actually functioned in the field.

St Felices, executed a raid on Colonel Beckwith's encampment at Barba del Puerco. Advancing under cover of darkness and with the sound of their movements drowned by the noise of the Agueda tumbling along its rocky bed, Ferrey's 600 grenadiers and *voltigeurs* crept to within a few

yards of the two British sentries at the northern end of the bridge over
the river. Then, having left a strong force to cover his retreat in the event
of a reverse, Ferrey, as Captain Kincaid explained,

> burst forth so silently and suddenly, that, of our double sentry on the bridge,
> the one was taken and the other bayonetted without being able to fire off
> their pieces.[26]

The French pressed onwards up the ravine that led to Barba del Puerco
itself and would probably have caught Beckwith's sleeping forces
completely unawares had it not been for a second small outpost of
riflemen which, in accordance with Jarry's *Instructions*,[27] had been posted
midway between the sentinels at the bridge and the main picket. This
'sergeant's party higher up the rocks', Kincaid recorded,

> had just time to fire off as an alarm, and even the remainder of the company
> on piquet under O'Hare had barely time to jump up and snatch their rifles
> when the enemy were among them. O'Hare's men, however, though borne
> back and unable to stop them for an instant, behaved nobly, retiring in a
> continued hand-to-hand personal encounter with their foes to the top of the
> pass, when the remaining companies under Sidney Beckwith having just
> started from their sleep, rushed forward to their support . . .[28]

Colonel Beckwith, dressed in a nightcap, dressing-gown and slippers,
now led his men in a counter-attack which quickly resecured the pass
and thrust the French back across the Agueda. Ferrey's units, breathless
and disordered, proved incapable of effective resistance and suffered
heavy losses. As one rifleman recalled, the lie of the land was in the
95th's favour and, whilst their own dark clothing largely hid them from
the enemy's view, the French had committed the error of wearing white
cross-belts – fastened with polished brass buckles – on top of their blue
greatcoats. Even at long range these made Ferrey's troops easy to see
and, furthermore, presented their opponents with an ideal guide-line for
aimed fire which, coming from riflemen, proved particularly effective.[29]
It was, as Kincaid commented, 'the first and last night-attempt which the
enemy ever made to surprise a British post in that army'.[30]

On 1 June, however, Marshal Ney's VI *Corps d'armée* finished building
building a new bridge over the Agueda at a point some one-and-a-half
miles to the north of Ciudad Rodrigo and, four days later, completed
another to the south of the fortress. Using these pontoons Massena's
army then crossed the river in strength and, completely encircling the
city, began siege operations in earnest. The marshal's cavalry, meanwhile, fanned out over the plateau to the west and, driving back the
German hussars, severed Craufurd's communications with the garrison.
But until Ciudad Rodrigo should have fallen, Massena did not intend to
advance further and, apart from exploring their outpost line with his
cavalry, made little effort to molest Craufurd's forces who fell back
across the Azava to Gallegos and Espeja. From here, they could continue
to give some encouragement to the beleaguered garrison of Ciudad

Rodrigo and, at the same time, bar the two roads that led from that city to the Coa and Almeida.

By the last days of June the defence of Ciudad Rodrigo was crumbling and the French began preparations for an advance over the Azava. Their cavalry, Leach recalled, 'were eternally in motion in large bodies towards our chain of posts, and we as often under arms waiting for them'.[31] However, there were no serious clashes. Indeed, two incidents which occurred during this period and which were witnessed by George Napier of the 52nd Light Infantry further illustrate the rather civil atmosphere that, throughout the Peninsular War, was generally maintained between opposing picket lines.

Napier was, at this time, in command of an outpost protecting a ford over the Azava near Gallegos and, on one occasion, Marshal Ney and his staff rode down to the river's northern edge to reconnoitre the crossing. Napier shouted to Ney that his suite must retire or risk being fired on and, when the marshal ignored this polite warning, had a soldier shoot one of their horses. Ney promptly wheeled his party about and rode away. A few days later, part of the French picket facing Napier's outpost across the Azava asked for permission to come across and get some tobacco from his troops as they had none of their own. Napier allowed two of them to come over on the condition that they should swim rather than try the ford. This they duly did and, as Napier concludes, 'got the tobacco, told us all the news from France, and returned quite happy'.[32]

Despite such niceties, the two sides were, after all, at war and each had to treat the other with caution. As the strength of the opposing forces on the Azava steadily rose, Craufurd became increasingly concerned that they might launch a sudden attack against him. Accordingly, whilst he continued to occupy Gallegos during daylight, every evening, Leach recalled, he

> marched his infantry to a wood on some heights behind the village, towards the river Duas Casas, where we bivouacked, and returned soon after daybreak to the village. This I presume was a precautionary measure, fearing the enemy might attempt a night attack on the village, which their extreme proximity rendered probable.[33]

This repeated manoeuvre, however, eventually drew Massena's attention and, as Leach explains, led to him making a major advance against Craufurd's forces on 4 July:

> From some commanding ground in the French lines, the return of our division from the heights of the village could plainly be perceived; and possibly being deceived on that point, mistaking us for reinforcements sent across the Coa to join General Craufurd, Massena ordered General Junot to cross the Azava . . . with, it was supposed, about fifteen thousand men: and, by a close reconnaissance, to ascertain how matters really stood.

We were, 'under arms, as usual, an hour before day-break, on the heights', Leach continues, when some shots were heard from our cavalry pickets . . . who shortly afterwards retired slowly and in excellent order, keeping up a continued skirmish. Captain Kraukenberg, of the 1st German Hussars, an officer of the highest merit, distinguished himself on this occasion. Forming his squadron on some eligible ground near a small narrow bridge over a rivulet which runs through Gallegos, he waited until as many of the French dragoons had crossed as he thought proper to permit, when he instantly charged and put them into confusion, killing and wounding many of them and bringing some prisoners with him to the heights, where General Craufurd had drawn out the Light Division in line. The horse artillery opened with effect on the head of Junot's troops, who advanced with caution; but General Craufurd having ascertained their great superiority of numbers, decided on retiring across the Duas Casas. This movement was covered by some cavalry and our battalion, who skirmished with the advance [guard] of the French until we had passed the river, which was effected with a very trifling loss on our part. Two hundred riflemen were left on the heights of Fort Conception as a picket, the remainder being placed in a position . . . behind the . . . Turon . . .[34]

Six days after this incident, Ciudad Rodrigo finally fell to the French and, on that same morning, Craufurd's forces also suffered a reverse while carrying out a typical *petite guerre* operation. Noting that French foraging parties were combing the countryside between the Azava and the Duas Casas, Craufurd decided to strike at some of them and, during the night of 9 July, assembled nine companies of infantry, six squadrons of cavalry and two guns at the village of Barquilla.

At first light, these troops spotted a small French detachment on the horizon and Craufurd promptly sent three squadrons of cavalry into the attack. But after galloping for over a mile through enclosed countryside, the disordered Allied horsemen found the 200 French infantry had formed a square and, whilst some of their supporting dragoons were taken prisoner, defied all attempts to break them. The Allied cavalry were repulsed with heavy losses and the French infantry slipped away before another attack could be mounted. Captain Leach, who was present at the action, was critical of Craufurd's handling of the affair and regarded the general's failure to support his horsemen with the light infantry and horse artillery as a fatal oversight. 'A few discharges of grape-shot would', he pointed out, 'either have annihilated the square in ten minutes or caused it to surrender.'[35] Wellington, however, rejected any criticism of Craufurd and, in a letter to him some days later, expressed the belief that the cavalry attack would have succeeded despite 'the gallantry and steadiness of the French infantry, if various accidents had not prevented the execution of the plan as first formed . . . I have stated this,' he concluded, 'as my opinion, in the report which I have made upon the business.'[36]

This abortive affair proved to be the last notable *petite guerre* operation that Craufurd's troops mounted in the Coa campaign. The fall of Ciudad Rodrigo had obliged Wellington to redraft his strategy and, on 11 July, he told Craufurd that

. . . I don't wish you to risk anything beyond the Coa; and indeed . . . I don't see why you should remain any longer at such a distance in front of Almeida. It is desirable that the communications with Almeida should be kept open as long as possible, in order that we may throw into that place as much provisions as possible; and therefore I would not wish you to fall back beyond that place, unless it should be necessary. But it does not appear that you should be so far, and it will be safer that you should be nearer, at least with your infantry.[37]

Accordingly, on 16 July, Craufurd pulled his infantry back to a position by the Coa at Almeida. Over the next few days Massena's troops moved forward in overwhelming numbers and, destroying the fortifications at Ford Concepcion, the Allied cavalry and horse artillery also retired; a few vedettes being left to observe the various roads to the east of Craufurd's new position.[38] The morning of 24 July saw Craufurd's division preparing to continue its withdrawal when, as William Napier of the 43rd Light Infantry recalled, '. . . Some pistol shots in front, followed by an order for the cavalry reserves and the guns to advance, gave notice of the enemy's approach'.[39] A general action ensued in which Ney's VI Corps succeeded in pushing Craufurd's force back across the Coa. The Light Division, however, repulsed Ney's attempts to pass troops over the river in pursuit and the French turned their attention to besieging Almeida.[40]

Thus concluded Craufurd's campaign on the Coa. It provides an exceptionally good example of the work of light troops in the *guerre des postes*, and the accomplished manner in which Craufurd and his Light Division carried out these duties adequately demonstrates the skill which, by the early days of the Pensinsular War, British light troops had acquired in this field. As Captain Kincaid concluded about the campaign:

The light division, and the cavalry attached to it, was at this period so far in advance of every other part of the army that their safety depended on themselves alone . . .

Their force consisted of about four thousand infantry, twelve hundred cavalry and a brigade of horse artillery – and yet with this small force did Craufurd, trusting to his own admirable arrangements, and the surprising discipline of his troops, maintain a position which was no position, for three months, within an hour's march of six thousand horsemen, and two hours' march from sixty thousand infantry, of a brave, experienced, and enterprising enemy, who was advancing in the confidence of certain victory.[41]

The light infantry in battle

As we saw in Chapter I, in the aftermath of the Revolution the French Army had adopted a new tactical system that ideally suited the blend of professional soldiers and barely trained yet enthusiastic volunteers that the French Army had become. This system revolved around the skilful coordination of troops deployed in the regular but versatile formations suggested in Guibert's *Essai de Tactique* with substantial numbers of light infantry who generally acted upon their own initiative. As a prelude to attacks mounted by columns of infantry who relied primarily on shock action for their success, swarms of these skirmishers, using aimed fire and screening themselves behind any cover that presented itself, would join with artillery in weakening the enemy's defensive line. Dispersed and sheltered, they were virtually immune to the inaccurate volley fire that Frederickian school foot troops were taught to deliver, and merely retired if subjected to attack; returning at the earliest opportunity to harry the opposition further.

This system generally proved very successful in the war between the armies of the *ancien régime* and the new republic, and was to form the basis of French battlefield tactics throughout the period we are concerned with. At Jena in 1806, for example, large numbers of French troops were deployed in skirmish order, and completely overwhelmed the Prussian Army that had carried the execution of the old order tactics and evolutions to such perfection.[42] Similarly, at the Battle of Thann in 1809 whole brigades of French line infantry were dispersed as skirmishers and subsequently bewildered and routed their Austrian opponents with a dazzling display of open-order movements and aimed fire.[43] Likewise, in their accounts of the Waterloo campaign, fought six years later, Allied officers were to speak of French attacks being 'carried on by Columns of Infantry, covered by a numerous body of light troops . . . '.[44] Indeed, such soldiers, Duhesme concluded in his *Essai Historique sur l'Infanterie légère*, had, by the early 1800s, regained the importance they had enjoyed

> in the tactics of the ancients, by taking a glorious part, not only in those battles fought in wooded and rugged country, but also in those fought upon the most open of plains.[45]

In analysing the French system of tactics and its success, Baron Gross had concluded that 'Nothing can be effected against this disposition, but by opposing light troops to light troops'.[46] This was the conclusion that other theorists like Scharnhorst, Money and the Archduke Charles eventually came to, and all of the various European powers steadily added more light units to their Armies to counter the French *voltigeurs* and *tirailleurs*. However, whilst they rather lagged behind the continental states in introducing substantial numbers of light infantry into their forces, it was the British above all who, particularly during the Peninsular War, were successfully to neutralize the French tactical system. As early as June 1808, some weeks before he took command of the British Army in Portugal, Sir Arthur Wellesley – later the duke of Wellington – told a friend that, 'If what I hear of . . . [the French] system of manoeuvres be true, I think it is a false one against steady troops.'[47] Throughout the next seven years the underlying truth of this statement was to be demonstrated time and again, as Wellington perfected a tactical system of his own that proved more than a match for that of the hitherto victorious French.

Wellington's system had three main elements. Firstly, the British, as one French general noted, 'generally occupied well chosen defensive positions having a certain command, and they showed only a part of their forces'.[48] Such concealment tactics not only prevented the French from weakening the defending forces with aimed artillery fire, they also made the exact positions and extent of Wellington's regiments difficult to ascertain. Consequently, at Bussaco in 1810, for example, General Reynier was to attack the Anglo-Portuguese centre, mistakenly believing it to be their right flank; and at Salamanca two years later, Marshal Marmont was to make a similar error.

The second element in Wellington's defensive system consisted of those parts of his forces that were invariably deployed on the forward slope of his ridge. These would consist of artillery, arrayed along the crest of the hill from where they could observe and fire down on any advancing hostile forces, and a strong cordon of light troops posted some distance in front of the guns. The orders issued to these skirmishers rarely varied and were, as one officer recalled:

> To cover and protect our Batteries. To establish ourselves at all times as much in advance as might be compatible with prudence. To preserve considerable intervals between our extended files for greater security from the fire of the Enemy's Batteries. To show obstinate resistance against Infantry of the same description, but to attempt no formation or offer useless opposition to charges of Cavalry, but to retire in time upon the Squares in our rear, moving in a direct line without any reference to Regiments . . . When the charge was repulsed, to resume our ground.[49]

Lastly, deployed out of the enemy's sight on the reverse slope of the ridge would be the main body of Wellington's forces, formed in line.

Whenever a French force endeavoured to attack a corps of Anglo-Portuguese troops deployed in this manner, the following sequence of events invariably ensued. To begin with, the French, following their usual method, would send forward their *voltigeurs* and attempt to weaken the defence with a preliminary artillery bombardment. However, with most of Wellington's troops screened from such fire, the effectiveness of the cannonade was greatly diminished. Captain Powell of the 1st Foot Guards recalled how, at Waterloo for instance, Napoleon's artillery

> were ordered to concentrate their whole fire on the intended point of attack. That point was the rise of the position about half-way between Hougoumont and La Haye Sainte . . . There ran along this part of the position a cart road, on one side of which was a ditch and a bank, in and under which the Brigade sheltered themselves during the cannonade, which might have lasted three-quarters of an hour. Without the protection of this bank every creature must have perished.[50]

Next, as the *voltigeurs* crept forward, the cordon of Allied light infantry, ordered 'to show obstinate resistance to such troops', would come into action. Making full use of the superior range and accuracy of their rifled weapons,[51] detachments from the 95th Regiment, the Fifth Battalion of the 60th, the Portuguese *cacadore* battalions and the

Brunswick *Jäger* would open fire first, picking off their targets at distances of up to 300 yards. As the range decreased, the musketeers of the various regimental light companies and light regiments would also commence firing, helping to generate a constant discharge that pinned down the *voltigeurs* on the forward slope of the Allied position. From here of course they were quite unable to molest Wellington's main line, or indeed to reconnoitre it and gather detailed information to assist their general in the planning of his main attack.

The French efforts to pave the way for an assault with skirmisher and cannon fire having been successfully thwarted, it only remained for the Allies to deal with the heavy infantry columns that eventually came forward intending to administer the *coup de grâce*. As these advanced, they came under an increasingly destructive artillery fire; the gunners changing from round shot to canister as the range diminished. In such densely packed formations, a solitary shot was quite capable of cutting down 20 men.[52] Concentrated artillery fire inevitably inflicted heavy casualties and caused mounting confusion in the ranks of the column.

The Allied skirmishers, having halted the progress of the French *voltigeurs* and driven them back, would also turn their attention increasingly to the enemy's columns. 'Our rifles', Captain Kincaid recalled in writing of the first French infantry assault at Waterloo,

> . . . opened such a fire on the advancing skirmishers as quickly brought them to a standstill; but their columns advanced steadily through them, although our incessant *tiralade* was telling in their centre with fearful exactness.[53]

Similarly, at the Battle of Toulouse the previous year, General Taupin's division had advanced in column against elements of the British Fourth and Sixth Divisions. Before the main bodies of the opposing forces clashed, 'the light company of the 42nd regiment,' recalled one soldier, 'by a well directed fire, brought down some of the French officers of distinction, as they rode in front of their respective corps'.[54]

Maintaining a constant fire, the Allied skirmishers would retire up the hill and file through the intervals in Wellington's front line of heavy infantry. Meanwhile, that formation would be preparing to receive the advancing columns and would either move up to the crest of the ridge as the light infantry screen retired, or hold its ground waiting for the French formations to appear over the brow of the hill.

In the columns, the sudden appearances of a line of enemy troops, evidently untouched by the preliminary bombardment or skirmisher fire, had dramatic effects. 'The men became excited', recalled General Bugeaud,

> called out to one another and increased the speed of their march; the column becoming a little confused. The English remained quite silent with ordered arms and from their steadiness appeared to be a long red wall . . . Very soon we got nearer, crying 'Vive l'Empereur! En avant! A la baionnette!' Shakos were raised on the muzzles of muskets, the march became a run, the ranks fell into confusion, shots were fired as we advanced. The English line remained

silent, still and unmoved, with ordered arms . . . and appeared to ignore the storm that was about to break. The contrast was striking; . . . we all felt that the enemy was taking a long time in firing and that this fire . . . would be very unpleasant when it came. Our ardour cooled. . . . At this moment of painful expectation, the English wall shouldered arms; an indescribable feeling would fix many of our men to the spot; they began an uncertain fire. The enemy's steady, concentrated volleys swept our ranks; decimated, we turned round seeking to recover our equilibrium; then three . . . cheers broke the silence of our opponents; at the third they were on us, pushing our disorganised flight.[55]

Such a result was fairly predictable: 'Columns do not break through lines', Napoleon once remarked to General Foy, 'unless they are supported by a superior artillery fire which prepares the attack.'[56] With that supporting fire effectively neutralized by Wellington's skilful dispositions, the comparatively narrow, deep column was no match for infantry deployed in a formation that permitted every man to see and fire at the target. As one British officer observed in his description of a French infantry assault at Waterloo:

The Enemy's Column, near which I was, on arriving at the crest of the position seemed very helpless, had very little fire to give from its front or flanks, was incapable of deploying, must have already lost many of its Officers in coming up, was fired into, close, with impunity, by stragglers of our Infantry who remained behind. As we approached at a moderate pace the front and flanks began to turn their backs inwards; the rear of the columns had already begun to run away.[57]

Given the fact that many French officers were apparently aware of the futility of attacking unshaken lines with heavy columns[58] – a practice Wellington once described as 'very contemptible'[59] and which was also condemned by many French military thinkers in the post Napoleonic era[60] – the question of why they persisted in doing so arises. The answer lies principally in the effectiveness of Wellington's policy of screening his formations with terrain features and light infantry. The Guibert-inspired *ordonnances* of 1791 provided a highly versatile tactical system in which troops advanced in column prior to deploying into line on contact with the enemy.[61] This was done, for example, at Castrillo in 1812, where, according to a lieutenant of the 43rd Light Infantry, 'The French moved up . . . in close column & deployed'.[62] But if the enemy were hidden from view, knowing exactly when to deploy their men could pose major problems for the French officers. All too often their columns would suddenly find themselves confronted by a solid line of enemy troops, when there was neither time nor space to reform. The worst case of this occurred at the Battle of Bussaco in 1810, where, having fought their way through hundreds of Allied light troops up an extraordinarily steep slope, Loison's division of Ney's *corps d'armée* had all but reached the crest of Wellington's ridge. There seemed to be nothing left for them to overthrow other than a few batteries, and they were rapidly closing in on these when, at Robert Craufurd's command, the British 43rd and 52nd Light Infantry Regiments suddenly rose out of a sunken lane only a few yards in front of the French formation. Their *voltigeur* screen having long since been driven in by the Allied skirmishers, Loison's battalions had no warning of the presence of Craufurd's line and were given no opportunity to deploy into a more suitable formation for a mustketry duel. Riddled with fire at almost point-blank range they turned and fled, losing over a thousand men. Craufurd's two regiments sustained a total of only 23 casualties in the battle.[63]

On other occasions, French columns did attempt to deploy into line on coming into sudden contact with the enemy. But redeploying under their very nose was an immensely difficult undertaking, requiring enormous courage and discipline. Often, the mixture of apprehension and excitement generated in the column by the sight of the enemy would, as General Bugeaud's account confirms, lead to growing confusion which made redeployment increasingly difficult. If the enemy then, as they usually did, raked the column with volleys, it became almost impossible. At the Battle of Albuera in 1811, for instance, one French officer on the staff of the V Corps witnessed an attack by General Gerard's division. Gerard, he recalled,

> having passed the rivulet at the head of the 5th Corps, in close column, and having forced the Allies, by the vigor of his attack, to abandon their first position, . . . continued his advance in the same order, fully convinced that the manoeuvres of the enemy . . . were a movement of retreat. . . . This . . . determined . . . Gerard not to stop to deploy his columns [and he] . . . committed the fatal imprudence of advancing the 5th Corps still in close column, and of attacking the enemy in that order. . . . [The enemy's] numerical superiority, and the false measures already taken by the French in their attack, insured an incalculable advantage to the Allies, which they did not fail to seize. They began, with coolness, from two ranks, a continued and well-directed fire: No shot is lost on our close column, which can only oppose the insufficient and badly maintained fire of its two front ranks. . . . The officers in vain attempt to restore confidence to the troops, and animate them by their example. General Pepin falls, mortally wounded; . . . the Generals Maransin and Brayer . . . are carried off dying; General Gazan, *Chéf de l'état Major*, is also wounded. General Gerard . . . attempts . . . to deploy his troops; . . . but deployment into line, which requires space and coolness, cannot be effected under so violent a fire. . . . Discouragement is at its height; and the soldiers . . . consider themselves as victims led to the slaughter. In this situation, . . . a most marked movement of fluctuation was perceptible, which soon became a disorderly retreat.

Amongst the Allied troops opposing the French column was one soldier who noticed

> their gallant officers vainly using every effort to deploy . . . [their men] into line. Sometimes a company or more filed out; but the fire of the Allies was so severe, that they ran back into the column as to shelter. After several abortive efforts, the attempt to move them was given up . . .[64]

Similarly, at Waterloo, Lieutenant Sharpin of the Royal Artillery saw the infantry of d'Erlon's French corps advance

> in close columns of Grand Divisions, and upon reaching the crest of our position they attempted to deploy into line, but the destructive fire of our guns loaded with canister shot, and the well-directed volleys from the Infantry, prevented their regular formation.[65]

Such eye-witness accounts, when taken in conjunction with the use of simple columnar formations by seasoned troops like the Imperial Guard at Waterloo, completely contradict the theory put forward by some historians that the steady deterioration in the quality of Napoleon's troops compelled French generals to rely on columns as the only formation their troops could effectively fight in.[65] Whilst it can be argued that the influx of new recruits into Napoleon's armies proceeded at such a rate that training standards inevitably suffered, it is an over-simplification to dismiss the use of columns by French generals as a mere symptom of the deterioration in the quality of their troops. To function and survive on a Napoleonic battlefield, infantry had to be able to perform the basic evolutions of the drill manual. These included the formation of lines, columns and squares. Furthermore, they had to be able to perform these manoeuvres under battlefield – rather than parade-ground – conditions: shrouded in dense smoke and often under fire.[67] Indeed, right up to the conclusion of the Napoleonic Wars, French infantry regularly displayed a capability for tactical flexibility which contradicts the simple notion that they were lacking in training.[68]

Thus, the French 'policy' of assailing unshaken British lines with ponderous columns was brought about more by accident than design, and was due more to errors of judgement by French commanders baffled by Wellington's dispositions than to any tactical inability on the part of the troops themselves. The failure to penetrate Wellington's defensive cordon of light troops was of crucial significance. The reconnaissance and the psychological and material weakening of the defending lines prior to the launching of what were intended as decisive assaults by the heavy infantry were the vital functions of the *voltigeurs* and artillery, though when circumstances permitted, Napoleon himself frequently called on the latter arm alone to fulfil these tasks. In his account of Waterloo, for example, one member of the 71st 'Highland' Light Infantry reveals that

> The [French] artillery had been tearing away since daybreak in different parts of the line. About twelve o'clock we . . . marched up to our position, where we lay on the face of a brae, covering a brigade of guns. . . . The cannonballs, plunging in amongst us killed a great many. . . . We lay thus, about an hour and a half, under a dreadful fire, which cost us about 60 men, while we had never fired a shot.[69]

However, in their battles against Wellington, the French usually found the opportunity for using cannon in this manner to be few. Wellington –

unlike most continental commanders who, like Blücher and Gneisenau at Ligny, insisted that their men 'liked to see the enemy' and deployed them in full view of Napoleon's forces[70] – invariably placed most of his troops under cover and the French had to rely on skirmishers to prepare the way for the attacks by their heavy infantry. However, Wellington effectively countered this strategem too, by throwing forward a dense screen of his own light troops to protect his main line from the enemy skirmishers and to silence any cannon that the French should bring forward.[71]

As we saw in Chapter I, the other Allied powers also increased the strength of their light infantry forces to try to match those of the French on the battlefield. But the British generally enjoyed far more success with this policy than their continental allies. From time to time, French *voltigeurs* would penetrate Wellington's skirmisher cordon and inflict great damage on his close-order formations. At Waterloo, for instance, this happened on a number of occasions. In his account of an attack against d'Erlon's corps, Lieutenant Weymouth of the Life Guards recalled a charge along a sunken lane, the banks of which were 'crowned by Chasseurs, who fired down upon the Life Guards, . . . killing great numbers of them.'[72] Similarly, Lieutenant-Colonel Taylor of the 10th Hussars was leading his horsemen forward in support of an infantry charge when they encountered 'A cloud of tiralleurs . . . close up to our Infantry, behind which we were, and keeping up a heavy fire'. The hussars sustained heavy losses: 'We had many casualties here,' Taylor confessed, '. . . Captain Curwood was struck in the knee, . . . Captain Wood was shot through the thigh, and . . . Captain Grey was wounded here.'[73]

The Third Battalion of the 1st Foot Guards also came under heavy attack from *voltigeurs* at one stage in the fighting. 'During the Cavalry attacks on the centre', recalled Lord Saltoun, then a captain in the battalion, 'a great number of the enemy's sharpshooters . . . crept up the slope of the hill, and galled the 3rd Battalion, who were in square, very severely'.[74] Likewise, the fall of the farmhouse of La Haye Sainte in the very centre of Wellington's position proved, in the words of one officer of the 95th,

> highly disastrous to the troops of Picton and Lambert, for the French instantly filled the house with swarms of sharpshooters, whose deadly fire precluded the possibility of our holding . . . the ground immediately about it, and they established also a strong . . . line of Infantry, extending along the front of Kempt's Brigade. These Frenchmen, however, *knelt down*, and exposed only their heads and shoulders to our fire . . .[75]

Generally, however, the French skirmishers were kept at a safe distance from Wellington's main line by his own light troops. The very high proportion of light infantry in his forces enabled him to deploy screens of extraordinary strength as a matter of regular practice. Out of the eight divisions he ultimately had at his disposal in the Peninsula, two

– the Light and Seventh Divisions – usually consisted entirely of light troops.[76] In addition to these forces there were regimental light companies, detachments of riflemen, and several other battalions of Portuguese and British light infantry spread throughout the army. Occasionally, line troops were also called on to reinforce the specialist skirmishers.[77]

Thus, of Waterloo, for example, Lieutenant Pratt of the British Third Division recalled how;

> The Artillery was advanced . . . on the exterior slope, and the Light Troops of the Division moved to the front to cover and support it. This force consisted . . . in the following details: Four British Light Companies formed into a Battalion under Lieutenant-Colonel Vigoureux, 30th Regiment; 1st and 2nd Light Battalions, K.G.L.; . . . a Light Hanoverian Battalion and the Jagers von Kilmansegge (Rifles).[78]

This meant that out of a total of 14 battalions in the division,[79] no fewer than five were deployed as skirmishers. Similarly, at the Battle of Orthez in 1813, the Third Division had 14 companies of light troops protecting its front: seven battalion light companies, three companies of the Fifth Battalion of the 60th (riflemen) and four of Portuguese *cacadores*.[80] Likewise, during the action at Tarbes in 1814, all three battalions of the 95th Regiment were sent in skirmish order to dislodge a French brigade from its position,[81] while at Bussaco Loison's ill-fated division had to advance through nearly 2000 Allied riflemen before encountering the 43rd and 52nd Light Infantry on the crest of Wellington's position.[82] Again, in his account of the Battle of Quatre Bras in 1815, Major Forbes of the 79th Foot recalled how:

> The Light Companies of the 8th Brigade, to which were added the 8th Company and marksmen of the 79th Regiment, were immediately thrown out, when the Action commenced. This movement was ordered by . . . Wellington in person, who was here present with his Staff. . . . These troops maintained their situation for an hour against the constantly increasing numbers of the Enemy.[83]

Faced with screens of such density, it is not surprising that some French generals mistakenly believed the Allied light infantry cordon to be the enemy's front line, and claimed to have broken through it before being repulsed by a 'second line of infantry'.[84] Nor is it surprising that the outnumbered French *voltigeurs* were invariably either pinned down on the forward slope of Wellington's ridge or driven back on the supporting columns of heavy infantry. For example, in writing of the famous charge executed by the Union Brigade against d'Erlon's infantry corps at Waterloo, Lieutenant-Colonels Straton and Miller of the 'Inniskilling' Dragoons observed that 'The French skirmishers [had] rejoined their columns before or at the moment of our clearing the hedge [on the crest of the position]. We do not recollect seeing them'.[85] Prior to this charge, Private Cruikshank of the 79th Foot had seen the French 'sharpshooters which came up the hill, . . . quickly driven back'.[86]

Similarly, Captain Ross of the 51st Light Infantry recalls elements of his regiment being sent out to meet 'the Enemy's skirmishers who were moving forward at the head of their columns';[87] whilst Major-General Adam of the Third Infantry Brigade observed a 'very sharp tussle' between the 71st Light Infantry and the *tirailleurs* preceding the columns of the Imperial Guard.[88] As is well known, the Imperial Guard columns were subsequently surprised and destroyed by the British 1st Foot Guards who were lying in wait for them, concealed behind the crest of Wellington's ridge. Had the *tirailleurs* penetrated the cordon formed by the 71st, things might have gone differently in the ensuing clash between the opposing Guards.

The degree of success the British enjoyed in thwarting the French light troops contrasts sharply with that of other Allied armies. The French *voltigeurs* largely maintained their supremacy over the skirmishers of Russia, Austria and Prussia, and Colonel Moscoso of the Spanish service, for example, noted in 1812 that the skirmishing lines of his compatriots were always too feeble to keep the French *tirailleurs* at bay. The latter

> invariably pushed their way close up to the Spanish main body and, whilst presenting in their scattered formation no definite mark for volleys, were yet numerous enough to shoot down so many of their opponents as to shake the Spanish formation before the columns in the rear came up.[89]

As Wellington had observed, the French system of attacks in column *was* 'a false one against *steady* troops'; but when, as was more usually the case, the defending forces had been shaken beforehand by *tirailleurs* and artillery, it invariably proved deadly.

However, in the Peninsular War, the French themselves tended to use a relatively small number of troops as skirmishers. Even their light infantry regiments were usually deployed in close-order formations like ordinary line troops[90] and, indeed, the only forces consistently employed in skirmishing duties were the *voltigeur* companies of line regiments. Each battalion had one such company, along with one of grenadiers and four centre companies. Thus, a typical French division of eight battalions would field around 800 light troops.

This was a far smaller proportion than that found in one of Wellington's divisions where the battalion light companies were reinforced by whole battalions of riflemen and other light infantry. Thus, in accounts of Peninsular engagements, one finds numerous incidents where the French *voltigeurs* were thrust back by overwhelming numbers of Anglo-Portuguese light infantry. At the Battle of Salamanca, for instance, Wellington directed the Seventh Division to send 'two whole battalions' against the eight *voltigeur* companies of Foy's division. These were 'the 68th and the 2nd *Cacadores*, who formed a very powerful screen of light troops, and pushed back the French . . .',[91] In the same battle, the leading brigade of Pakenham's division deployed their flank companies, three companies of riflemen detached from the 60th, and the entire 12th *Cacadores* against the eight *voltigeur* companies of Thomières division.[92] Similarly, at the Battle of Sabugal in 1811, half of Beckwith's brigade, some 1500 men, were deployed as skirmishers against General Merle's four *voltigeur* companies. The French skirmish line was 'at once driven in by the Rifles and Cacadores' and Merle's four supporting columns were badly mauled.[93]

The Battle of Sorauren in 1813 provides an interesting contrast with this state of affairs. Here, General Lecamus sent his brigade against the Allied line with both the *voltigeur* and grenadier companies deployed as skirmishers in front of the battalion columns.[94] Further along the front, his colleague General Vandermaesen did the same. Interestingly enough, both of the French formations enjoyed considerable success over their adversaries: Campbell's Allied brigade was routed by Lecamus, and Vandermaesen was only driven off by a counter-attack launched against his flank by Wellington's reserves.[95]

Thus, the relative strengths of the opposing light infantry screens played a major role in the clashes between British lines and French columns. But the success of the British skirmishers was attributable more to their large numbers than their quality: the French *voltigeur* were invariably greatly outnumbered by their Anglo-Portuguese counterparts, and with the notable exception of the regiments trained at Shorncliffe by Moore and Mackenzie, many of the British light infantry were not particularly skilled in their art when compared with the French *tirailleurs*. Lieutenant Blakiston of the 43rd Light Infantry, for example, confessed that

> Certainly I never saw such skirmishers as the 95th . . . They could do the work much better and with infinitely less loss than any of our best Light troops. They possessed an individual boldness, a mutual understanding and a quickness of the eye in taking advantage of the ground, which taken altogether, I never saw equalled. They were in fact, *as much superior to the French Voltigeurs as the latter were to our skirmishers in general*. As our regiment was often employed in supporting them, I think I am fairly well qualified to speak of their merits.[96]

Blakiston and other officers also wrote most critically of the British light troops' apparent failure to make use of cover on the battlefield, a point that even the scanty clauses relating to skirmishing found in the 1792 *Regulations* had emphasized.[97] In his account of the Battle of the Nive in 1813, Blakiston recalled how

> The brigade of guards was on this occasion brought forward to bear the brunt of the action during which their light companies received a dreadful mauling from the French *voltigeurs*. The great John Bulls had no notion of screening themselves from the fire of their more cautious adversaries, and suffered accordingly.[98]

This peculiar failing of the British light infantry was noted as early as 1807 by Colonel Stewart of the 95th, during the abortive expedition against the Turks. 'The Mahometans', he wrote, are more calculated for this desultory warfare than any of the European nations will ever be, whose ideas are perpetually fixed to lines, columns and close movements. . . . The natural result of this mode of fighting obliges every man to act very independently . . . The Mohamedan troops . . . certainly take their positions and cover the persons . . . with a degree of intelligence and alertness that we are perpetually endeavouring to teach and drive into our soldiers' brains, and generally in vain. The comparison of the conduct of our men in most of our rencontres with the enemy was by no means in our favour. While the Turks would gain a sandhill, and, with their turbans only visible, keep up the hottest fire on us, our officers would be indifferent whether it was hill or hollow that they were in or on; and our men would stand erect and expose their whole persons in the most useless manner.[99]

Similarly, at the Battle of Fuentes de Oñoro in 1811, Edward Costello of the 95th saw the 85th Light Infantry 'very roughly handled by the enemy'. This was, he explained, 'the first time since their arrival in the . . . [Peninsula], that they had been engaged. Opposed', he continued – echoing General Money's warning of the advantages of camouflage in skirmisher warfare[100] –

with their conspicuous red dresses, to the old trained French tirailleurs, . . . the 85th suffered . . . severely. When we came up, however, our practised fellows, in their dark clothing, from the murderous nature of our arms, soon turned back the advancing French . . .[101]

In the same action, Costello had also seen a demonstration of the inability of British line troops to fight effectively in anything other than their usual close-order formations – despite War Office attempts to introduce more flexibility into their tactical capabilities.[102] After witnessing a clash between the 79th Highlanders and some French voltigeurs in the vicinity of Fuentes de Oñoro itself, '. . . The place', he recalled,

was strewn about with their bodies. Poor fellows! they had not been used to skirmishing, and instead of occupying the houses in the neighbourhood, and firing from the windows, they had exposed themselves [to the French snipers] by firing in sections.[103]

Likewise, in 1810 Lieutenant-General Sir Thomas Graham had written to the Adjutant-General complaining that:

It must be allow'd by all, that the system of modern warfare requires a much larger proportion of light troops, or at least of men, *acquainted with the true principles of acting as such* than formerly and that in point of fact we possess none that deserve to be so class'd, *as so instructed* except those Brit. Regt's. formerly in our friend Sir J. Moore's Brigade at Shorncliffe . . . & some of the German Corps. Let anyone belonging to this army speak to this fact, & say, whether there is any comparison whatever between the Batt'ns. of Crawford's (sic) Lt. Div. & any other Brit. Batt'ns. in point of instruction, *as exemplify'd in practice before the Enemy*. We have other Brit. Batt'ns. called Lt.

Infantry that know no more of the matter than my gallant friends of the Guards here, & consequently expose themselves improperly & unnecessarily to be knocked in the head when they might & ought to be under cover.[104]

However, whatever they may have lacked in skill, the British light infantry made up for it by their weight of numbers. In one battle after another they succeeded in containing the attacks of the French *voltigeurs*, and thus enabled Wellington effectively to counter the tactical system which had secured the French a score of major victories over the continental powers. In 1799, General John Money had written:

> I know that it is to this new system of bringing more Irregulars into the field than their opponents, that the French owe chiefly their success . . . Let us learn to fight them by land in the manner they have found out and adopted; never let us be above or ashamed following the example even of an enemy, when we see it is a good one.[105]

As we have seen, the British Army gradually responded to this plea and over the next decade introduced light infantry regiments on the French model. By September 1813, with the Peninsular War drawing to a triumphant conclusion, Lieutenant George Hennell of the 43rd Light Infantry was able to tell his brothers: 'Soult* says the French have made us good soldiers by example. So they have but unfortunately for them (like Mr Hennell teaching me chess) they have taught us rather too long & we beat them in every game.'[106]

---

*Marshal Nicolas Jean de Dieu Soult (1769–1851) was Commander-in-Chief of the French Imperial forces in Spain, 1813.

CHAPTER VII

Light forces yesterday and tomorrow

In 9 A.D., in the Teutoburg Forest to the east of the River Emms, three of the five legions that made up the Roman Army in the Rhineland were surrounded and surprised by lightly armed *Cherusci* tribesmen. Prevented from deploying and fighting according to their traditional methods by the wooded, marshy and mountainous terrain, the Roman troops were utterly routed; some 20,000 legionaries and auxiliaries, along with their commander, P. Quinctilius Varus, were massacred. It was one of the greatest reverses ever sustained by the mighty Roman Empire's formidable armed forces, and it provoked intense interest amongst the military historians of the time: that three entire legions could be defeated by relatively undisciplined opponents, fighting with neither formal tactical drill nor heavy weapons and armour, certainly seemed incredible.[1]

But such spectacular successes continued to occur as the history of light forces unfolded. As we have seen, General Braddock's defeat in 1755 and the collapse of the Prussian war machine at Jena both led to significant reappraisals of military doctrine – despite the insistence of some 'die hard' conservative soldiers and theorists that the established tactical methods of the time stood in no need of modification. The need for substantial numbers of light troops to perform both specialist, *petite guerre* operations and select roles on major battlefields was gradually recognized; and, by the conclusion of the Napoleonic Wars, every European state had incorporated permanent bodies of light troops into the structure of its armed forces.

Interest in light troops, however, continued to follow its cyclical course and, as long periods of relative peace descended on Europe, many of the lessons of war were forgotten and had to be relearnt whenever conflict returned. Although light forces played a significant role in various colonial campaigns and the American Civil and Franco-Prussian Wars, it was not until the closing stages of World War I that they again drew attention on the scale they had during the struggle against Revolutionary and Napoleonic France. General Oscar von Hutier's Riga offensive of September 1917 heralded new developments in German tactics: the lengthy artillery bombardments that had characterized most battles of the war were discarded in favour of a sudden, short, concentrated preparation which immediately preceded attacks mounted by specially trained storm-troopers. Backed by light artillery, these *Angriffsgruppen* – mixed-arm combat teams, like those advocated by Dumouriez – bypassed centres of resistance and penetrated deep into the enemy's rear, while the German reserves exploited the breakthrough and subdued any remaining strongpoints. Further refined during the Battle of Caporetto (October – November 1917), 'Hutier Tactics' proved so successful that, in his five great offensives of 1915, Ludendorff made them the basis of his attacks.[2]

But whilst these German thrusts made considerable headway, the problem of maintaining continuity of advance was never solved during the First World War; Ludendorff's light force spearheads invariably ground to a halt as their logistical support faltered and the Allies, grasping their opportunity, sealed off any salient with reserves and defences in depth. By the outbreak of World War II, however, improved technology and the resultant progress in military aircraft and vehicle design had greatly reduced the constraints on forces attempting rapid, sustained advances. The result was the German concept of the *Blitzkrieg*; and, between 1939 and 1941, it was to wreak havoc with a series of opponents whose armed forces had failed to keep abreast of changes in military thought.

Whilst differing in detail because of improved technology, the *Blitzkrieg* was, in principle, virtually identical to Napoleonic strategy and, as in his time, light troops played a crucial role both on and around the main battlefields. Amongst their forces, the Germans had a number of 'shock divisions'. Each of these consisted of nine large battalions of light infantry – trained like the storm-troopers of World War I – with a brigade of motorized artillery for close support. Furthermore, each *Panzer* division had, besides two tank regiments (which included numerous light tanks), three battalions of *Jäger* – again, trained for infiltration operations. Whilst two of these battalions used various forms of personnel carrier, the other was mounted on motorcycles. They were backed by 18 highly mobile artillery pieces, and a large company of anti-tank and machine-gun units. A reconnaissance battalion consisting of motorcyclists and some 50 armoured cars was also attached to the divisional headquarters, as was a squadron of light aircraft.[3]

Similarly, in their civil war and the 1920s conflict with the Poles, the Russians saw the value of cavalry armies, mobile groups and 'forward detachments'. Commanded by men like Budienny, the cavalry armies – whose wide, quasi-independent sweeps were reminiscent of General J.E.B. Stuart's operations in the American Civil War, or Napoleonic cavalry corps-level activities – embodied the cossack tradition of mobile warfare which played a central role in Russian military thought in the 1930s and continues to be felt in their doctrine today. But it was not until 1942 that the emergence of this doctrine was clearly seen: Stalin's purges and the disputes over the lessons of the Spanish Civil War crippled the

Red Army in the late 1930s and, with Hitler's sudden attack in 1941, the Russians were forced into a series of desperate defensive campaigns, with no opportunity to launch the 'deep operations' that had been planned for the start of any conflict.

Indeed, in World War II, the one major offensive operation the Russians did undertake prior to 1942 nearly ended in catastrophe and clearly demonstrated the value of light forces. In November 1939, Russian armies nearly 1,000,000 men strong invaded Finland. To oppose them the Finns had just 300,000 troops – 80 per cent of whom were reservists. Many of these men were formed into mobile units of battalion or smaller size, accustomed to operating in the wooded terrain of eastern Finland and its intensely cold weather. Clad in warm, camouflaged clothing and mostly mounted on skis, they were ideally suited to lightning *kleiner Krieg* operations on the flanks and rear of the invaders' forces.

But, particularly when supported by heavy units, they could also prove devastatingly effective in open battle and, at Suomussalmi in December 1939, for example, obliterated two enemy divisions, including a motorized formation: the Russians lost 27,500 dead and 1,300 prisoners, along with 50 tanks and all their equipment and vehicles; Finnish casualties totalled 900 killed and 1,770 injured. Indeed, by the February of 1940, the Russian offensive had been completely halted by a series of astounding reverses.

In desperation, the Red Army flung 54 divisions with massive air and military support against the Mannerheim Line – system of World War I fortifications in the Karelian Isthmus. The Finns beat off four or five major assaults a day for nearly two weeks but, on 13 February, finally had their lines breached. By this stage of the war, Finland's casualties were nearing 68,000 and, too exhausted to continue the struggle, she conceded Russia's territorial demands. However, the Red Army had sustained appalling casualties in the six-month war: 200,000 men had been killed and perhaps 400,000 wounded; equipment losses were also severe. This, of course, only served to further enfeeble the general condition of the Russian armed forces and, when Hitler struck, the USSR came dangerously close to experiencing the utter military and political collapse suffered by France in 1940.[4]

The Russians' counter-offensive of early 1942 and their eventual victory at Stalingrad led, however, to the overstretched Germans increasingly taking up defensive postures, initially based on scattered strongpoints. Unlike the system proposed by Dumouriez, these defensive networks lacked depth and powerful mobile reserves that pivoted on the strongpoints in a battle of manoeuvre. Consequently, the Red Army, by launching concentrated attacks through gaps and other selected weakpoints, often managed to breach them. But having yet to develop sufficient mobility in their own units, the Russians proved unable to gain much tangible operational success from these localized tactical victories: like Ludendorff in 1918, they were incapable of exploiting any breakthroughs they might make.

Over the next two years, the Germans developed defensive systems that were deeper and more elaborate and, in turn, the Russians had to formulate more effective ways of breaching them. The *Wehrmacht*'s defensive mode became a genuine mixture of 'sword and shield' tactics, with aggressive counter-attacks at every level being combined with staunch defensive actions. Flowing round 'Islands of Resistance', powerful, highly manoeuvrable forces led the counter-strokes and covered withdrawals. To combat these, the Russians formed 'tank armies' – mobile groups, capable of intercepting enemy thrusts and sweeps, and maintaining contact with hostile forces that were retreating at high speeds. By 1945, a typical tank army totalled some 50,000 men, with 1000 tanks and assault guns, 850 mortars and artillery pieces, and 5300 supporting vehicles.[5]

By the end of the Second World War, such formations were implementing 'deep operations' which, in East Prussia and Manchuria, for instance, involved sustained advances of between 350 and 600 kilometres. Indeed, the sheer scale of the Red Army's strategic operations, when compared with those of the *Wehrmacht*, for example, largely accounts for the Russian success in the campaigns of 1943–45. But whilst the Germans might be dislodged by grand strategic movements, on a tactical level their 'Island of Resistance' network frequently proved impenetrable. In the 'Epsom' and 'Goodwood' Operations of the summer of 1944, for instance, powerful Allied armoured forces backed by immense air and artillery support were pitted against relatively flimsy German units. But the outnumbered German forces – mostly infantry anti-tank teams, ably supported by a few batteries and squadrons of tanks – made the most of the advantages offered by the local terrain. The *bocage* – the network of dense, embanked hedges that breaks much of this region of France up into numerous enclosures – both slowed down and channelled the Allies' advance and, together with villages, farm buildings, ditches, orchards and other forms of cover, provided the German light infantry combat teams with a perfect environment in which to function. Both operations dragged on for far longer than had been anticipated and, worse still, the Allies' losses were out of all proportion to their gains. Despite their massive superiority in armour, artillery and air support, they struggled to overcome their seemingly weak opponents and suffered heavy casualties in the process.[6]

Such incidents clearly show the potential of light forces when imaginatively and properly deployed; and the battle for Suez city in the Yom Kippur War of 1973 demonstrates the point still further: a single brigade of lightly equipped Egyptian infantry successfully defended the city against the Israeli armoured and mechanized units that attacked it on 24 October. The Israelis were repulsed with severe losses, largely inflicted with weapon systems of considerably less sophistication than those currently available to light forces fulfilling an anti-tank role.[7]

Indeed, interest in the potential uses of light troops and in their traditional fields of service – *petite guerre* operations, and urban and mobile warfare – has recently intensified. As both NATO and the Warsaw Pact seek answers to what are largely old problems, the solutions suggested by former generations become of increasing interest and importance. With both sides faced by the threat of tactical nuclear weapons and emerging technology, moves towards more dispersed modes of fighting based on enhanced arm integration, speed and mobility are pre-eminent. The Russians, for example, are incorporating thousands of *Spetsnaz* – specialist light troops – into their armed forces and are developing an operational doctrine which has the Operational Manoeuvre Group (OMG) – a highly manoeuvrable, deep-penetration force – as its core. But the OMG is nothing especially new; it has its roots in the cavalry armies, mobile groups, tank armies and forward detachments that have long played a role in Russian military thought. The Soviets are merely drawing on their past wartime experience and updating the concept to incorporate allowances for improved technology; the basic principles, however, remain the same.

At the same time, the USA is evolving the 'Air Land Battle' doctrine as enunciated in FM 100–5 and the more futuristic studies *Air Land Battle 2,000* and *Focus 21*. FM 100–5 provides for three distinct but interlocking types of engagements in all of which flexibility, speed, manoeuvre and mobility play an important part: there is the 'deep battle' against the enemy's follow-up forces; the battle in one's own rear areas against OMGs and *Spetsnaz*; and the 'close in' engagement. Light forces – and the US Army, for example, is currently forming a number of light divisions, whilst other NATO states already possess small bodies of specialist light troops – are clearly of immense potential value in all of these spheres of operation and could, as they have been throughout history, be employed either in independent groups or alongside heavy units according to circumstances. Looking to their long tradition in the *Jäger* field and their experience in past wars, the West Germans, for instance, seem to be reviving the 'Island of Resistance' concept. In a recent article, for example, Lieutenant-General von Sandrart – Chief-of-Staff of the *Bundeswehr* – stressed the importance of mobile defence based on settlements, minefields and other barriers. Such positions, he concluded, 'could be used by light infantry, giving them better protection and serving as a cornerstone in a highly mobile defence battle'.[8]

As we have seen, the notion of using light forces in this manner and, indeed, the whole concept of mobile defence, can be traced back through Second World War engagements like Operation 'Goodwood' to the Napoleonic-period writings of General Dumouriez. He and his contemporaries were the first generation of military thinkers to confront the basic problems that face current-day defence specialists interested in light forces; and it is regrettable that the various NATO states have not drawn more on the wealth of relevant military history that is available when shaping their responses to these 'new' challenges. Certainly, in their military journals the Soviets pay far more attention to the practical lessons of past conflicts – notably the Great Patriotic War – and are far less concerned about the managerial and technological dimensions of defence that feature so prominently in similar Western periodicals.

One particular regrettable point – and a suitable one on which to end this study – is the current neglect of the British Army's light forces. A number of the distinguished light infantry regiments originally formed at the beginning of the nineteenth century do remain on the *Army List*; but, as has happened to such units on earlier occasions, they have been subjected to a process of 'standardization' and are, to all intents and purposes, heavy infantry. Indeed, other than a few airborne battalions, the only bodies of true light infantry to be found in the British armed forces today are the Gurkhas, the Special Air Service Regiment, and small, *élite* naval units such as the Special Boat Service and the Arctic Warfare Cadre of the Royal Marines.

These troops are probably the finest of their kind in the world and clearly demonstrated their value in the *petite guerre* operations of the recent Falklands campaign. In any conflict with the Warsaw Pact they would doubtlessly be employed in missions behind enemy lines and promise to distinguish themselves once again. But the need for substantial bodies of light infantry as integral parts of the British 'Army of the Rhine' remains. What few resources are available in these times of mounting financial stringency are being committed to the strengthening of heavy, mechanized units;[9] and, whilst any increase in expenditure on conventional – rather than on nuclear – defence is to be applauded, at least some of these resources could be better devoted to the revival of true light infantry units, capable of operating in the increasingly enclosed and urbanized terrain of West Germany. The peacetime neglect of light forces has been an error repeated throughout history and, as we have seen, has often ended in disaster on the battlefield, with appalling political repercussions. When much the same challenge first faced the British Army in the late eighteenth and early nineteenth centuries, its response, although a sluggish and often painful process, was ultimately successful. It remains to be seen if our own generation's will prove as good.

REFERENCES

Index of Abbreviations

BL   The British Library, London
DPD   Department of Palaeography and Diplomatic, Durham
            University
KAV   *Kriegsarchiv*, Vienna
KROM   Kent County Record Office, Maidstone
MFF   *Militärgeschichtliches Forschungsamt*, Freiburg im Breisgau,
            West Germany
NLS   The National Library of Scotland, Edinburgh
PRO   The Public Records Office, Kew
ULS   The University Library, Southampton

Chapter I: The European Powers and the introduction of light forces, *c.* 1740–1815

1. See J. Colin, *L'Infanterie au XVIIIe siècle: la tactique* (Paris, 1907), pp. 180–184.

2. W.O. Shanahan, *Prussian Military Reforms, 1786–1813* (New York, 1945), p. 22.

3. See C. Jany, *Die Gefechtsausbildung der Preussischen Infanterie von 1806* (Berlin, 1903), pp. 4–16.

4. Frederick II of Prussia, *Oeuvres de Frédéric le Grand* (edited by J.D.E. Preuss, Berlin, 1846–1857), II, p. 42.

5. Gen. J. Money, *To the Right Honourable William Windham on a Partial Reorganization of the British Army* (London, 1799), p. 49.

6. J.A.H. de Guibert, *General Essay on Tactics* (English edition, London, 1781), I, p. 300.

7. Ibid., p. 301.

8. See G.E. Rothenberg, *The Military Border in Croatia. 1740–1881* (Chicago, 1966), pp. 1–103.

9. See J. Colin, op. cit., pp. 135–184.

10. M.F.F. *Nachlass* Scharnhorst, B.

No. 170: 'Essay on the need to have Light Troops' (*c.* 1794), p.1. Also see W. Rüstow, *Die Lehre vom kleinen Kriege* (Zurich, 1864), p. 3; and Capt. de Grandmaison, *La Petite guerre* (Paris, 1756), pp. 7–8.

11. See S.M. Pargellis, 'Braddock's defeat', *American Historical Review*, XLI (1935–36); and R.L. Yaple, 'Braddock's defeat: the theories and a reconsideration', *J.S.A.H.R.*, XLVI (1968), pp. 194–201.

12. S.M. Pargellis, *Lord Loudoun in North America* (New Haven, 1933), pp. 299–300.

13. See K.L. Parker, 'Anglo-American wilderness campaigning, 1754–1764: Logistical and Tactical Developments' (Columbia Univ. Ph.D. thesis, 1970), pp. 60–70.

14. S.M. Pargellis, *Lord Loudoun*, p. 304.

15. See E.E. Curtis, *The Organisation of the British Army in the American Revolution* (New Haven, 1926), pp. 14–15. Also see W. Wheeler, *The Letters of Private W. Wheeler, 1809–28* (edited by B. Liddell-Hart, London, 1951), p. 112.

16. E. Robson, 'British light infantry in the mid 18th century: the effect of American conditions', *The Army*

Quarterly, LXIII, No. 2 (1952), p. 212.

17.   See T. Mante, *The History of the Late War in North America and the Islands of the West Indies, Including the Campaigns of 1763 and 1764 Against His Majesty's Indian Enemies* (London, 1772), *passim*; and W.A. Smith, *A Historical Account of the Expedition Against the Ohio Indians in the Year MDCCLXIV Under the Command of Henry Boquet* (London, 1776), *passim*.

18.   See H.M. Chichester and G. Burges-Short, *The Records and Badges of Every Regiment and Corps in the British Army* (London, 1900), pp. 666–667.

19.   Gen. J. Money, *Partial Reorganization*, p. 21.

20.   Gen. J. Money, op. cit., p. 26.

21.   See Lt.–Col. J. Simcoe, *A Journal of the Operations of the Queen's Rangers From the End of the Year 1777, to the Conclusion of the late American War* (New York, 1844 edition), p. 38.

22.   Lt.–Col. B. Tarleton, *A History of the Campaigns of 1780 and 1781 in the Southern Provinces of North America* (London, 1787).

23.   Lt.-Col. A. Emmerich, *The Partisan in War: Or the Use of a Corps of Light Troops to an Army* (London, 1789), p. 9.

24.   Ibid., pp. 10–12.

25.   PRO War Office Papers, 28/5: Report on the 'King's Rangers' by Maj. James Rogers (undated, but covers period 1781–83).

26.   WO 28/4: Report on 'Jessup's Loyal Rangers', 24 Feb. 1783.

27.   WO 28/4: Report on 'Butler's Rangers', 26 March 1779.

28.   E. Robson, 'British Light Infantry in the mid 18th Century' (see Bibliography), pp. 218–220.

29.   See H.M. Chichester and G. Burgess-Short, *Records and Badges*, pp. 384–385, 646 and 666–667.

30.   See H. Strachan, *European Armies and the Conduct of War* (London, 1983), p. 29.

31.   See the presentation copy of Simcoe's *Journal* in the King's Library (BL).

32.   Gen. J. Money, *Partial Reorganization*, pp. 16–26. Also see Capt. T. H. Barber, *Instructions for the Formation and Exercise of Volunteer Sharpshooters* (London, 1804), pp. iv–v.

33.   Gen. J. Money, op. cit., pp. 26–27.

34.   See Gen. J. Money, op. cit., p. 43; and J.A. Houlding, *Fit for Service: The Training of the British Army, 1715–1795* (Oxford, 1981). p. 374.

35.   C.T. Atkinson, 'The Highlanders in Westphalia 1760–62 and the development of light infantry', *J.S.A.H.R.*, xx (1941), pp. 208–223.

36.   See H.M. Chichester and G. Burges–Short, *Records and Badges*, pp. 384–385 and 646.

37.   F. Vanicek, *Specialgeschichte der Militärgrenze* (Vienna, 1875), II, p. 403.

38.   G.E. Rothenberg, *Napoleon's Great Adversaries: The Archduke Charles and the Austrian Army, 1792–1814* (London, 1982), p. 109.

39.   C. Jany, *Geschichte der Königlich Preussischen Armee* (Berlin, 1928–33), III, p. 160.

40.   W.O. Shanahan, *Prussian Military Reforms*, p. 69; and P. Paret, *Yorck and the Era of Prussian Reform, 1807–1815* (Princeton, 1966), pp. 56–57.

41.   See P. Paret, op. cit., p. 40; and M.F.F. *Nachlass* Scharnhorst, B. No. 101: 'Essay on infantry tactics' (1811), section II, p. 1.

42.   J. Colin, *L'Infanterie au XVIIIe siècle*, pp. 274–275 ; and Capt. de Grandmaison, *La Petite guerre*, pp. 7–8.

43.   G.E. Rothenberg, *Napoleon's Great Adversaries*, p. 59.

44.   See J.A. Houlding, *Fit for Service*, p. 288.

45.   K.R.O.M. U.1350 (Lord Amherst Papers), MSS. 073/21, f.l: Lord Townshend to Lord Amherst, 19 June, 1775.

46.   *Oberst–Lt.* von Ewald, *Abhandlung von dem Dienst der leichten Truppen* (Flensburg, Schleswig and Leipsiz, 1790), p. 3.

47.   E. Werheimer, 'Erzherzog Karl und die 2 Koalition bis zum Frieden von Lunéville, 1798–1801', *Archiv für österreichische Geschichte*, LXVII (1886), p. 231.

48.   Gen. P.G. Duhesme, *Die leichte Infanterie* (Berlin, 1829), p. 44.

49.   See J. Canski, *Tableau statistique politique et moral du système militaire de la Russie* (Paris, 1833), pp. 222–255.

50.   W. Surtees, *Twenty-five Years in the Rifle Brigade* (London, 1833), pp. 8–9.

51.   See C. von Roeder, *Für Euch, meine Kinder! Erinnerungen aus dem Leben des Königlichen General-Leutnants Carl von Roeder* (Berlin, 1861), p. 30; E. von Conrady, *Geschichte des Königlich Preussischen Sechsten Infanterie Regiments* (Berlin, 1857), p. 52.

52.   G.E. Rothenberg, *Napoleon's Great Adversaries*, p. 109; and W. Rüstow, *Geschichte der Infanterie* (Nordhausen, 1964), II, p. 328.

53.   See P.G. Griffiths, 'Military thought in the French Army, 1815–1851' (Oxford Univ. D.Phil. thesis, 1975), p. 169; and D.G. Chandler, *The Campaigns of Napoleon* (London, 1966), p. 344.

54.   J. Colin *L'Infanterie au XVIIIe siècle*, p. 275.

55.   See C. Kling, *Geschichte der Bekleidung, Bewaffnung, und Ausrüstung des Königlich Preuss* (Weimar, 1901–12), I, p. 157; and C. Jany, *Geschichte der Königlich Preussischen Armee*, III, p. 160.

56.   M. de Saxe, *Les Rêveries, ou mémoires sur l'art de guerre* (The Hague, 1756), p. 44.

57.   *Oberst-Lt.* von Ewald, *Abhandlung*, p. 3.

58.   Ibid., pp. 2–3 and 36.

59.   Ibid., p. 35.

60.   Ibid., p. 5.

61.   J.A.H. de Guibert, *General Essay on Tactics*, I, pp. 309–310.

62.   Ibid.

63.   P.G. Duhesme, *Essai historique sur l'infanterie légère* (third edition, Paris, 1864), pp. 66–67.

64.   Ibid., p. 71.

65.   See P. Paret, *Yorck and the Era of Prussian Reform*, pp. 85–87, 103–104, 139–140 and 190.

66.   *Exercier-Reglement für die kaiserlich-königliche Infanterie* (Vienna, 1807), Preamble, Book III. Also see A.L.S.D. de Fonseca, *The Theory of the Infantry Movements* (London, 1825), I, p. 38.

67.   *Krieg 1809* (K.A.V., Vienna 1907–10), I, pp. 17–18.

68.   Lt. Col. A. Emmerich, *The Partisan in War*, pp. 197–198.

69.   Col. G. Hanger, *A Letter to Lord Castlereagh* (London, 1808), p. 81.

70.   J. Macdonald, *Instructions for the Conduct of Infantry on Actual Service* (London, 1807), II, p. 9.

71.   DPD Earl Grey Papers, f. 1599: Duke of York to Grey and others, 11 Oct. 1798.

72.   See Maj. J. Cunninghame, *The Tactics of the British Army* (London, 1804), p. 66.

73.   *Manual for Volunteer Corps of Infantry* (London, 1803), p. iii.

74.   NLS MSS. 8028 (Mackenzie Papers), f. 34: Sir Thomas Graham to General Calvert, 15 Oct. 1811.

75.   *Manual for Volunteer Corps of Infantry*, pp. iii.iv.

76.   DPD Grey Papers, f. 1599: Duke of York to Grey and others, 11 Oct. 1798.

77.   NLS MSS. 8028 (Mackenzie Papers), ff. 34–35: Graham to Calvert, 15 Oct. 1811.

78.   See, for example, G.E. Rothenberg, 'Nobility and military careers: The Hapsburg officer corps, 1740–1918', *The Journal of Military Affairs*, XL, (1976), pp. 182–183; S.F. Scott, *The Response of the Royal Army to the French Revolution* (Oxford, 1978), pp 19–26.

79.   See P. Paret, *Yorck and the Era of Prussian Reform*, pp. 263–266.

80.   See O. Heilbrunn, *Warfare in the Enemy's Rear* (London, 1963), p. 74.

81.   *Oberst-Lt.* von Ewald, *Abhandlung*, pp. 2 and 6.

82.   Frederick II of Prussia, *Die Instruktion Friedrichs des Grossen für seine Generale von 1747* (edited by R. Foster, Berlin, 1936), p. 93. Also see Ibid., p. 143.

83.   KAV *Nachlass* Mayer von Heldenfeld, B. 857–80.

84.   JAH de Guibert, op. cit., I, pp. 306–308.

85.   JAH de Guibert, op. cit., I, pp. 301–304.

86.   A. Graydon, *Memoirs of a Life Chiefly Passed in Pennsylvania* (Edinburgh, 1822), p. 210. Also see P.D. Nelson, 'Citizen soldiers or regulars: the views of the American General Officers on the Military Establishment, 1775–1781', *Journal of Military Affairs*, XLIII, No. 3 (1979), pp. 126–132.

87.   Capt. T.H. Barber, *Instructions for Sharpshooters*, p. i. Also see Capt. T.H. Cooper, *A Practical Guide for the Light*

Infantry Officer (London, 1806), pp. xvii–xviii and vi.

88.   M. de Jeney, *The Partisan: Or the Art of Making War in Detachments* (London, 1760 edition), p. 2.

89.   Ibid., pp. 6–7.

90.   MFF *Nachless* Scharnhorst, B. No. 170: 'Essay on the Need to Have Light Troops' (*c.* 1794). In W.O. 30/72: to York, 1 Sept., 1803, Gen. Dumouriez remarks: 'Experience proves that there are two principal bodies which are the nursery of excellent generals: The Etat Major of the army, . . . and the *petite guerre* . . .'. In his Notes sur les Chasseurs, Dumouriez also describes light units as 'practical schools destined to form officers' and urges that two officer cadets be attached to each company for training in logistics, tactics, reconnoitring and field fortification. See W.O. 30/72: *Notes sur les Chasseurs*, Summer, 1803.

91.   M. de Jeney, op. cit., p. 4. Gen. Dumouriez, for example, also commented that light infantry were not to be taught 'what they have to execute in war'. See W.O. 30/72: *Notes sur les chasseurs*, Summer, 1803.

92.   Gen. J. Money, *Partial Reorganization*, pp. 21–22 and 45.

93.   See Lt.-Gen. Sir W. Stewart, *The Cumloden Papers: The Correspondence of Lt.-Gen. Sir W. Stewart* (Edinburgh, 1871), p 23; and NLS MSS. 3835 (Melville Papers), f.181: 'Hints on improving the military system of Great Britain, by Sir John Sinclair.'

94.   MFF *Nachlass* Scharnhorst, B. No. 101: 'Essay on infantry tactics', (1811).

95.   M. de Jeney, op. cit. pp. 13–14.

96.   F.L. Petre, *Napoleon and the Archduke Charles* (London, 1976 edition), p. 31.

97.   Ibid., p. 341.

98.   F.L. Petre, *Napoleon's Last Campaign in Germany, 1813* (London, 1974 edition), p. 20.

99.   P.G. Duhesme, *Die leichte Infanterie*, p. 44.

100.   KAV *Feldakten* 1813, *Hauptarmee*, F/10–436b.

101.   KAV *Schriftgut Militärgrenze*, F/30, Maj.-Gen. Klein, 'Gedanken über Eigenschaften und Widmung der Militär Grenzer'. Also see G.R. Rothenberg, *The*

Military Border in Croatia, pp. 94–95.

102.   C. von Muffling, *Marginalien zu den Grundsätzen der Höheren Kriegskunst für die Generäle der österreichischen Armee* (Weimar, 1810), pp. 93–94.

103.   KAV *Feldakten* 1813, *Deutschland*, F/10–436b.

104.   *Krieg 1809*, I, pp. 76–77.

105.   P. Paret, *Yorck and the Era of Prussian Reform*, p. 18.

106.   MFF *Nachlass* Scharnhorst, B. No. 101: 'Essay on Infantry Tactics', (1811).

107.   Ibid.

108.   *Grundsätze der Höheren Kriegs-Kunst für die Generäle der Österreichisch-Armee* (Vienna, 1806), pp. 89–91.

109.   W. Wagner, *Von Austerlitz bis Königgrätz: Österreichische Kampftaktik im Spiegel der Reglements, 1805–1864* (Osnabrück, 1978), pp. 4–5.

110.   J. Gallina, *Beiträge zur Geschichte des österreichische Heerwesens* (Vienna, 1872), I, pp. 137–139.

111.   Ibid., I, pp. 143–144.

112.   *Grundsätze der Höheren Kriegs-Kunst*, pp. 85–88.

113.   See P. Paret, *Yorck and the Era of Prussian Reform*, p. 149. Gen. Dumouriez also observed: 'One must never allow an officer . . . to beat a *chasseur*, or abuse him with degrading remarks. The superior officer must severely punish any officer or N.C.O. who indulges in [such] a brutality . . .'. WO 30/72: Gen. Dumouriez's *Notes sur les Chasseurs*, Summer, 1803.

114.   See P.G. Mackesy, *The War for America, 1775–83* (London, 1964), p. 518. 518.

115.   Col. D. Dundas, *Principles of Military Movements, Chiefly Applied to Infantry* (London, 1788). Also see B.L. MSS. 27597–27600 (Papers of Sir David Dundas).

116.   Col. D. Dundas, *Principles*, p. iii.

117.   Ibid., p. 14.

118.   Ibid., pp. 13–14.

119.   Ibid., p. 13.

120.   Ibid., p. 14.

121.   See P.G. Mackesy, *War for America*, p. 518; and G.E. Rothenberg, *Napoleon's Great Adversaries*, p. 108.

122.   MFF *Nachlass* Scharnhorst, B. No. 101: 'Essay on Infantry Tactics', (1811).

123.   Gen. J. Money, *Partial*

Reorganization, pp. 37–41.

124. Maj.-Gen. G. Rigaud, *Celer et Audax: A Sketch of the Services of the 5th Battalion of the 60th Regiment (Rifles)* (Oxford, 1879), p. 69.

125. MFF *Nachlass* Scharnhorst, B. No. 101: 'Essay on Infantry Tactics'.

126. Quote in J.F.C. Fuller, *British Light Infantry in the Eighteenth Century* (London, 1925), pp. 179–80.

127. See P. Paret, op. cit., pp. 62–63.

128. See S.F. Scott, *The Response of the Royal Army*, pp. 170–182.

129. See S.F. Scott, op. cit., pp. 19–26.

130. Ibid., p. 172.

131. See J. Lynn, 'Esquisse sur la tactique de l'infanterie des Armées de la République', *Annales Historiques de la Révolution Française*, No. 210 (1972), pp. 537–566.

132. See R.S. Quimby, *The Background of Napoleonic Warfare: The Theory of Military Tactics in 18th Century France* (New York, 1957), pp. 328–329.

133. See J.W. Croker, *The Croker Papers: The Correspondence and Diaries of J.W. Croker* (Edited by L. Jennings, London, 1884), I, pp. 12–13.

134. Gen. M.S. Foy, *Histoire de la Guerre de la Péninsule sous Napoleon* (Paris, 1827), I, pp. 102–104.

135. MFF *Nachlass* Scharnhorst, B. No. 170: 'Essay on the need to have Light Troops', (*c.* 1794).

136. MFF *Nachlass* Scharnhorst, B. No. 101: 'Essay on infantry tactics', (1811).

137. See P. Paret, op. cit., pp. 78–92 and 112–113.

138. Ibid., pp. 182–190 and 121–140.

139. Gen. J. Money, op. cit., p. 47.

140. Baron Gross, *Duties of an Officer in the Field and Principally of Light Troops* (London, 1801), p. vii.

Chapter II: The British Army and the shortage of light infantry, *c.* 1790–1799

1. C.M. Clode, *Military Forces of the Crown: Their Administration and Government* (London, 1869), II, pp. 181–188 and 254–260.

2. J.A. Houlding, *Fit for Service*, pp. 46–90; and C.M. Clode, op. cit., I, p. 275.

3. J.A. Houlding, op. cit., p. 95.

4. C.M. Clode, op. cit., II, pp. 254–260 and 320–321.

5. See J. Watkins, *A Biographical Memoir of His Late Royal Highness Frederick Duke of York and Albany* (London, 1827), pp. 307–308.

6. Ibid., pp. 58–69.

7. W. Blackstone, *Commentary on the Laws of England* (fourth edition, London, 1777), I, p. 412.

8. See J. Macdonald, *Instructions for the Conduct of Infantry*, I, p. 4.

9. See C.M. Clode, op. cit., I, pp. 273–275.

10. King George III, *The Latter Correspondence of George III* (edited by A. Aspinall, Cambridge, 1962–70), II, pp. 381 and 384.

11. See T. Pakenham, *The Year of Liberty: The Great Irish Rebellion of 1798* (London, 1969), *passim*.

12. Lt.-Gen. Sir H. Bunbury, *Narratives of Some Passages in the Great War with France* (London, 1854), pp. xix-xx.

13. C.M. Clode, op. cit., I, pp. 273–275 and II, p. 436.

14. Sir J.W. Fortescue, *The British Army, 1783–1802* (London, 1905), p. 37.

15. Capt. T. Reide, *A Treatise on the Duty of Infantry Officers and the Present System of British Military Discipline* (London, 1795), pp. 2–3.

16. Sir H. Bunbury, *Great War with France*, p. vii.

17. Historical Manuscripts Commission, *Dropmore Papers*, IV, 264, Dundas to Grenville, 21 July, 1798.

18. The duke of York was appointed Field Marshal on the Staff, 10 Feb., 1795; Commander-in-Chief in Great Britain, 3 April 1798; Commander-in-Chief of the forces in Great Britain and Ireland, 9 June 1801.

19. Sir J.W. Fortescue, *The British Army, 1783–1802*, p. 109.

20. J. Watkins, *A Biographical Memoir of York*, pp. 306–308.

21. See A.H. Burne, *The Noble Duke of York: The Military Life of Frederick Duke of York and Albany* (London, 1949), pp. 231–234.

22. A.H. Burne, op. cit., pp. 229–230.

23. J. Watkins, op. cit., p. 308.

24. Sir J.W. Fortescue, *The British Army, 1783–1802*, p. 52.

25.   BL Addit. MSS. 57327 (Sir John Moore Papers): Moore to his father, Aug. (?), 1796.

26.   BL MSS. 57327 (Moore Papers): Moore to Abercrombie. 2 Sept. 1796.

27.   BL MSS. 57548 (Moore Papers): Moore to Calvert, 4 Sept. 1803.

28.   'The Author of Waverly' (sic), 'Memoirs of the Duke of York', *The Naval and Military Magazines*, (1827), p. 6.

29.   *Advice to Officers of the British Army* (edited by B. Ferguson, London, 1846 edition), pp. 32 and 59–60.

30.   WO 40/10: Letters of Commission for the Royal Military College, 12 Dec. 1798.

31.   See WO 1/943 for details of the establishment and early work of the Royal Military College. Also see J. Watkins, *A Biographical Memoir of York*, pp. 309–313.

32.   See R.E. and T.N. Dupuy, *The Encyclopedia of Military History, From 3,500 BC to the Present* (Revised edition, London, 1977), pp. 619–620.

33.   See Brigadiers M. Calvert and P. Young, *A Dictionary of Battles, 1715–1815* (London, 1979), p. 195.

34.   See R.E. and T.N. Dupuy, op. cit., pp. 185, 174 and 172.

35.   Capt. J. Knox, *An Historical Journal of the Campaigns in North America for the Years 1757, 1758, 1759 and 1760* (edited by A.G. Doughty, Toronto, 1915–16), I, pp. 487–488.

36.   See, for example, *Oberst-Leutnant von Ewald*, op. cit., p. 39.

37.   Col. D. Dundas, *Principles*, p. 13.

38.   Ibid., p. 12.

39.   See WO 27/61: Inspection returns on the 17th, 34th and 38th Regiments of f Foot, May, 1788; and WO 27/64: Inspection returns on the 17th, 34th and 38th Regiments of Foot, May 1789.

40.   Col. D. Dundas, *Principles*, pp. ii and 2.

41.   Ibid., p. 11.

42.   See J.A. Houlding, *Fit for Service*, p. 231.

43.   Gen. F. von Saldern, *Elements of Tacticks, and Introduction to Military Evolutions for the Infantry* (English edition, translated by I. Landmann, London, 1787).

44.   Lt.-Col. W. Dalrymple, *Tacticks* (London, 1781), p. viii.

45.   Col. D. Dundas, *Principles*, p. 13.

46.   Ibid., pp. 13–14.

47.   Ibid., p. 13

48.   Ibid., pp. 13–14.

49.   See, for example, A. von Montbé, *Die Chursächsischen Truppen im Feldzuge 1806*–7 (Dresden, 1860), II, p. 16; and A. von Seydlitz, 'Aus den Akten der Militär-Reorganisationskommission von 1808' (edited by F. Meinecke), *Forschungen zur Brandenburgischen und Preussischen Geschichte*, V (1892), pp. 487–495.

50.   See WO 3/10: Fawcett to Dundas, 4 Feb., 1792; and WO 3/10: Fawcett to Lord Harrington and others, 3 March 1792.

51.   *Rules and Regulations for the Formulations, Field Exercises and Movements of His Majesty's Forces* (London, 1792). Also see WO 3/27: General Order from Fawcett, 23 March 1792.

52.   *By His Majesty's Command: The Manual and Platoon Exercise* (London, 1792).

53.   Capt. Dominicus, *General Dundas' XVIII Manoeuvres* (London, 1798).

54.   R. Smirke, *Review of a Battalion of Infantry, Including the Eighteen Manoeuvres* (London, 1799).

55.   Lt.-Gen. Sir H. Bunbury, *Great War With France*, pp. 45–46.

56.   See Maj. J. Cunninghame, *The Tactic of the British Army* (London, 1804).

57.   *General Orders and Observations on the Movements and Exercises of the Infantry* (London, 1804).

58.   Lt.-Gen. Sir H. Bunbury, *A Narrative of the Campaign in North Holland* (London, 1799), p. 38.

59.   A.M. Delavoye, *Life of Thomas Graham, Lord Lynedoch* (London, 1880), p. 80.

60.   WO 3/10: Fawcett to the colonel, 38th Foot, 10 Feb. 1792; and WO 3/27: Fawcett to the colonel, 4th Foot, 4 Feb. 1792.

61.   Cathcart Papers: Cathcart to his son, 12 May, 1834.

62.   A.M. Delavoye, *Records of the 90th Regiment* (London, 1880), p. 1.

63.   J.A. Houlding, *Fit for Service*, p. 251.

64.   See WO 5/58: Circulars from the Secretary at War to fourteen regiments, 14 July 1774 and 4 October 1774.

65.   R. Lamb, *Memoir of His Own Life by R.L.* (Dublin, 1811), p. 89.

66.   Ibid., p. 91.
67.   Capt. T. Reide, *A Treatise on the Duty of Infantry Officers*, pp. 229–230.
68.   For details of Howe's system, see Howe's manuscript in the National Army Museum, MS. 6807/157/6; and Col. Williamson, *Elements of Military Arrangement* (London, 1790), I, p. 210.
69.   Col. D. Dundas, *Principles*, p. 13.
70.   L. Butler, *Annals of the King's Royal Rifle Corps* (London, 1913), II, p. 4.
71.   *Règlement provisoire sur le service de l'infanterie en campagne du avril, 1792* (Paris, 1792), p. 124. Also see J. Colin, *L'Infanterie au XVIIIe siècle*, pp. 180–181.
72.   Gen. K. von Mack, 'Observationspünkte für die Generale bei der Armee in Deutschland im Jahre 1796', *Beiträge zur Geschichte des österreichischen Heerwesens, Der Zeitraum von 1757–1814* (Vienna, 1872), p. 139.
73.   See M.J.C. von Ditfurth, *Die Hessen in den Feldzügen, 1793, 1794 und 1795 in Flandern, Brabant, Holland und Westphalen* (Kassel, 1839), I, pp. 112–124.
74.   See Sir J.W. Fortescue, *British Campaigns in Flanders, 1690–1794* (London, 1918), p. 294.
75.   Gen. J. Money, *The History of the Campaign of 1792* (London, 1794), p. 294.
76.   Sir J.W. Fortescue, *History of the British Army* (London, 1899–1930), IV, (Part Two), p. 917.
77.   L. Butler, *Annals of the King's Royal Rifle Corps*, I, p. 237. Also see J.F.C. Fuller, *British Light Infantry*, pp. 183–84.
78.   Dept. of Palaeography and Diplomatic, *The Papers of First Earl Grey* (Durham, 1974), II, p. 415.
79.   DPD Earl Grey papers, f. 1279: Fawcett to Grey, 24 Dec., 1797.
80.   Gen. J. Money, *Partial Reorganization*, pp. 18–19.
81.   Lord Cornwallis, *Correspondence of Lord Cornwallis* (edited by C. Ross, London, 1859), II, p. 331.
82.   W. Windham, *The Diary of the Right Honourable William Windham* (Edited by H. Baring, London, 1866), p. 392.
83.   Lord Cornwallis, *Correspondence*, II, p. 332.
84.   Sir J. Moore, *Diary of Sir John Moore* (edited by F. Maurice, London, 1904), I, p. 267.

85.   W. Windham, *Diary*, pp. 395–396.
86.   NLS MSS. 3835 (Melville Papers), f. 181: Sir John Sinclair to Henry Dundas, 6 Oct., 1798.
87.   Ibid.
88.   Ibid., f. 176 and ff. 180–181.
89.   Ibid., f. 176.
90.   Gen. J. Money, *Partial Reorganization*, pp. 8–9.
91.   Ibid., pp. 13–14.
92.   Ibid., pp. 16–17.
93.   Ibid., p. 14.
94.   Ibid., pp. 34–38.
95.   Ibid., pp. 7–9.
96.   Ibid., pp. 17–18.
97.   Ibid., p. 18.
98.   Gen. J. Money, *History of the Campaign of 1792*, p. 292.
99.   Gen. J. Money, *Partial Reorganization*, pp. 9–11.
100.   Ibid., p. 10.
101.   Ibid., pp. 11–12.
102.   Ibid., pp. 38–39.
103.   Ibid., p. 53.
104.   Ibid., p. 54.
105.   Ibid., pp. 51–53.
106.   Ibid., p. 54.
107.   Ibid., p. 8.
108.   Ibid., pp. 54–55.
109.   Gen. F. Jarry, *Instruction Concerning the Duties of Light Infantry in the Field* (second edition, London, 1803), Preface, pp. vi–vii.
110.   J. Macdonald, *Instructions for the Conduct of Infantry*, I, pp. lxxxi–lxxxii.
111.   Ibid., II, p. 9.
112.   See NLS MSS. 3835 (Melville Papers), f. 176: Sinclair to Henry Dundas, 6 Oct. 1798.
113.   Ibid., f. 177: Henry Dundas to Sinclair, 14 Nov. 1798.
114.   DPD Earl Grey Papers, f. 1764a: Circular from York to Earl Grey and others, 11 April 1799.
115.   See Ibid., f. 1764c: Lords Euston, Hardwick, and Sloane to Henry Dundas, 20 March 1799; f. 1764d: Henry Dundas to Earl Fitzwilliam, 26 March 1799; and f. 1764e: Lords Carnavon, Belgrave and Granville to Henry Dundas, 30 March 1799.
116.   Ibid., f. 1765e: Lords Carnavon, Belgrave and Granville to Henry Dundas, 30 March 1799.
117.   Ibid., f. 1778b: Grey to York, 18

April 1799.
118.   Ibid., f. 1777: Grey to York, 17
April 1799.
119.   Ibid.
120.   Ibid., f. 1784: Brownrigg to Grey,
20 April 1799.
121.   Ibid., f. 1378a: Brownrigg to
Grey, 14 April 1798.
122.   See Ibid., f. 928: York to Grey, 7
Nov. 1796; f. 933: Grey to York, 14 Nov.
1796; f. 945: Fawcett to Grey, 21 Nov.
1796.
123.   See Ibid., f. 1856: Circular from
York to Grey and others, 24 June 1799.
124.   Ibid., f. 1865: Brownrigg to Grey,
29 June 1799. Also see f. 1872: Brownrigg
to Grey, 3 July 1799.
125.   Ibid., f. 1966: Brownrigg to Grey,
26 Aug. 1799.
126.   See A. Emmerich, *The Partisan in
War*, p. 10.
127.   Se Sir J.W. Fortescue, *History of the
British Army*, IV (Part Two), p. 916.
128.   See WO 40/12: York to
Brownrigg, 29 July 1799.
129.   Lt.-Gen. Sir H. Bunbury, *A
Narrative of the Campaign in North Holland,
1799* (London, 1849), p. 3.
130.   W. Surtees, *Twenty-five Years in the
Rifle Brigade*, pp. 16–17.
131.   J. Watkins, *A Biographical Memoir
of York*, p. 361.
132.   Ibid., p. 364.
133.   C.G. Gardyne, *The Life of a
Regiment: The History of the Gordon
Highlanders* (London, 1901), I, p. 67.
134.   Lt.-Gen. Sir H. Bunbury,
Campaign in North Holland, p. 22.
135.   J. Watkins, op. cit., pp. 364–365.
136.   *Information and Instructions for
Commanding Generals and Others* (London,
1800), p. 13.

Chapter III: The light infantry units of the British Army, *c*. 1790–1815

1.   See WO I/60: Williamson to
Dundas, 13 Sept. 1794.
2.   BL MSS. 57320 (Moore Papers):
Moore to his father, 10 Jan. 1797.
3.   WO 6/5: Henry Dundas to
Simcoe, 25 April 1796.
4.   See WO 6/131: Henry Dundas to
York, 8 Dec. 1795.
5.   See Gen. P. Bourcet, *Principes de la
Guerre des Montagnes* (Paris, 1775).
6.   WO 1/60: Williamson to Dundas,
1 Aug. 1794.
7.   See WO 6/5: Dundas to
Williamson, 17 April, 1795; and WO
1/83: Dundas to Vaughan, 17 April 1795.
8.   See WO 4/337: Windam to Col's.
Howe, Keppel, Nicolls and Whitelocke,
29 May 1795; and Lewis to Col's Skerret
and Lewes, 15 Sept. 1795.
9.   See WO 6/131: Huskisson to
Brownrigg, 7 Jan. 1800; and WO 1/623:
Brownrigg to Henry Dundas, 4 May
1801. Also see WO 40/25: Gordon to F.
Moore, 17 Nov. 1806.
10.   For a more comprehensive
examination of the West Indian regiments
during this period, see R.N. Buckley,
*Slaves in Red Coats: The British West India
Regiments, 1795–1815* (London and New
Haven, 1979).
11.   See Col. G. Hanger, *A Letter to
Lord Castlereagh*, p. 68.
12.   See C. von Roeder, *Für Euch,
meine Kinder!* p. 30; and E. von Conrady,
*Geschichte des Königlich Preussischen
Sechsten Infanterie-Regiments*, p. 62.
13.   See Lt.-Col. J. Simcoe, Journal,
pp. 189 and 213.
14.   See, for example, F. Redlich, *The
Military Enterpriser and his Work Force*
(Wiesbaden, 1954); and M. Mallett,
*Mercenaries and their Masters: Warfare in
Renaissance Italy* (London, 1974).
15.   See Sir J. Fortescue, *British
Campaigns in Flanders, 1690–1794*
(London, 1918), pp. 213–14; and J.F.C.
Fuller, *British Light Infantry*, pp. 182–85.
16.   See WO 6/131: Henry Dundas to
York, 8 Dec. 1795.
17.   WO 6/131: Henry Dundas to
York, 25 Oct. 1797; and WO 40/11: York
to Windham, 9 Jan. 1798.
18.   WO 1/940: Plan to establish a
regiment of infantry (chasseurs), 6 Nov.
1799.
19.   WO 6/131: Henry Dundas to
York, 25 Oct. 1797.
20.   WO 133/9: Brownrigg to
Manningham, 8 Oct. 1800.
21.   See L. Butler, *Annals of the King's
Royal Rifle Corps*, II, p. 4.
22.   Maj.-Gen. J. Money, *Partial

Reorganization, pp. 22–23; also see L. Butler, *Annals of the King's Royal Rifle Corps*, II. p. 4.

23.   These were the *Regulations for the Exercise of Riflemen and Light Infantry* (London, 1798) and Gen. F. Jarry, *Instructions Concerning the Duties of Light Infantry in the Field* (London, 1801). In WO 30/72: *Notes sur les chasseurs*, 1803, Gen. Dumouriez urges York to include in all new light regiments 'some foreign officers who, having carried out the duties of the light troops on the continent [would be useful] for the formation and instruction of the Regiments . . .' Also see WO 30/72: Dumouriez to York, 1 Sept. 1803.

24.   WO 1/1109: Col. Ramsay to Charles Yorke, 3 June 1803.

25.   See p. 71.

26.   Col. H.C.B. Rogers, *Wellington's Army* (London, 1979), p. 80.

27.   See W. Wheeler, *Letters*, pp. 67–8.

28.   WO 1/623: Maj.-Gen. Dundas to Calvert, 11 Sept. 1801.

29.   Ibid.

30.   See WO 40/25: Windham to York, 31 July 1806.

31.   *The Army List* (Published by the War Office, London, 1795 edition), p. 234.

32.   See BL MSS. 57547 (Moore Papers): Moore to Brownrigg, 14 July 1802; and the *Diary of Sir John Moore*, II, p. 62.

33.   *The Army List* (London, 1807 edition), p. 292.

34.   See *The Army List*, (London, 1817 edition), p. 456.

35.   See J.F.C. Fuller, *British Light Infantry*, p. 185.

36.   Lt.-Col. R.E.F.G. North, 'The raising and organising of the King's German Legion', *J.S.A.H.R.*, XXXIX (1961), p. 78.

37.   D.S. Gray, 'Prisoners, wanderers and deserters', *J.S.A.H.R.*, LIII (1975), p. 192.

38.   See A. Wellesley, First Duke of Wellington, *Supplementary Dispatches and Memoranda, 1797–1818* (Edited by his son, London, 1858–72), VI, p. 640.

39.   See W.S. Moorsom, *Historical Record of the Fifty-Second Regiment* (London, 1860), p. 115.

40.   H.M. Chichester and G. Burges-Short, *The Records and Badges of Every Regiment and Corps in the British Army* (London, 1900), pp. 666–667.

41.   WO 40/11: York to Windham, 9 Jan. 1798.

42.   H.M. Chichester and G. Burges-Short, op. cit., po. 667; and Maj.-Gen. G. Rigaud, *5th Battalion of the 60th*, pp. 2–3.

43.   See WO 6/131: Henry Dundas to York, 25 Oct. 1797; and pp. 97–98.

44.   WO 6/131: Henry Dundas to York, 25 Oct. 1797.

45.   Capt. T.H. Barber, *Instructions for Sharpshooters*, p. 1.

46.   'A Corporal of Riflemen' (Capt. H. Beaufoy), *Scloppetara: or Considerations on the Nature and Use of Rifled Barrel Guns* (Richmond, 1971 edition), pp. 79–80.

47.   See Col. G. Hanger, *A Letter to Lord Castlereagh*, p. 78. Also see Chapter V.

48.   W. Surtees, *Twenty-five Years in the Rifle Brigade*, p. 42.

49.   See pp. 212–214.

50.   J.N. George, *English Guns and Rifles* (Plantersville, U.S.A., 1947), p. 133.

51.   See p. 16; and E. Robson, 'British 'British light infantry in the mid 18th century: the effect of American conditions', *The Army Quarterly*, LXIII, No. 2 (1952), p. 218.

52.   E. Baker, *Remarks on Rifle Guns* (London, 1829 edition), p. 9.

53.   G.E. Rothenberg, *Napoleon's Great Adversaries*, p. 52.

54.   WO 3/36: Calvert to Sir James Craig, 21 January 1804. In WO 30/72: *Notes sur les Chasseurs*, 1803, Gen. Dumouriez notes the shortages of rifles experienced by the British and suggests that up to 75 per cent of a unit could instead be armed with 'light muskets'. However, he continues: 'It is essential to give each *chasseur* a hunting knife and an axe; the axe would be useful . . . in clearing paths through thick woods and for attacking . . . houses.'

55.   WO 3/152: Calvert to F. Moore, 30 April 1804.

56.   E. Wheatley, *The Wheatley Diaries* (edited by C. Hibbert, London, 1964), p. 8; and Lt. Col. R.E.F.G. North, 'The raising and organising of the King's

German Legion', *Journal of the Society for Army Historical Research*, XXXIX (1961), p. 78.

57.   H.M. Chichester and G. Burges-Short, op. cit., p. 667.

58.   WO 40/12: York to Brownrigg, 29 July 1799.

59.   H.M. Chichester and G. Burges-Short, op. cit., p. 667.

60.   Communication from the Headquarters Museum of the Light Division, The Peninsula Barracks, Winchester, 5 June 1983.

61.   See Capt. T.H. Barber, *Instructions for Sharpshooters*, pp. 2–3.

62.   Ibid.

63.   'A Corporal of Riflemen' (Capt. H. Beaufoy), *Considerations on Rifled Barrel Guns*, p. 192.

64.   Col. G. Hanger, *A Letter to Lord Castlereagh*, p. 82.

65.   Ibid., pp. 74–75.

66.   Lord Cornwallis, *Correspondence*, III, p. 177.

67.   WO 3/591: Clinton to Weyland, 11 July 1803.

68.   WO 30/76: York to Lord Hobart, 12 Aug. 1803.

69.   WO 3/35: Clinton to Stewart, 22 Nov. 1803.

70.   Brig.-Gen. W. Stewart, *Outlines of a Plan for the General Reform of the British Land Forces* (second edition, London, 1806), p. 45.

71.   ⚫ Col. G. Hanger, *A Letter to Lord Castlereagh*, p. 68.

72.   Capt. T.H. Barber, *Instructions for Sharpshooters*, p. vi. Also see Gen. H.H.E. Lloyd, *A Political and Military Rhapsody on the Invasion and Defence of Great Britain and Ireland, by the late Gen. Lloyd* (edited by J. Drummond, London, 1798), p. 124.

73.   See WO 3/22: Calvert to Stewart, 14 May 1800; and WO 3/33: Calvert to Manningham, 14 May 1800.

74.   See WO 6/119: Huskisson (for Henry Dundas) to Stuart (sic), 13 Dec. 1799.

75.   Lt.-Gen. Sir W. Stewart, *The Cumloden Papers*, p. 22.

76.   Ibid., p. 23.

77.   NLS MSS. 3835 (Melville Papers), f. 176: Sir John Sinclair to Henry Dundas, 21 Oct. 1798. Also see p. 56.

78.   Lt.-Gen. Sir W. Stewart, op. cit.,

p. 23; and NLS MSS. 3835 (Melville Papers), f. 181: Sinclair to Henry Dundas, 6 Oct. 1798. Gen. Dumouriez in his *Notes sur les Chasseurs* (W.O. 30/72), enlarged on this point: '. . . One should raise more men for this service in Ireland and in Scotland than from England, not only because they are tougher, do not tire as easily and are more sturdy, but also because the Irish noblemen, above all, having more power over their peasants, enlist them with more ease and less expense.'

79.   See, for example, Lord Cornwallis, *Correspondence*, III, p. 177.

80.   See WO 133/7: Brownrigg to Manningham, 7 Jan. 1800.

81.   WO 3/32: Calvert to Manningham, 7 Jan. 1800.

82.   WO 3/21: Circular to fourteen regiments from Calvert, 9 Jan. 1800.

83.   Ibid.

84.   WO 3/21: Circular to six regiments from Calvert, 8 Feb. 1800.

85.   WO 3/22: Circular to five regiments from Calvert, 22 March 1800.

86.   WO 3/22: Circular to various regiments from Calvert, 22 March 1800.

87.   WO 3/22: Calvert to Lt.-Col. Stuart (sic), 1 April 1800.

88.   WO 3/32: Calvert to Stewart, 14 May 1800.

89.   Ibid.

90.   See WO 3/22: Calvert to Manningham, 9 May 1800.

91.   WO 3/33: Calvert to Manningham, 14 May 1800.

92.   WO 3/32: Calvert to Manningham, 9 May 1800.

93.   Sir W.H. Cope, *The History of the Rifle Brigade, Formerly the 95th* (London, 1877), p. 3.

94.   Ibid., p. 4.

95.   Ibid., p. 6; and WO 133/9: Brownrigg to Manningham, 14 Oct. 1800.

96.   WO 3/330: Calvert to Manningham, 20 Sept. 1800.

97.   See WO 133/9: Brownrigg to Manningham, 8 Oct. 1800.

98.   Lt.-Gen. W. Stewart, *The Cumloden Papers*, p. 23.

99.   WO 3/330: Calvert to Manningham, 7 Feb. 1801.

100.   WO 3/332: Calvert to Stewart, 26

April 1802.

101. WO 3/35: Calvert to Moore, 21 May 1802.

102. BL MSS. 57547 (Moore Papers): Moore to Stewart, 2 Oct. 1802.

103. Col. C. Manningham, *Military Lectures Delivered to the Officers of the 95th (Rifle) Regiment at Shorn-Cliff Barracks, Kent* (London, 1803). For details of these papers, see pp. 156–159.

104. WO 3/35: Calvert to Manningham, 3 Dec. 1802.

105. See WO 3/335: Calvert to Manningham, 28 Sept. 1803.

106. WO 3/334: Calvert to Manningham, 10 March 1803.

107. See, for example, J. Blakiston, *Twelve Years Military Adventure* (London, 1829), II, pp. 334–345.

108. J.C. Moore, *Life of Sir John Moore* (London, 1834), II, pp. 4–6.

109. BL MSS. 57547 (Moore Papers): Moore to Calvert, 30 Jan. 1803.

110. See pp. 63–65.

111. J.C. Moore, op. cit., II, p.5.

112. *Regulations for Riflemen and Light Infantry*, p. 1.

113. See pp. 19–20.

114. WO 133/12: Brownrigg to Moore, 18 Jan. 1803.

115. BL MSS. 57547 (Moore Papers): Moore to Brownrigg, 17 Jan. 1803; and Moore to Calvert, 28 Jan. 1803.

116. WO 3/35: Calvert to Moore, 18 Jan. 1803.

117. WO 3/36: Calvert to Smith, 12 July 1803.

118. See WO 3/37: 'W.W.' (for Calvert) to Moore, 1 Aug. 1804; and 'W.W.' (for Calvert) to Moore, 21 March 1804.

119. See WO 3/36: Calvert to Smith, 28 Sept. 1803; and BL MSS. 57544 (Moore Papers): Extra expense estimates on clothing the 52nd as light infantry, 25 Dec. 1803 – 25 Dec. 1804.

120. See BL MSS. 57548 (Moore Papers): Moore to Calvert, 10 Oct. 1803; and Maj. Gen. G. Rigaud, *5th Battalion of the 60th*, p. 69.

121. WO 40/29: Secretary at War to the colonels of the 68th and 85th, 10 Sept. 1808.

122. See WO 27/94: Inspection return by Rottenburg on the 71st, 4 May 1809; and Maj.-Gen. G. Rigaud, *5th Battalion of the 60th*, pp. 5–6.

123. H.M. Chichester and G. Burges-Short, *Records and Badges*, pp. 636 and 732.

124. See pp. 129–133.

125. BL MSS. 57547 (Moore Papers): Moore to Brownrigg, 17 Jan. 1803.

126. WO 27/94: Inspection return by Brig.-Gen. Baron de Rottenburg on the 71st, 4 May 1809.

127. Ibid., Inspection return on the 71st (Second Battalion), by Rottenburg, 12 June 1809.

128. Ibid., Inspection return on the 85th by Rottenburg, 9 May 1809.

129. A.M. Delavoye, *Life of Thomas Graham*, p. 84.

130. NLS MSS. 3605 (Papers of Thomas Graham, Lord Lynedoch), f. 156: Col. K. Mackenzie to Sir David Dundas, 17 June 1809, Mackenzie to Graham, 6 May 1799; and Ibid, MSS 3605, f. 156.

131. Ibid.

132. See H.M. Chichester and G. Burges-Short, *Records and Badges*, p. 385. Also see C. Oman, *Sir John Moore* (London, 1953), p. 242; and 'Obituary on Lt.-Gen. Sir Kenneth Douglas/ Mackenzie', *The Gentleman's Magazine* (April 1834), p. 442.

133. See NLS MSS. 3598 (Papers of Thomas Graham, Lord Lynedoch), f. 81: Mackenzie to David Dundas, 17 June 1809, Mackenzie to Graham, 6 May 1799; and ibid, MSS 3605, f. 156.

134. See A.M. Delavoye, *Life of Thomas Graham*, p. 92.

135. See 'Obituary on Mackenzie', *Gentleman's Magazine*, p. 442.

136. Cathcart Papers: Graham to Lord Cathcart, 28 Sept. 1803.

137. Ibid.

138. See, for example, WO 27/88: Inspection return on the 90th by Maj.-Gen. Boughton, 8 July 1805. Also see NLS MSS. 3612 (Graham Papers), f. 212: Official statistics on the establishment of the 90th Foot, 18 Dec. 1813.

Chapter IV: The architects and their works

1. Maj.-Gen. R. Rigaud *Fifth Battalion of the 60th*, p. 3.

2. WO 6/131: Henry Dundas to

York, 25 Oct. 1797.

3.   Maj.-Gen. G. Rigaud, op. cit., p. 5.

4.   This was the *Regulations for the Exercise of Riflemen and Light Infantry* (London, 1798). There were further editions in 1803 and 1808.

5.   Maj.-Gen. G. Rigaud, op. cit., pp. 5–6.

6.   *Regulations for the Exercise of Riflemen and Light Infantry* (second edition, London, 1803), p. 1.

7.   Maj.-Gen. G. Rigaud. op. cit., p. 20.

8.   *Regulations for Riflemen and Light Infantry*, p. 13.

9.   Ibid., p. 14; and Capt. T.H. Barber, *Instructions for Sharpshooters*, p. 16 and pp. 23–24.

10.   *Regulations for Riflemen and Light Infantry*, pp. 15–17.

11.   Maj.-Gen. G. Rigaud, op. cit., p. 69. Also see W.S. Moorsom, *Historical Record of the Fifty-Second Regiment*, p. 66.

12.   Capt. T.H. Cooper, *Guide for the Light Infantry Officer*, p. 17.

13.   A comprehensive list of bugle-calls can be found in the appendix to Capt. T.H. Cooper's *Guide for the Light Infantry Officer*.

14.   *Regulations for Riflemen and Light Infantry*, p. 15.

15.   See Capt. T.H. Cooper, op. cit., pp. 1–2.

16.   See Sir C. Oman, *History of the Peninsular War* (Oxford, 1900–1932), II, pp. 163–165; and IV, pp. 383–384. Also D. Gates 'The Spanish Ulcer': *A History of the Pensinular War* (London, 1986), pp. 120–23.

17.   See, for example, D. Rentzell, *Geschichte des Garde-Jäger-Bataillons* (second edition, Berlin, 1894), p. 13.

18.   *Regulations for Riflemen and Light Infantry*, pp. 11 and 18–20.

19.   Ibid., p. 20.

20.   Ibid., pp. 11 and 18–20.

21.   Ibid., p. 24.

22.   Ibid., pp. 24–25.

23.   Ibid., pp. 26–27.

24.   Maj.-Gen. G. Rigaud, op. cit., p. 16.

25.   Ibid., p. 5.

26.   Capt. T.H. Cooper, *Guide for the Light Infantry Officer*, pp. 14 and 16.

27.   Maj.-Gen. G. Rigaud, op. cit., p. 21.

28.   See p. 144.

29.   See Lt.-Gen. W. Stewart, *Cumloden Papers*, p. 23.

30.   J.A.H. de Guibert, *General Essay on Tactics*, I, p. 310; and Maj.-Gen. G. Rigaud, op. cit., p. 18.

31.   Maj.-Gen. G. Rigaud, op. cit., p. 20.

32.   See WO 3/35: Brownrigg to Manningham, 3 Dec. 1802.

33.   WO 40/10: York to Windham, 10 Dec. 1798.

34.   Ibid.

35.   Gen. F. Jarry, *Instructions Concerning the Duties of Light Infantry in the Field* (second edition, London, 1803), pp. 1–2.

36.   Ibid., pp. ii–iv.

37.   See M. de Jeney, *The Partisan*, pp. 6–7; and Lt.-Col. A. Emmerich, *The Partisan in War*, pp. 13–22.

38.   See Gen. F. Jarry, op. cit., p. viii.

39.   See, for example, *Oberst-Lt*. von Ewald, op. cit., pp. 16–17; and Lt.-Col. A. Emmerich, op. cit., pp. 13–24.

40.   Gen. F. Jarry, op. cit., pp. iv-vi.

41.   Ibid., pp. vi-vii.

42.   Ibid., pp. 37–40.

43.   Ibid., p. i.

44.   Ibid., p. 50.

45.   Ibid., p. 45.

46.   Ibid., pp. 39–45.

47.   Ibid., pp. 43 and 53.

48.   Ibid., pp. 197–98.

49.   Ibid., p. 195.

50.   Ibid., pp. 212–13.

51.   Ibid., pp. 199–200.

52.   Ibid., pp. 198–208.

53.   Ibid., p. 208.

54.   Ibid.

55.   See pp. 139–141.

56.   Gen. F. Jarry, op. cit., pp. 208–10. The standard infantry formation for resisting cavalry was a hollow square.

57.   See Maj.-Gen. W.C.E. Napier, *Outpost Duty by General Jarry* (London, 1869), p. vii.

58.   See Lt.-Gen. W. Stewart, *The Cumloden Papers*, p. 22.

59.   See WO 3/32: Calvert to Manningham, 7 Jan. 1800.

60.   See WO 3/335: Calvert to Manningham, 28 Sept. 1803.

61. This was his *Instruction Concerning the Duties of Light Infantry in the Field*.

62. See WO 3/35: Calvert to Manningham, 3 Dec. 1802.

63. Lt.-Gen. Sir W. Stewart, *The Cumloden Papers*, p. 23.

64. Brig.-Gen. Sir W. Stewart, *Outlines of a Plan for the General Reform of the British Land Forces* (second edition, London, 1806), pp. 10–11.

65. Ibid., p. 10.

66. Ibid., p. 13.

67. Ibid., p. 45.

68. See WO 3/335: Calvert to Stewart, 27 and 28 Dec. 1803.

69. WO 3/335: Calvert to Stewart, 2 Jan. 1804.

70. Col. C. Manningham, *Military Lectures*, pp. 1–2.

71. Ibid., p. 2.

72. Ibid.

73. See Lt.-Col. A. Emmerich, op. cit., p. 81.

74. See M. de Jeney, op. cit., pp. 73–130.

75. Col. C. Manningham, *Military Lectures*, p. 20.

76. WO 1/1137: General Order, 20 April 1801.

77. Col. C. Manningham, op. cit., pp. 71–72.

78. BL MSS. 57321 (Moore Papers): 'Instructions given to the Battalion of Lt. Infantry of Irish Militia under my command in Ireland in 1798 and 1799', p. 1.

79. See *The Diary of Sir John Moore* (edited by Maj.-Gen. J.F. Maurice, London, 1904), II, pp. 65–66.

80. See WO 3/35: Calvert to Moore, 21 May 1802; and WO 3/34: Calvert to Moore, 14 Dec. 1801.

81. BL MSS. 57329 (Moore Papers), f. X: Moore to Stewart, 2 Oct. 1802.

82. See *Diary of Sir John Moore*, II, p. 67.

83. See J.C. Moore, *Life of Sir John Moore*, II, pp. 4–6.

84. See pp. 84–88.

85. R. Glover, *Peninsular Preparation: The Reform of the British Army, 1795–1809* (Cambridge, 1963), p. 126.

86. W.S. Moorsom, *Historical Record of the 52nd*, p. 63.

87. BL MSS. 57329 (Moore Papers), f.

X: Moore to Brownrigg, 17 Jan. 1803.

88. 'Obituary of Lt.-Gen. Sir Kenneth Douglas (Mackenzie)', *The Gentleman's Magazine*, (April, 1834), p. 442.

89. See NLS MSS. 3605 (Graham Papers), ff. 155–156: Col. K. Mackenzie to Sir David Dundas, 17 June 1809.

90. Ibid., f. 136: Col. K. Mackenzie to Graham, 1 June 1809.

91. See, for example, J.F.C. Fuller, *Sir John Moore's System of Training* (London, 1924, *passim*.

92. Sir W.F.P. Napier, *The Life and Opinions of General Sir Charles James Napier* (London, 1857), I, pp. 58–9.

93. Gen. Sir G.T. Napier, *Passages in the Early Military Life of General Sir George T. Napier* (edited by W.C.E. Napier, London, 1884), p. 10.

94. Ibid., pp. 10–11.

95. See Sir W.F.P. Napier, *Life of General Sir W.F.P. Napier* (edited by H.A. Bruce, London, 1864), pp. 10–11 and 18–19.

96. R. Glover, op. cit., p. 129.

97. Ibid., pp. 127 and 129.

98. See, for example, Sir Charles' comments in his *History of the Peninsular War*, Preface, and IV, p. 374.

99. Anon., *Further Strictures on those Parts of Col. Napier's History of the Peninsular War which relate to the Military Opinions and Conduct of General Lord Viscount Beresford* (London, 1832), p. iv.

100. Ibid., pp. 3–5. Also see Gen. W.C. Beresford, *Refutation of Col. Napier's Justification of his Third Volume* (London, 1834); and *Strictures on Certain Passages of Lt.-Col. Napier's History of the Peninsular War which relate to the Military Opinions and Conduct of General Lord Viscount Beresford* (London, 1831).

101. W.F.P. Napier, *Life of General Sir W.F.P. Napier*, I, p. 21.

102. Ibid., p. 23.

103. Ibid., p. 22.

104. See W.S. Moorsom, *Historical Record of the 52nd*, pp. 63–4 and 66.

105. See pp. 189–190.

106. See W.O. 3/36: Calvert to Smith, 12 July 1803.

107. W.F.P. Napier, *Life of Gen. Sir W.F.P. Napier*, I, p. 19.

108. See, for example, BL MSS. 57547 (Moore Papers), *passim*.

109. NLS MSS. 3605 (Graham Papers), ff. 135–6: Mackenzie to Graham, 1 June 1809.

110. W.S. Moorsom, op. cit., p. 68. Also see the *Royal Military Calendar* (edited by J. Philipart, London, 1820 edition), III, pp. 184–5.

111. Gen. Sir G.T. Napier, *Early Military Life of George T. Napier*, pp. 12–13.

112. NLS MSS. 8028 (Mackenzie Papers), f. 33: Graham to Calvert, 15 Oct. 1811.

113. NLS MSS. 3605 (Graham Papers), ff. 135–136: Mackenzie to Graham, 1 June 1809.

114. 'Obituary on Mackenzie', *Gentleman's Magazine*, (April 1834), p. 443. Also see NLS MSS. 3605 (Graham Papers), f. 136: Mackenzie to Graham, 1 June 1809.

115. Lt.-Col. J. Leach, *Rough Sketches of the Life of an Old Soldier* (London, 1831), pp. 3–4.

116. See *Diary of Sir John Moore*, II, p. 85.

117. Also see NLS MSS. 3605 (Graham Papers), f. 136: Mackenzie to Graham, 1 June 1809.

118. Ibid., f. 203: Moore to Maj.-Gen. Mackenzie, Nov. 1803.

119. *Diary of Sir John Moore*, II, p. 94.

120. NLS MSS. 8028 (Mackenzie Papers), f. 33: Graham to Calvert, 15 Oct. 1811.

121. Capt. Cooke, *Memoirs of the Late War: The Personal Narrative of Captain Cooke of the 43rd Regiment, Light Infantry* (London, 1831), I, p. 5.

122. J.F.C. Fuller, op. cit., pp. 79–80. Also see J.F.C. Fuller, 'Two private letters from Maj.-Gen. Sir John Moore', *J.S.A.H.R.*, IX (1930), pp. 162–167.

123. Communication from the Archibald Stevens Alexander Library, Rutgers State University, New Brunswick, New Jersey, USA, 3 Feb. 1983.

124. See *Diary of Sir John Moore*, II, pp. 94–100; and J.F.C. Fuller, *Sir John Moore's System of Training*, p. 33.

125. See NLS MSS. 8028 (Mackenzie Papers), f. 7: Moore to Mackenzie, 1 Sept. 1805; and Ibid., f. 90: Mackenzie to Wellington, May 1815.

126. See NLS MSS. 3605 (Graham Papers), ff. 135–136: Mackenzie to Graham, 1 June 1809.

127. Ibid., MSS. 3609, ff. 191–192: Calvert to Graham, 26 Nov. 1811.

128. See J.F.C. Fuller, op. cit., pp. 79–80.

129. Ibid., p. 80.

130. Ibid., pp. 78–84.

131. Also see *Sir John Moore's System of Training*, p. 83, where Fuller makes further comments that suggest he had never actually read Rottenburg's drill manual.

132. See p. 129.

133. See Lt.-Col. J. Leach, *Life of an Old Soldier*, pp. 3–4; and Capt. Cooke, *Memoirs of the Late War*, I, p. 5.

134. NLS MSS. 8028 (Mackenzie Papers), f. 38: Mackenzie to Gen. Gross, 27 Feb. 1812.

135. Ibid., f. 41: Mackenzie to Graham, 22 May 1812.

136. BL MSS. 57547 (Moore Papers): Moore to Calvert, 30 Jan. 1803.

137. See W.S. Moorsom, op. cit., pp. 68–69.

138. WO 40/29: The Secretary at War to the colonels of the 68th and 85th Regiments, 10 Sept. 1808. Also see W.S. Moorsom, op. cit., p. 71.

139. See p. 121.

140. NLS MSS. 8028 (Mackenzie Papers), f. 33: Graham to Calvert, 15 Oct. 1811.

141. Lt.-Col. J. Leach, *Life of an Old Soldier*, pp. 3–4.

142. W.F.P. Napier, *The Life of General Sir Charles James Napier*, I, p. 59.

143. Gen. Sir G.T. Napier, *Early Military Life of George T. Napier*, pp. 13–14.

144. Capt. Cooke, *Memoirs of the Late War*, I, 32–33. Gen. Dumouriez, for example, also stressed the importance of company-based discipline: '[It] establishes a mutual confidence between officer and soldier, more necessary in [a light force] . . . than in any other, since the fate of an expedition, of even an army, can depend on the rashness or on the desertion of a single man.' WO 30/72: *Notes sur les chasseurs*, 1803.

145. Lt. G. Hennell, *A Gentleman Volunteer: The Letters of George Hennell*

From the Peninsular War, 1812–13 (edited by M. Glover, London, 1979), p. 49.

146. Gen. Sir. G.T. Napier, *Early Military Life of George T. Napier*, p. 14.

147. See *Diary of Sir John Moore*, II, pp. 84–85.

148. Gen. Sir G.T. Napier, *Early Military Life of George T. Napier*, p. 13.

149. R. Glover, *Peninsular Preparation*, p. 129.

150. See BL MSS. 57547 (Moore Papers): Moore to Brownrigg, 17 Jan. 1803.

151. R. Glover, op. cit., p. 127.

152. See pp. 123–124.

153. W.F.P. Napier, *Life of Gen. Sir W.F.P. Napier*, I, p. 21.

154. See p. 42.

155. *Diary of Sir John Moore*, I, p. 236.

156. Gen. Sir G.T. Napier, *Early Military Life of George T. Napier*, p. 13.

157. Ibid.

158. W.F.P. Napier, *The Life of General Sir Charles James Napier*, I, p. 59.

159. See J.C. Moore, *Life of Sir John Moore*, II, pp. 4–6.

160. Ibid.

161. See p. 90.

162. See p. 91.

163. R. Glover, op. cit., p. 129.

164. Ibid.

165. BL MSS. 57547 (Moore Papers): Moore to Brownrigg, 17 Jan. 1803.

166. See p. 172.

167. See p. 179.

168. See p. 192.

169. See W.S. Moorsom, op. cit., p. 63.

170. *Diary of Sir John Moore*, II, pp. 78–79.

171. NLS MSS. 8028 (Mackenzie Papers), f. 90: Mackenzie to Wellington, May 1815.

172. See WO 30/72 and WO 30/116: *Memoir (sic) militaire sur l'Angleterre*. A translation, with commentary, of this manuscript can be found in: J.H. Rose and A.M. Broadley, *Dumouriez and the Defence of England Against Napoleon* (London and New York, 1909).

173. Ibid.

174. Ibid.

175. Ibid. Dumouriez speaks particularly highly of Jarry's study: 'I could add nothing to the details in this excellent work', he comments in his *Notes sur les Chasseurs*. '[They] . . . contain all one has to know . . .' See WO 30/72: *Notes sur les Chasseurs*, 1803.

176. See p. 179.

177. See pp. 94–95.

178. WO 30/72.

179. Ibid.

180. Ibid.

181. See D. Gates, 'Light forces in western defence planning: some parallels from the past', *Centrepiece*, No. 8 (Centre for Defence Studies, Aberdeen University, autumn, 1985); T. Velocci, 'The new Light Division: will it work?' *National Defense* (Nov. 1984, pp. 56–60; D.H. Petraeus, 'Light infantry in Europe: strategic flexibility and conventional deterrence', *Military Review* (Dec. 1984), pp. 35–55; Gen. J.A. Wickham, 'Light infantry divisions in defense of Europe', *NATO's Sixteen Nations*, Special (Jan. 1985), pp. 100–107.

182. P. Bracken, 'Urban sprawl and NATO Defence', *Survival*, (Nov.–Dec. 1976), pp. 254–60; and D.H. Petraeus, op. cit., p. 40.

183. WO 30/72.

184. Ibid.

185. See, for example, D.H. Petraeus, op. cit., T. Velocci, op. cit.; and F.C. Berry, 'The U.S. Army's 9th Infantry Division', *International Defense Review* (Sept. 1984), pp. 1224–1229.

186. For details of Dumouriez's career see Rose and Broadley, pp. 512–513.

187. A.H. Craufurd, *General Craufurd and his Light Division* (London, 1891).

188. See Lt.-Col. J. Leach, *Life of an Old Soldier*, p. 71.

189. See W.S. Moorsom, *Historical Record of the 52nd Regiment*, p. 117.

190. Sir C. Oman, *History of the Peninsular War*, II, p. 303.

191. Gen. Sir G.T. Napier, *Early Military Life of George T. Napier*, p. 225.

192. Capt. Sir J. Kincaid, *Adventures in the Rifle Brigade and Random Shots from a Rifleman* (Glasgow, 1981 edition), p. 195.

193. Ibid., pp. 255–266.

194. Ibid., pp. 225–226.

195. *Standing Orders as Given Out and Enforced by the late Major-General Robert Craufurd, for the use of the Light Division* (edited by Brevet-Major Campbell and

Capt. Shaw, London, 1852), pp. v and 255–256.
196.   Capt. T.H. Cooper, *Guide for the Light Infantry Officer*, p. vi.

Chapter V: Aimed fire

1.   See P. Paret, *Yorck and the Era of Prussian Reform*, pp. 14–15. Also see W.O. Shanahan, *Prussian Military Reforms, p. 22; and Exercier-Reglement für die Kaiserlich-Königliche Infanterie* (Vienna, 1807), p. 15.
2.   P. Paret, op. cit., p. 158.
3.   See R. Scurfield, 'British military smoothbore firearms', *Journal of the Society for Army Historical Research*, XXXIII (1955), pp. 147–160.
4.   W.W. Greener, *The Gun and its Development* (London, 1972 edition), p. 624.
5.   J.A.H. de Guibert, *General Essay on Tactics*, I, p. 160.
6.   Ibid.
7.   Col. G. Hanger, *A Letter to Lord Castlereagh*, p. 78.
8.   W.S. Moorsom, *Historical Record of the Fifty-Second Regiment*, p. 137. Also see *A Soldier of the 71st* (edited by C. Hibbert, London, 1975 edition), p. 69.
9.   Maj.-Gen. Sir G. Bell, *Soldier's Glory* (edited by B. Stuart, London, 1956), p. 169.
10.   W.S. Moorsom, op. cit., p. 137.
11.   WO 27/94: Inspection return on the 1/95th Regiment or Rifle Corps, 12 May 1809, by Maj.-Gen. T. Graham.
12.   See p. 82.
13.   *Soldier of the 71st*, p. 61.
14.   C.W. Sawyer, *Firearms in American History, 1600–1800* (Boston, 1910), p. 99.
15.   Maj.-Gen. Sir G. Bell, *Soldier's Glory*, p. 72.
16.   R. Henegan, *Seven Years Campaigning in the Peninsula and the Netherlands* (London, 1846), pp. 344–346. Also see J.A.H. de Guibert, op. cit., I, p. 164.
17.   See *Exercier-Reglement für die Kaiserlich-Königliche Infanterie* (Vienna, 1807), p. 15.
18.   J.F.C. Fuller, *British Light Infantry*, p. 64.
19.   See, for example, P. Paret, 'Colonial experience and european military reform at the end of the 18th

century', *Bulletin of the Institute of Historical Research*, XXXVII, No. 95 (1964), p. 47.
20.   See *Instructions for the Drill, Manual and Platoon Exercise Directed by His Majesty* (Edinburgh, 1800 edition), plates facing p. 20.
21.   See J.A. Houlding, *Fit for Service*, p. 262.
22.   J.A.H. de Guibert, op. cit., I, p. 161.
23.   Capt. T.H. Cooper, *Guide for the Light Infantry Officer*, p. 30.
24.   J.A.H. de Guibert, op. cit., I, pp. 162–163.
25.   *Oberst.-Lt* von Ewald, op. cit., p. 3.
26.   Gen. J. Money, *The History of the Campaign of 1792*, pp. 292–293. Also see F. von Meerheimb, 'Berenhorst und Bülow', *Historische Zeitschrift*, VI (1861), pp. 61–71.
27.   Capt. T.H. Barber, op. cit., p. 120.
28.   WO 1/1109: Lt.-Col. Robertson to Lord Hobart, 25 Aug. 1803.
29.   See *Drill, Manual and Platoon Exercise* (Edinburgh, 1800 edition), p. 23.
30.   See, for example, *The Manual and Platoon Exercises by His Majesty's Command* (London, 1807 edition), pp. 33–34.
31.   Ibid., p. 39.
32.   WO 1/1137: General Order, 20 April 1801.
33.   J. Macdonald, *Instructions for the Conduct of Infantry*, I, p. lix.
34.   Ibid., I, p. lxviii.
35.   Ibid., I, pp. lxxxi-lxxxiii.
36.   Ibid., II, p. 9.
37.   Capt. T.H. Barber, *Instructions for Sharpshooters*, pp. 17–18.
38.   See, for example, WO 3/35: 'W.W.' to Gen. John Moore, 25 Jan. 1803.
39.   WO 27/94: Inspection return on the Second Battalion, 95th Regiment, by Rottenburg, 22 May 1809.
40.   See pp. 96.
41.   See p. 139.
42.   See, for example, NLS MSS. 3620 (Graham Papers), ff. 310–311: Mackenzie to Graham, 24 July 1832.
43.   NLS MSS. 8028 (Mackenzie Papers), f. 40: Circular by Mackenzie, (undated, but probably 1811).
44.   Ibid., f. 17: Mackenzie to Moore, 28 Jan. 1808.

45. Ibid., f. 40: Circular by Mackenzie (undated).
46. Ibid., f. 17: Mackenzie to Sir John Moore, 28 Jan. 1808.
47. See S.G.P. Ward, *Faithful: The Story of the Durham Light Infantry* (London, 1963), pp. 98–99.
48. See p. 67.
49. W. Wheeler, *Letters*, p. 172.
50. Col. G. Hanger, *Reflections on the Menaced Invasion* (London, 1804), pp. 159–60.

Chapter VI: The British light infantry at war, *c.* 1809–1815

1. M. de Jeney, *The Partisan*, pp. 1–2.
2. Baron Gross, *Duties of an Officer*, p. vi.
3. Lt. G. Hennell, *A Gentleman Volunteer*, p. 151.
4. Capt. Sir J. Kincaid, *Adventures in the Rifle Brigade*, p. 17.
5. Ibid., p. 18.
6. Ibid., pp. 18–19.
7. Capt. Cooke, *Memoirs of the Late War*, II, p. 60.
8. *A Soldier of the Seventy-First*, pp. 95–96.
9. Capt. Sir J. Kincaid, *Adventures in the Rifle Brigade*, pp. 20–25.
10. W.S. Moorsom, *Historical Record of the 52nd*, p. 117.
11. A.H. Craufurd, *General Craufurd and his Light Division*, pp. 83–84.
12. Ibid., p. 84.
13. Ibid., pp. 86–88.
14. Ibid., pp. 82–83.
15. See A.H. Craufurd, op. cit., pp. 88–91.
16. Capt. Sir J. Kincaid, *Adventures in the Rifle Brigade*, p. 196.
17. Ibid.; and Lt.-Col. J. Leach, *Life of an Old Soldier*, p. 124.
18. Ibid., pp. 124–25.
19. A.H. Craufurd, op. cit., pp. 88–92.
20. Ibid., pp. 96–97.
21. W.F.P. Napier, *War in the Peninsula*, II, pp. 404–405.
22. See p. 136.
23. See p. 136.
24. Capt. Sir J. Kincaid, op. cit., pp. 194–95.
25. Ibid., p. 195.
26. Ibid., p. 197.
27. See p. 102.
28. Capt. Sir J. Kincaid, op. cit., p. 197.
29. See Maj. G. Simmons, *A British Rifleman: The Journals and Correspondence of Major G. Simmons, Rifle Brigade, During the Peninsular War and the Campaign of Waterloo* (edited by Lt.-Col. W. Verner, 1899), pp. 53–54.
30. Capt. Sir J. Kincaid, op. cit., p. 198.
31. Lt.-Col. J. Leach, op. cit., p. 134.
32. W.F.P. Napier, op. cit., II, pp. 114–115.
33. Lt.-Col. J. Leach, op. cit., p. 137.
34. Ibid., pp. 137–139.
35. Ibid., pp. 111–112.
36. See A. Wellesley, First Duke of Wellington, *The Dispatches of Field Marshal The Duke of Wellington During his Various Campaigns* (8 vols. Compiled by Lt.-Col. J. Gurwood, London, 1844), IV, pp. 164–167.
37. A.H. Craufurd, op. cit., p. 122.
38. Lt.-Col. J. Leach, op. cit., pp. 144–145.
39. W.F.P. Napier, op. cit., II, pp. 411–412.
40. See D. Gates, 'The Spanish Ulcer': *A History of the Peninsular War* (London, 1986).
41. Capt. Sir J. Kincaid, op. cit., p. 200.
42. See A. von Montbé, *Die Chursächsischen Truppen im Feldzuge 1806–1807*, II, p. 16.
43. See F.L. Petre, *Napoleon and the Archduke Charles*, pp. 112–117.
44. *The Waterloo Letters: A Selection from Original and Hitherto Unpublished Letters Bearing on the Operations of the 16th, 17th and 18th June, 1815, by Officers who Served in the Campaign* (edited by Maj.-Gen. H.T. Siborne, London, 1983 edition), p. 25.
45. P.C. Duhesme, *Essai historique sur l'infanterie légère*, p. 315.
46. Baron Gross, *Duties of an Officer*, p. vii.
47. J.W. Croker, *The Croker Papers*, I, pp. 12–13.
48. Count H. d'Ideville, *Memoirs of*

Marshal Bugeaud, From his Private Correspondence and Original Documents, 1784–1849 (edited by F. Yonge, London, 1884), I, pp. v–vi.

49.   *Waterloo Letters*, p. 327. Also see the General Order for 4 May 1809, in Duke of Wellington, *Supplementary Dispatches*, VI, p. 251.

50.   *Waterloo Letters*, p. 254.

51.   See *Oberst-Lt.* von Ewald, *Abhandlung*, pp. 68–70.

52.   See, for example, *Waterloo Letters*, p. 401; and Lt. G. Hennell, *A Gentleman Volunteer*, pp. 89–90.

53.   Capt. Sir J. Kincaid, *Adventures in the Rifle Brigade*, p. 166.

54.   J. Malcolm, 'Reminiscences of a campaign in the South of France', *Constables Miscellany*, XXVII (1828), p. 293. Also see Capt. Sir J. Kincaid, op. cit., p. 166.

55.   Count H. d'Ideville, op. cit., I, pp. v–vi. Also see E. Lapene, *Conquête de l'Andalousie: Campagne de 1810 et 1811 dans le Midi de l'Espagne* (Paris, 1823), pp. 382–4.

56.   M. Girod de l'Ain, *Vie Militaire du General Foy* (Paris, 1900), p. 111.

57.   *Waterloo Letters*, p. 61.

58.   See, for example, E. Lapene, *Campagnes de 1813 et de 1814 sur l'Ebre, les Pyrénées et la Garonne* (Paris, 1823), pp. 382–384; and E. Lapene, *Conquête de l'Andolousie*, pp. 382–4.

59.   Duke of Wellington, *The Dispatches of Field Marshal The Duke of Wellington During His Various Campaigns* (compiled by Lt.-Col. Gurwood, London, 1834–1839), VII, p. 415.

60.   See P. Griffith, 'Military thought in the French Army', p. 157.

61.   See R.S. Quimby, *The Background of Napoleonic Warfare*, pp. 328–329.

62.   Lt. G. Hennell, op. cit., p. 28. Also see, for example, C.L.I.V. Londonderry, *Narrative of the Peninsular War from 1808 to 1813* (second edition, London, 1828), p. 231.

63.   D. Gates, *Peninsular War*, p. 235.

64.   E. Lapene, *Conquete de l'Andelousie, pp. 382–4; and Further Strictures on those Parts of Col. Napier's History of the Peninsular War which relate to the Military Opinions and Conduct of Viscount Beresford* (London, 1832), p. 175.

65.   *Waterloo Letters*, p. 229.

66.   See, for example, H. Strachan, *European Armies and the Conduct of War*, p. 52. Columns were, after all, theoretically composed of battalions deployed in line one behind the other.

67.   See, for example, *Waterloo Letters*, pp. 390–391; and *A Soldier of the Seventy-First*, p. 108.

68.   See R.S. Quimby, op. cit., pp. 334–338. Also see P.G. Duhesme, *Essai sur l'infanterie légère*, p. 177; and J. Colin, *La Tactique et la discipline dans les armées de la Révolution* (Paris, 1902), p. lxlvi.

69.   *A Soldier of the Seventy-First*, p. 107.

70.   See P.H. Stanhope, *Notes on Conversations with the Duke of Wellington* (London, 1899), p. 109.

71.   See, for example, Capt. Sir J. Kincaid, op. cit., p. 168.

72.   *Waterloo Letters*, p. 44.

73.   Ibid., p. 172.

74.   Ibid., p. 247.

75.   Ibid., p. 365.

76.   For details of the 7th Division, see ULS Wellington Papers, 9/1/2/4: General Order, 5 March 1811. Also see W. Wheeler, *Letters*, p. 53.

77.   See, for example, *Waterloo Letters*, p. 358.

78.   Ibid., p. 327.

79.   Wellington Papers, 9/7/2: Weekly Returns of Forces, 1815–1818, Report on Third Division, 11 June 1815.

80.   Sir C. Oman, *History of the Peninsular War*, VII, p. 360.

81.   Capt. Sir J. Kincaid, op. cit., p. 143.

82.   See D. Gates, *'The Spanish Ulcer': A History of the Peninsular War*, p. 235.

83.   *Waterloo Letters*, p. 358.

84.   See Col. Vigo-Roussillon, *La Guerre d'Espagne: Fragments des Mémoires Militaires du Colonel Vigo-Roussillon* (Paris, 1891), pp. 7–9.

85.   *Waterloo Letters*, p. 86. Also see Ibid., p. 89.

86.   Ibid., p. 361.

87.   Ibid., p. 315.

88.   Ibid., p. 277.

89.   G. de Arteche, *Guerra de la Independencia Historia Militar de Espána de 1808 a 1814* (Madrid, 1868–1903), II, p. 394.

90. See D. Gates, op. cit., p. 24.
91. Sir C. Oman, op. cit., V. p. 422.
92. Ibid., V. pp. 442–443.
93. Ibid., IV, p. 192.
94. B. Smyth, *History of the 20th Regiment, 1688–1898* (London, 1889), p. 400.
95. D. Gates, op. cit., pp. 415–17.
96. J. Blakiston, *Twelve Years Military Adventure*, II, pp. 344–345 (author's italics). Also see Lt. G. Hennell, op. cit., p. 136.
97. See the *1792 Regulations*, pp. 335–336.
98. J. Blakiston, op. cit., II, p. 312.
99. Lt.-Gen. Sir W. Stewart, *The Cumloden Papers*, p. 45.
100. See p. 60.
101. E. Costello, *The Adventures of a Soldier* (London, 1841), pp. 121–122.
102. See WO I/1137: General Order, 20 April, 1801.
103. E. Costello, op. cit., p. 124.
104. NLS MSS. 8028 (Mackenzie Papers), f. 33: Graham to Calvert, 15 Oct. 1811.
105. Gen. J. Money, *Partial Reorganization*, p. 55.
106. Lt. G. Hennell, *A Gentleman Volunteer*, p. 131.

Chapter VII: Light forces yesterday and tomorrow

1. See L. Keppie, *The Making of the Roman Army From Republic to Empire* (London, 1984), pp. 168–169.
2. See D. Gates, 'Light forces in western defence planning: parallels from the past', *Centrepiece*, No. 8 (Aberdeen University Centre for Defence Studies, autumn, 1985).
3. Ibid., p. 39.
4. Ibid., p. 39–41.
5. Ibid., p. 42.
6. Ibid., pp. 43–45 and 48.
7. Ibid., p. 49.
8. See Gen. H. von Sandrart, 'Forward defence: mobility and the use of barriers', *NATO's Sixteen Nations*, Special, Vol. 30 (Jan. 1985), pp. 37–43.
9. See *Statement on the Defence Estimates, Presented to Parliament by the Secretary of State for Defence by Command of Her Majesty, 1985* (H.M. Stationery Office, London, 1985), I, paragraphs 215, 418, 419. 420, 522.

BIBLIOGRAPHY

(Printed sources published in London unless otherwise indicated)

MANUSCRIPT SOURCES

University Library, Southampton
The Wellington Papers, 1809–1815:
9/1 Records of the Adj.-Gen. in the Peninsula and South of France.
9/2 Records of the Military Secretary.
9/4 Military Records for the Peninsular Campaigns.
9/5 Records of the Adj.-Gen. in Germany, the Low Countries and France.

The Public Records Office, Kew
War Office Papers:
WO 1 War Office In Letters.
WO 2 Indexes of Correspondence.
WO 3 Out Letters, Commander-in-Chief.
WO 4 Out Letters, Secretary at War.
WO 6 Out Letters, Secretary at State, War Office.
WO 17 Monthly Returns.
WO 26 War Office Miscellany Books.
WO 27 Inspection Returns.
WO 28 Headquarters Records.
WO 30 War Office Miscellanea.
WO 34 Papers of General Sir J. Amherst.
WO 40 Selected Unnumbered Papers.
WO 64 Manuscript Army Lists.
WO 133 Papers of General Sir R. Brownrigg.

Department of Palaeography and Diplomatic, Durham University
The Papers of First Earl Grey.

Kent County Record Office, Maidstone
U. 1350 Lord Amherst Papers.

The National Army Museum, Chelsea
MS. 6807/157/6 Maj.-Gen. Howe's Light Infantry Discipline, 1774.

The Light Division's Museum, Winchester
Manuscript copy of the 'Green Book', the Standing Orders devised for the Experimental
Rifle Corps, Blatchington, 1800.

The British Library
Addit. MSS. 57320–57332 Sir John Moore Papers.
MSS. 2597 and 27599–27600 Papers of Sir David Dundas.

The National Library of Scotland
MSS. 3590–3645 Papers of Thomas Graham, Lord Lynedoch.
MSS. 16001–16434 Addit. Papers of Thomas Graham, Lord Lynedoch.
MSS. 8028 Mackenzie Papers.
MSS. 3835 Melville Papers.

Cathcart Collection (privately owned)
The Papers and Correspondence of the First Earl Cathcart.

Historical Manuscripts Commission, Reports
HMC *Dropmore Papers* (1906)

Militärgeschictliches Forschungsamt, Freiburg im Breisgau
Nachlass Scharnhorst.

Kriegsarchiv, Vienna
B./573 *Nachlass* Mack.
B./857 *Nachlass* Mayer.
A./1 *Nachlass* Radetzky.
Hofkriegsrat Akten, 1788–1814.
Feldakten, 1792–1813.

PRINTED PRIMARY SOURCES

Advice of Officers of the British Army (Edited by B. Ferguson, 1946 edition).
Army List (War Office, 1785–1815 editions).
'Author of Waverly' (sic) 'Memoirs of the Duke of York', *Naval and Military Magazine* (1827).
Baker, E. *Remarks on Rifle Guns* (1829 edition).
Barber, T.H. Capt. *Instructions for the Formation and Exercise of Volunteer Sharpshooters* (1804).
Beresford, Gen. W.C. *Refutation of Col. Napier's Justification of his Third Volume* (1834).
Bell, Maj.-Gen. Sir G. *Soldier's Glory* (edited by B. Stuart, 1956).
Blakiston, J. *Twelve Years Military Adventure, or Memoirs of an Officer* (2 vols. 1829).
Boothby, C. *Under England's Flag, 1804–9* (1900).
Bourcet, Gen. P. *Principes de la guerre des montagnes* (Paris, 1775).
Bunbury, Lt.-Gen. Sir H. *A Narrative of the Campaign in North Holland, 1799* (1849).
Bunbury, Lt.-Gen. Sir. H. *Narratives of Some Passages in the Great War with France 1799–1810* (1854).
Bunbury, Lt.-Gen. Sir H. *A Narrative of Military Transactions in the Mediterranean* (1851).
By His Majesty's Command: The Manual and Platoon Exercises (1792)
Cadell, Lt.-Col. C. *Narrative of the Campaigns of the 28th Regiment Since Their Return From Egypt in 1802* (1835).
Canski, J. *Tableau statistique, politique et moral du système militaire de la Russie* (Paris, 1833).
Chambray, G. de. *De l'Infanterie* (Paris, 1824).
Chambray, G. de *Oeuvres* (5 vols. Paris, 1839–40).
Cooke, Capt. *Memoirs of the Late War: The Personal Narrative of Captain Cooke of the 43rd Regiment, Light Infantry* (2 vols., 1831).
Cooper, Capt. T.H. *A Practical Guide for the Light Infantry Officer* (1806).
Cornwallis, Lord. *Correspondence of Lord Cornwallis* (3 vols. edited by C. Ross, 1859).
'Corporal of Riflemen' (Capt. H. Beaufoy). *Scloppetaria: Or Considerations on the Nature and Use of Rifled Barrel Guns* (Richmond, 1971 edition).
Costello, E. *The Adventures of a Soldier, or Memoirs of Edward Costello* (1841).
Croker, J.W. *The Croker Papers: The Correspondencee and Diaries of J.W. Croker* (2 vols. edited by L. Jennings, 1884).
Cunningham, Maj. J. *The Tactic of the British Army* (1804).
Dalrymple, Lt.-Col. W. *Tacticks*(1781).
Decker, C. von *Der kleine Krieg* (Berlin, 1828).
Ditfurth, M.J.C. von. *Die Hessen in den Feldzügen in der Champagne, am Maine und Rheine während der Jahre 1792, 1793 und 1794* (2 vols. Kassel, 1839).
Dominicus, Capt. G. *General Dundas' XVIII Manoeuvres* (1798).
Duhesme, P.G. *Die leichte Infanterie* (Berlin, 1829).

Duhesme, P.G. *Essai historique sur l'infanterie légère* (third edition, Paris 1864).

Dumas, M. *Précis des evénements militaires, ou essais historiques sur les campagnes de 1799 à 1814*)19 vols. Paris, 1817–1826).

Dundas, Col. D. *Principles of Military Movements, Chiefly Applied to Infantry* (1788).

Emmerich, Lt.-Col. A. *The Partisan in War: Or The Use of a Corps of Light Troops to an Army* (1789).

Ewald, *Oberst-Leutnant* von. *Abhandlung von dem Dienst der leichten Truppen* (Flensburg, Schleswig & Leipzig, 1790).

Exerzir-Reglement für die Infanterie der Königlich Preussischen Armee (Berlin, 1812).

Exercier-Reglement für die Kaiserlich-Königliche Infanterie (Vienna, 1807).

Fonseca, A.L.S.D. de *The Theory of the Infantry Movements* (2 vols. 1825).

Foy, Gen. M.S. *Histoire de la guerre de la Péninsule sous Napoleon* (4 vols. Paris, 1827).

Frederick II of Prussia. *Militärische Schriften* (edited by A. von Taysen, Dresden, 1893).

Frederick II of Prussia. *Oeuvres de Frédéric le Grand* (31 vols. Edited by J.D.E. Preuss, Berlin, 1846–1857).

Frederick II of Prussia. *Die Instruktion Friedrichs des Grossen für seine Generale von 1747* (edited by R. Foster, Berlin, 1936).

Fririon, F.N. *Considérations sur l'Infanterie Française* (Paris, 1822).

Further Strictures on those Parts of Col. Napier's History of the Peninsular War which relate to the Military Opinions and Conduct of Viscount Beresford (1832).

Gavin, W. *The Diary of William Gavin, Ensign and Quartermaster of the 71st Highland Regiment 1806–1814* (edited by Sir C. Oman. Oxford, 1921).

General Orders and Observations on the Movements and Field-Exercise of the Infantry (1804).

General Regulations and Orders for the Army (1811 and 1822 editions).

George III of England. *The Later Correspondence of George III* (edited by A. Aspinall, Cambridge, 1962–1970).

Grandmaison, Capt. de *La Petite Guerre* (Paris, 1756).

Graydon, A. *Memoirs of a Life Chiefly Passed in Pennsylvania* (Edinburgh, 1822).

Gross, Baron. *Duties of an Officer in the Field and Principally of Light Troops* (1801).

Grundsätze der Höheren Kriegs-Kunst für die Generale der österreichisch-Armee (Vienna, 1806).

Guibert, Comte de J.A.H. *General Essay of Tactics* (English edition, 2 vols., 1781).

Hanger, Col. G. *A Letter to Lord Castlereagh* (1808).

Hanger, Col. G. *Reflections on the Menaced Invasion* (1804).

Henegan, R. *Seven Years Campaigning in the Peninsula and the Netherlands from 1808 to 1815* (1846).

Hennell, Lt. G. *A Gentleman Volunteer: The Letters of George Hennell from the Peninsular War* (edited by M. Glover, 1979).

Hessen-Casselisches Militär-Reglement für die Infanterie, Artillerie, und leichten Truppen (Cassel, 1802).

Ideville, Comte H. d'. *Memoirs of Marshal Bugeaud. From his Private Correspondence and Original Documents 1784–1849* (edited by F. Yonge, 1884).

Information and Instructions for Commanding Generals and Others (1800).

Instructions for the Drill, Manual and Platoon Exercise Directed by His Majesty (1800 and 1803 editions).

Instruction für sämtliche Infanterie Regimenter und Fusilier Bataillone, Exercieren der Schützen betreffend (Berlin, 1789).

Jarry, Gen. F. *Instruction Concerning the Duties of Light Infantry in the Field* (second edition, 1803).

Jeney, M. de *The Partisan: Or the Art of Making War in Detachments* (English edition, 1760).

Kincaid, Capt. Sir J. *Adventures in the Rifle Brigade and Random Shots from a Rifleman* (1981 edition, Glasgow).

Knesebeck, K.F. von. *Betrachtungen über den jetzigen Krieg* (Berlin, 1794).

Knox, Capt. J. *An Historical Account of the Campaigns in North America for the Years 1757, 1758, 1759 and 1760* (3 vols, edited by A.G. Doughty, Toronto, 1915–1916).

Lamb, Sergeant R. *A Narrative of His Own Life by R.L.* (Dublin, 1811).

Lapene, E. *Campagnes de 1813 et 1814 sur l'Ebre, les Pyrénées et la Garonne* (Paris, 1823).

Lapene, E. *Conquête de l'Andalousie: Campagne de 1810 et 1811 dans le Midi de l'Espagne* (Paris, 1823).

Leach, Lt.-Col. J. *Rough Sketches of the Life of an Old Soldier* (1831).

Lecointe, M. *The Science of Military Posts, for the use of Regimental Officers who Frequently Command Detached Parties* (1761).

Lloyd, Maj.-Gen. H. *A History of the Late War in Germany; Between the King of Prussia, and the Empress of Germany and Her Allies* (revised edition, 2 vols., 1766–1781).

Lloyd, Maj.-Gen. H. *A Political and Military Rhapsody on the Invasion and Defence of Great Britain and Ireland, by the late General Lloyd* (edited by J. Drummond, 1798).

Macdonald, J. *Rules and Regulations for the Field Exercise and Manoeuvres of the French Infantry, Issued August 1st, 1791. Translated by J. Macdonald with Explanatory Notes, and Illustrative References to the British and Prussian Systems of Tactics* (2 vols., 1803).

Macdonald, J. *Instructions for the Conduct of Infantry on Actual Service* (2 vols., 1807).

Malcolm, J. 'Reminiscences of a campaign in the South of France', *Constables' Miscellany*, XXVII (1828).

Manningham, Col. C. *Military Lectures Delivered to the Officers of the 95th (Rifle) Regiment at Shorn-Cliff Barracks, Kent* (1803).

Mante, T. *The History of the Late War in North America and the Islands of the West Indies, Including the Campaigns of 1763 and 1764 Against His Majesty's Indian Enemies* (1772).

Manual for Volunteer Corps of Infantry (1803).

Manual and Platoon Exercises by His Majesty's Command (1805 and 1807 editions).

Military Tracts (1806).

Money, Gen. J. *To the Right Honourable William Windham on a Partial Reorganization of the British Army* (1799).

Money, Gen. J. *The History of the Campaign of 1792* (1794).

Moore, Lt.-Gen. Sir J. *The Diary of Sir John Moore* (2 vols. edited by Maj.-Gen. J.F. Maurice, 1904).

Moore, J.C. *Life of Sir John Moore* (2 vols., 1834).

Muffling, C. von. *Marginalien zu den Grundsätzen der Höheren Kreigskunst für die Generäle der österreichischen Armee* (Weimar, 1810).

Napier, Sir G.T. *Passages in the Early Military Life of General Sir George T. Napier* (1884).

Napier, Sir W.F.P. *Life of General Sir W.F.P. Napier* (edited by H.A. Bruce, 1864).

Napier, Sir W.F.P. *History of the War in the Peninsula and in the South of France, 1807–14* (6 vols., 1851 edition).

'Obituary on Lieutenant-General Sir Kenneth Douglas (Mackenzie)', *The Gentleman's Magazine* (April, 1834).

Ochs, A.L. von. 'Ein kleiner Beitrag zur Berichtigung der Taktik für leichte Truppen', *Mars III*, No 2 (1805).

Règlement concernant l'exercise et les manoeuvres de l'infanterie du premier août 1791 (Paris, 1791).

Regulations for the Exercise of Riflemen and Light Infantry (1803 edition).

Reglement für die leichte Infanterie (Berlin, 1788).

Règlement provisoire sur le service de l'infanterie en campagne du 5 avril 1792 (Paris, 1792).

Reide, Capt. T. *A Treatise on the Duty of Infantry Officers and the Present System of British Military Discipline* (1795).

Roeder, C. von. *Für Euch, meine Kinder! Erinnerungen aus dem Leben des Königlichen General-Leutnant Carl von Roeder* (Berlin, 1861).

Royal Military Calendar (edited by J. Philipart, 1815 and 1820 editions).

Rules and Regulations for the Formations, Field-Exercises, and Movements of His Majesty's Forces 1792, 1801 and 1807 editions).

Rules and Regulations for the Manual and Platoon Exercises, Formations, Field-Exercise and Movements of His Majesty's Forces (1807).

Russell, Lt. J. *A Series of Military Experiments Made in Hyde Park, in 1802, Under the*

Sanction of H.R.H. The Commander-in-Chief (1806).

Russell, Lt. J. *A Series of Military Experiments of Attack and Defence* (1806).

Saldern, Maj.-Gen. F. von. *Elements of Tacticks, and Introduction of Military Evolutions for the Infantry* (English edition translated by I. Landmann, 1787).

Saxe, Marshal M. de. *Les Rêveries, ou mémoires sur l'art de guerre* (Le Hague, 1756).

Simcoe, Lt.-Col. J.G. *A Journal of the Operations of the Queen's Rangers From the End of the Year 1777, to the Conclusion of the Late American War* (Exeter, 1787).

Simmons, Maj. G. *A British Rifleman: The Journals and Correspondence of Major G. Simmons, Rifle Brigade, During the Peninsular War and the Campaign of Waterloo* (edited by Lt.-Col. W. Verner, 1899).

Smirke, R. *Review of a Battalion of Infantry, Including the Eighteen Manoeuvres* (1799).

Smith, W.A. *A Historical Account of the Expedition against the Ohio Indians in the Year MDCCLXIV Under the Command of Henry Boquet* (1766).

Soldier of the Seventy-First: The Journal of a Soldier of the Highland Light Infantry, 1806–15 (edited by C. Hibbert, 1975 edition).

Standing Orders as Given Out and Enforced by the late Major-General Robert Craufurd, for the use of the Light Division During the Years 1809, 1810 and 1811 (edited by Brevet-Maj. Campbell and Capt. Shaw, 1852).

Stanhope, P.H. *Notes on Conversations with the Duke of Wellington* (1899).

Stewart, Brig.-Gen. *Outlines of a Plan for the General Reform of the British Land Forces* (second edition, 1806).

Stewart, Lt.-Gen. Sir W. *The Cumloden Papers: The Correspondence of Lieutenant-General Sir William Stewart* Edinburgh, 1871).

St-Cyr, Gen. L. *Mémoires sur les campagnes des armées du Rhin et du Rhinet-Moselle, de 1792 jusqu'a la Paix de Campo-Formio* (Paris, 1829).

Strictures on Certain Passages of Lt.-Col. Napier's History of the Peninsular War which relate to the Military Opinions and Conduct of Gen. Lord Viscount Beresford (1831).

Surtees, W. *Twenty-Five Years in the Rifle Brigade* (1833).

Tarleton, Lt.-Col. B. *History of the Southern Campaigns of 1780 and 1781, in the Southern Provinces of North America* (1787).

Vigo-Roussillon, Col. *La Guerre d'Espagne: fragments des mémoires militaires du Colonel Vigo-Roussillon* (Paris, 1891).

'Versuch con der kriegeszucht', *Krieges-Bibliothek*, I (Breslau, 1755).

Waterloo Letters: A Selection from Original and Hitherto Unpublished Letters Bearing on the Operations of the 16th, 17th and 18th June, 1815, by Officers who Served in the Campaign (edited by Maj.-Gen. H.T. Siborne, 1983 edition).

Watkins, J. *A Biographical Memoir of His Late Royal Highness Frederick Duke of York and Albany* (1827).

Wellesley, A. First Duke of Wellington. *Supplementary Dispatches and Memoranda of Field-Marshal Arthur Duke of Wellington* (15 vols. edited by his son, 1858–1872).

Wellesley, A. First Duke of Wellington. *The Dispatches of Field Marshal The Duke of Wellington During his Various Campaigns* (12 vols. Compiled by Lt.-Col. J. Gurwood, 1834–1839, and 8 vols., 1844).

Wellesley, A. First Duke of Wellington. *The General Orders of Field-Marshal the Duke of Wellington* (Edited by Lt.-Col. J. Gurwood, 1832).

Wheatley, E. *The Wheatley Diaries* (edited by C. Hibbert, 1964).

Wheeler, W. *The Letters of Private W. Wheeler, 1809–28* (edited by B. Liddell Hart, 1951).

Williamson, Col. *Elements of Military Arrangement* (2 vols., 1790).

Windham, Rt. Hon. W. *The Diary of the Right Honourable William Windham* (edited by Mrs H. Baring, 1866).

Secondary sources:

Arteche, G. de *Guerra de la Independencia Historia Militar de España de 1808 a 1814* (vol. II, Madrid, 1868–1903).

Atkinson, C.T. 'The Highlanders in Westphalia 1760–2 and the development of light infantry', *Journal of the Society for Army Historical Research*, XX (1941), 208–223).

Becke, Capt. A.F. *An Introduction to the History of Tactics 1740–1905* (1909).

Berry, F.C. 'The U.S. Army's 9th Infantry Division', *International Defense Review*, (September, 1984), 1224–1229.

Bertaud, J.P. *La Révolution Armée* (Paris, 1979).

Blackstone, W. *Commentary on the Laws of England* (fourth edition, 1777).

Bracken, P. 'Urban Sprawl and NATO Defence', *Survival*, (Nov.–Dec. 1976), 254–60.

Brownrigg, B. *The Life and Letters of Sir John Moore* (Oxford, 1923).

Buckley, R.N. *Slaves in Red Coats: The British West India Regiments, 1795–1815* (London and New Haven, 1979).

Burne, A.H. *The Noble Duke of York: The Military Life of Frederick Duke of York and Albany* (1949).

Butler, L. *The Annals of the King's Royal Rifle Corps* (vols. 1 and 2, 1913).

Calvert, Brig. M. & Young, Brig. P. *A Dictionary of Battles, 1715–1815* (1979).

Carrias, E. *La Pensée Militaire Française* (Paris, 1960).

Chandler, D.G. *The Campaigns of Napoleon* (1966).

Chichester, H.M. and Burges-Short, G. *The Records and Badges of Every Regiment and Corps in the British Army* (1900).

Childs, J. *Armies and Warfare in Europe, 1648–1789* (Manchester, 1982).

Clark, Lt.-Col. W. 'The maintenance of discipline', *The 43rd and 52nd Light Infantry Chronicle*, III (1894), 206–212.

Clode, C.M. *Military Forces of the Crown: Their Administration and Government* (2 vols., 1869).

Colin, J. *The Transformation of War* (trans. by L.H.R. Pope-Hennessy, 1912).

Colin, J. *L'Infanterie au XVIIIe siècle: la tactique* (Paris, 1907).

Colin, J. *La Tactique et la discipline dans les armée de la Révolution* (Paris, 1902).

Conrady, E. von. *Geschichte des Königlich Preussischen Sechsten Infanterie-Regiments* (Berlin, 1857).

Cope, Sir W.H. *The History of the Rifle Brigade, Formerly the 95th* (1877).

Craufurd, A.H. *General Craufurd and his Light Division* (1891).

Criste, O. *Erzherzog Carl von Österreich* (3 vols. Vienna, 1912).

Curtis, E.E. *The Organisation of the British Army in the American Revolution* (New Haven, 1926).

Delavoye, A.M. *The Life of Thomas Graham, Lord Lynedoch* (1880).

Delavoye, A.M. *The Records of the 90th Regiment* (1880).

Delbrück, H. *Geschichte der kriegskunst im Rahmen der politischen Geschichte* (vol. 4. Berlin, 1900–36).

Duffy, C. *The Army of Frederick the Great* (Newton Abbot, 1974).

Duffy, C. *The Army of Maria Theresa* (Newton Abbot, 1977).

Dupuy, R.E. and T.N. *The Encyclopedia of Military History from 3500 B.C. to the Present* (revised edition, 1977).

Ernstberger, A. *Die deutschen Freikorps 1809 in Böhmen* (Berlin, Vienna and Amsterdam, 1942).

Fortescue, Sir J. *British Campaigns in Flanders, 1690–1794* (1918).

Fortescue, Sir J. *History of the British Army* (vol. iv, 1899–1930).

Fortescue, Sir J. *The British Army, 1783–1802* (1905).

Förster, S. von. *Das Tiraillement im coupirten Terrain nach der Instruction des General von Yorck* (Berlin, 1851).

Fuller, J.F.C. 'Sir John Moore's light infantry instructions of 1798–99', *Journal of the Society for Army Historical Research*, XXX (1952), 68–75.

Fuller, J.F.C. 'Two private letters from Maj.-Gen. Sir John Moore', *Journal of the Society for Army Historical Research*, IX (1930), 162–167.

Fuller, J.F.C. *British Light Infantry in the Eighteenth Century* (1925).

Fuller, J.F.C. *Sir John Moore's System of Training* (1924).

Gallina, J. *Beiträge zur Geschichte des österreichischen Heerwesens* (2 vols. Vienna, 1872).

Gardyne, C.G. *The Life of a Regiment: The History of the Gordon Highlanders* (vol. I., 1901).

Gates, D. *'The Spanish Ulcer': A History of the Peninsular War* (1986).

Gates, D. 'Light Forces in Western Defence Planning: Some Parallels From The Past', *Centrepiece*, No. 8, (Aberdeen University Centre for Defence Studies, Autumn, 1985).

George, J.N. *English Guns and Rifles* (Plantersville, USA, 1947).

Girod de l'Ain, M. *Vie Militaire du General Foy* (Paris, 1900).

Glover, R. *Peninsular Preparation: The Reform of the British Army, 1795–1809* (Cambridge, 1963).

Gray, D.S. 'Prisoners, wanderers and deserters', *Journal of the Society for Army Historical Research*, LIII (1975).

Greener, W.W. *The Gun and its Development* (1972 edition).

Griffiths, P.G. 'Military thought in the French Army, 1815–51' (Oxford Univ. D. Phil. thesis, 1975).

Heilbrunn, O. *Warfare in the Enemy's Rear* (1963).

Higginbotham, D. *The War of American Independence* (New York, 1971).

Houlding, J.A. *Fit for Service: The Training of the British Army, 1715–1795* (Oxford, 1981).

Jany, C. *Geschichte der Königlich Preussischen Armee* (4 vols. Berlin, 1928–33).

Jany, C. *Die Gefechtsausbildung der Preussischen Infanterie von 1806* (Berlin, 1903).

Kling, C. *Geschichte der Bekleidung, Bewaffnung, und Ausrüstung der Königlich Preuss* (3 vols. Weimar, 1902–12).

Krieg 1809 (Published by the Kriegsgeschichtliche Abteilung des k. und k. Kriegsarchives, 6 vols., Vienna, 1907–10).

Levinge, Sir R. *Historical Records of the Forty Third, Monmouthshire, Light Infantry* (1868).

Luvas, J. *Frederick the Great on the Art of War* (New York, 1966).

Lynn, J. 'Esquisse sur la tactique de l'infanterie des armées de la République', *Annales Historiques de la Révolution Française* No. 210 (1972), 537–566.

Mackesy, P.G. *The Strategy of Overthrow, 1798–1799* (1974).

Mackesy, P.G. *The War for America, 1775–83* (1964).

Mallett, M. *Mercenaries and their Masters: Warfare in Renaissance Italy* (1974).

Meerheimb, F. von. 'Berenhorst und Bülow', *Historische Zeitschrift*, VI (1861).

Montbé, A. von. *Die Chursächsischen Truppen im Feldzuge 1806–7* (2 vols. Dresden, 1860).

Moorsom, W.S. *Historical Record of the Fifty-Second Regiment, 1755–1858* (1860).

Napier, Maj.-Gen. W.C.E. *Outpost Duty by General Jarry* (1869).

Napier, Sir W.F.P. *The Life and Opinions of General Sir Charles James Napier* (vol. I. 1857).

Nelson, P.D. 'Citizen Soldiers or Regulars? The views of the American General Officers on the Military Establishment, 1775–1781', *Journal of Military Affairs*, XLIII, No. 3 (1979), 126–32.

North, Lt.-Col. R.E.F.G. 'The Raising and Organising of the King's German Legion', *Journal of the Society for Army Historical Research*, XXXIX, (1961).

Oman, Sir C. *Wellington's Army, 1809–1814* (1912).

Oman, Sir C. *History of the Peninsular War* (7 vols. Oxford, 1900–32).

Oman, Sir C. *Column and Line in the Peninsular War* (Oxford, 1910).

Oman, C. *Sir John Moore* (1953).

Pakenham, T. *The Year of Liberty: The Great Irish Rebellion of 1798* (1969).

Paret, P. 'Colonial experience and military reform in the late eighteenth century', *Bulletin of the Institute of Historical Research*, XXXVII, (1964).

Paret, P. *Yorck and the Era of Prussian Reform, 1807–1815* (Princeton, 1966).

Pargellis, S.M. 'Braddock's defeat', *American Historical Review*, XLI, (1935–36).

Pargellis, S.M. *Lord Loudon in North America* (New Haven, 1933).

Parker, K.L. 'Anglo–American Wilderness Campaigning, 1754–63: Logistical and Tactical Developments', (Columbia Univ. Ph.D. thesis, 1970).

Pertz, G.H. and Delbrück, H. *Das Leben des Feldmarschalls Grafen Neithardt von Gneisenau* (Berlin, 1864).

Petraeus, D.H. 'Light infantry in Europe: strategic flexibility and conventional deterrence', *Military Review*, (Dec., 1984), 35–55.

Petre, F.L. *Napoleon and the Archduke Charles* (1976 edition).

Petre, F.L. *Napoleon's Last Campaign in Germany, 1813* (1974 edition).

Quimby, R. *The Background of Napoleonic Warfare; The Theory of Military Tactics in 18th Century France* (New York, 1957).

Redlich, F. *The Military Enterpriser and his Work Force* (2 vols. Wiesbaden, 1954).

Rentzell, D. *Geschichte des Garde-Jäger Bataillons* (second edition, Berlin 1894).

Rigaud, G. *Celer et Audax: A Sketch of the Services of the Fifth Battalion of the 60th Regiment (Rifles)* (Oxford, 1879).

Robertson, Lt. 'Notes on the first three parts of the "Field Exercises and Evolutions of the Army"', *Colburn's United Service Magazine*, Part One, (1845), 427–39.

Robson, E. 'British light infantry in the mid eighteenth century: the effect of American conditions', *The Army Quarterly*, LXIII, No. 2, (1952), 209–22.

Roger, A.B. *The War of the Second Coalition 1798–1801: A Strategic Commentary* (Oxford, 1964).

Rogers, Col. H.C.B. *Wellington's Army* (1979).

Rothenburg, G.E. *The Military Border in Croatia, 1740–1881* (Chicago, 1966).

Rothenburg, G.E. *Napoleon's Great Adversaries: The Archduke Charles and the Austrian Army, 1792–1814* (1982).

Rothenburg, G.E. 'Nobility and military careers: The Hapsburg officer corps, 1740–1918', *The Journal of Military Affairs*, XL (1976).

Russell, P.E. 'Redcoats in the wilderness: British officers and irregular warfare in Europe and America, 1740–1760', *The William and Mary Quarterly*, Third Series, XXXV, No. 4 (1978), pp. 629–652.

Rüstow, W. *Die Lehre vom kleinen Kriege* (Zurich, 1864).

Rüstow, W. *Geschichte der Infanterie* (2 vols. Nordhausen, 1864).

Sawyer, C.W. *Firearms in American History, 1600–1800* (Boston, 1910).

Scott, S.F. *The Responses of the Royal Army to the French Revolution* (Oxford, 1978).

Scurfield, R. 'British military smoothbore firearms', *Journal of the Society for Army Historical Research*, XXXV (1955).

Seydlitz, A. von. 'Aus den Akten der Militär-Reorganisationskommission von 1808', (edited by F. Meinecke), *Forschungen zur Brandenburgischen und Preussischen Geschichte*, V (1892).

Seymour, W. *British Special Forces* (1985).

Shanahan, W.O. *Prussian Military Reforms, 1786–1813* (New York, 1945).

Smyth, B. *History of the 20th Regiment, 1688–1888* (1889).

Sparks, Brevet-Major. 'Observations upon infantry drill', *Colburn's United Service Magazine*, Part Three (1845), 97–106.

Strachan, H. *European Armies and the Conduct of War* (1983).

Thiry, Commandant. *Histoire de la tactique de l'infanterie français, 1791–1905* (Paris, 1905).

Vanicek, F. *Specialgeschichte der Militärgrenze* (4 vols. Vienna, 1875).

Velocci, T. 'The New Light Division: will it work?' *National Defense*, (Nov. 1984), 56–60.

Wagner, W. *Von Austerlitz bis Königgrätz: Österreichische Kampftaktik im Spiegel der Reglements. 1805–1864* (Osnabrück, 1978).

Ward, S.G.P. *Faithful: The Story of the Durham Light Infantry* (1963).

Weighley, R.F. *The American Way of War* (New York, 1973).

Wertheimer, E. 'Erzherzog Karl und die 2 Koalition bis zum Frieden von Lunéville,

1798–1801', *Archiv für österreichische Geschichte*, LXVII.

Wheeler, H.F.B. and Broadley, A.M. *Napoleon and the Invasion of England: The Story of the Great Terror* (1907).

Wickham, Gen. J.A. 'Light Infantry Divisions in Defense of Europe', *NATO's 16 Nations*, Special, (Jan. 1985), 100–107.

Yaple, R.L. 'Braddock's defeat: the theories and a reconsideration', *Journal of the Society for Army Historical Research*, XLVI (1968), 194–201.

INDEX